GOD OF THE LOWLY

SOCIO-HISTORICAL INTERPRETATIONS OF THE BIBLE

Edited by
Willy Schottroff and Wolfgang Stegemann

Translated from the German by
Matthew J. O'Connell

ORBIS BOOKS
Maryknoll, New York 10545

The Catholic Foreign Mission Society of America (Maryknoll) recruits and trains people for overseas missionary service. Through Orbis Books Maryknoll aims to foster the international dialogue that is essential to mission. The books published, however, reflect the opinions of their authors and are not meant to represent the official position of the society.

Originally published as *Der Gott der kleinen Leute: Sozialgeschichtliche Bibelauslegungen*, vol. 1, *Altes Testament*, and vol. 2, *Neues Testament*, copyright © 1979 by Chr. Kaiser Verlag, Munich, and Borckhardthaus-Laetare Verlag, Gelnhausen/Berlin/Stein.

Except where otherwise indicated, Bible quotations are from the Revised Standard Version (JB = Jerusalem Bible; NAB = New American Bible).

Manuscript Editor: William E. Jerman

Index compiled by James Sullivan

Library of Congress Cataloging in Publication Data

Gott der kleinen Leute. English.
  God of the lowly.

  Translation of: Der Gott der kleinen Leute.
  Includes bibliographical references and index.
    1. Bible—Criticism, interpretation, etc.—Addresses,
essays, lectures. I. Schottroff, Willy. II. Stegemann,
Wolfgang. III. Title.
BS540.G7713   1984   220.6   84-5152
ISBN 0-88344-153-5 (pbk.)

Contents

PART TWO
NEW TESTAMENT

Part One

Old Testament

Introduction to Part One

WILLY SCHOTTROFF

"Truth is concrete." According to Walter Benjamin, these words were painted on a ceiling beam of the study Bertolt Brecht used during his Danish exile at Svendborg. This brief sentence is better suited than almost any other to bring out the special character of the Bible and its truth.

Such a claim may surprise readers when they first hear it. After all, ever since childhood a long training in matters ecclesiastical and theological has accustomed us to think that, on the contrary, the truth of the Bible is to be found in its timeless generality and universal validity, which meant that its contents could become the basis for binding principles of faith—dogmas.

According to the common way of thinking, the Bible has to do with the relationship between God and the human person as such. These two entities are thought of always the same in every age and little subject to change by history and the vicissitudes of life. Consequently, only one type of concreteness seems possible in principle—namely, the existential application of the Bible to me as the particular person I am. But even here I am thinking of myself as an abstract individual whose relationship to God is independent of the concrete circumstances of my life. And even when my relationship to my neighbor is brought into the picture, this relationship itself is usually limited to those basic aspects of human life that are timeless and recurrent in character.

The reflections on and interpretations of biblical texts that are offered in the present volume, from both the Old Testament and the New, are intended to counteract this kind of "idealist" misunderstanding of the Bible.

The contributions assembled here come from a study group on the "materialist" interpretation of the Bible; it met for the first time at Villigst in the fall of 1977. The word "materialist" in this description is not meant to reflect a philosophical concept of materialism. Much less does it express a commitment to a particular ideological position, such as dialectical and historical materialism. "Materialist interpretation" is rather the name given to an approach to the Bible that has become widespread, especially in the Romance-language countries; Kuno Füssel gives a detailed account of it in chapter 2 of the present volume.

Despite differences due to the dissimilar scientific traditions that provide the background in each country, there is extensive agreement at least regarding the basic intention of this effort to interpret the Bible. In the Romance-language countries the "materialist" reading of the Bible relies less on the critical historical method than on a structuralist view of the approach to biblical texts. The agreement on intention extends not least to acceptance of the view that the underlying concept of materialism is primarily a practical one and based on the materialism of the Bible itself.

What is meant by speaking of a materialism proper to the Bible is explicitly brought out by Aurel von Jüchen in chapter 1 of this volume. He points out that the Bible does not see the human person in "idealist" terms, as an "abstract entity squatting apart from the world" (to use a very apt saying of Karl Marx). Rather it takes all of human corporeality very seriously. In other words, the spiritual nature of the human person is neither denied nor so one-sidedly absolutized that it appears to be a spiritual being and nothing more. Instead, the Bible presents human persons as they really are: in all the manifestations of their lives, but also in the concrete, historically and socially differentiated relationships that make up their lives. This does not mean that the biblical presentation aims at a pseudo-objective neutrality. On the contrary, the Bible shows so great a partiality for the weak members of society, the underprivileged and the poor, as to justify the title given to this book, *The God of the Lowly*.

If exegesis is to meet the expectations voiced by Aurel von Jüchen and be capable of helping our contemporaries to recognize and deal with their situation in the light of what the Bible intends, it must not imitate traditional biblical scholarship by treating the texts of scripture almost exclusively as literary productions and in the light of the perspectives offered by the literary sciences. On the contrary, the primary need is that of a socio-historical approach that will re-create the real life of a given era in a very concrete way. Against this background the texts will acquire a wholly new vitality; at the same time it will be shown how biblical experience, biblical faith, and biblical hope were not only shaped by reality but also shaped reality in their turn.

The three examples, in part 1, of the interpretation of Old Testament texts are to be understood as experiments in achieving the goals just described. Of course it has not been possible in these essays to describe completely the social reality of Israel in the Old Testament period, but only to point out certain aspects of this reality by way of example. Willy Schottroff uses the writings of Amos as an example of the prophetic criticism of society and thus shows the social relevance of prophecy against the background of the socio-economic development of Israel at the time of the monarchy. Jürgen Kegler's chapter on Jeremiah takes a concrete case that brings out with special clarity the political implications and public nature of prophecy.

Of the three figures dealt with in these three essays, the first—Amos—is the clearest representative of the idea of God that is expressed in the book's title. The last of the three—Solomon the Preacher (Koheleth), whom Frank Crüsemann studies from the socio-historical viewpoint against the background of his thinking—provides a complete contrast to Amos and his "God of the Lowly." Yet it is both meaningful and necessary to deal with the strangely fascinating personality of the Preacher, not only that we may grasp the differences that exist within the Bible, but also for the sake of the insights this essay gives us for understanding the social background of the attitude of extreme skepticism that is expressed in the Book of Koheleth.

Editors and authors alike hope that the chapters offered here will be taken for what they are meant to be: attempts to give expression to the writers' deep love of the Bible by communicating a vivid picture of real life in the biblical period, and, at the same time, modest contributions to the humanization of our present reality along the lines of the humanity of God that finds expression in the scriptures.

REFLECTIONS

1

What a Pastor Expects from a Materialist Reading of the Bible: A Letter

AUREL VON JÜCHEN

Dear friends,

I understand that you're thinking of publishing some thoughts on a materialist exegesis of the Bible and some examples of this type of thing. Allow me to speak for the community and to tell you something of what we expect from an exegesis and a theology that no longer speaks in an idealist way of "man," or "the old and the new Adam," or "the sinner" and "the justified person," while forgetting that the contemporaries of Jesus Christ, no less than our own contemporaries, experienced quite specific socio-historical threats, temptations, hopes, and expectations.

It would be a mistake to suppose that contemporary Christian communities are "at home" in biblical thinking. When we enter the world of the Old or the New Testament, we are entering a *foreign* country. The exhortation to "read your Bible every day" betrays a lack of real-life contact with those who take encouragement from such advice. Even daily reading by itself does not make the Bible any less alien to us. The contemporaneousness of which Kierkegaard speaks remains a fiction unless exegetes are unable to build bridges between the present and the past. Reader and hearer of a passage from the Bible must *un*learn their habitual ways of thinking, their preformed judgments, if they are to understand the faith and the thinking of the Bible.

Materialist exegesis is inspired by a twofold love: one that looks back to persons of a past age, and another that reaches out to persons of the present and tries to make them "contemporaneous" with those from the past. But we cling stubbornly to our idealist and individualist thought categories, and as a result our alienation from that distant past is not eliminated; it is intensified.

7

The way that the Christian faith has been "naturalized" in our everyday life is due to the fact that in its proclamation the church has not succeeded in building a bridge of love between the twentieth century and the century in which Jesus Christ lived. Only those who stop speaking the language of their own country for a while can learn the language of another country. The difficult work of *un*learning is always a prerequisite for learning.

I should like to give a few examples of what we expect from a materialist exegesis. The examples have only one thing in common: they deal with questions that an idealist exegesis or an exegesis bent solely on edification cannot answer.

1) Jesus Christ came into the world of human events at a time when vast numbers of persons were anxiously awaiting some cataclysmic occurrence in the immediate future. Many advent sermons today continue to dwell on the "stillness that prevailed on the earth." But the gospels record something very different. Practically all the inhabitants of Palestine shared in the throbbing expectancy. The Pharisees, the Zealots, the Essenes, the apocalyptics, the baptism community of John the Baptist, and other baptism communities—all were looking ahead in great expectation.

All that the gospels had to say to the contemporaries of Jesus was: "When the time was fulfilled . . . ," and this was enough. But we who are strangers to that time ask why a great number of messiahs appeared just before, during, and after his lifetime. Why was there such an intense expectation for something momentous to happen very soon? Why were some believers expecting an imminent coming of the judgment of God, others an imminent coming of the reign of God?

I suspect that there were widespread material conditions that gave rise to those movements. Here it is possible to see that a materialist approach to history has nothing in common with determinism. Yet it is this anxious worry about determinism that causes many to shrink from a materialist approach. The phenomenon of widespread expectations that something momentous was soon to happen makes it clear that the same material situation that led some to opt for Jesus and the kingdom of God led others to opt for his execution.

2) Another example. There are parables that both preachers and congregations are happy to meditate on: the parables of the field that yields a fourfold harvest, the seed that grows by itself, the lilies of the field that take no concern over their raiment, the birds of the sky that take no concern over their food supply. With these parables we do not feel at a loss. But there are less idyllic parables: the master who demands a financial reckoning of his housekeeper; the creditors who order their debtors to be tortured; the vineyard keepers who kill the owner's son in order to seize his inheritance for themselves.

Do these parables not have a *Sitz im Leben*? Do they not reflect a real-life situation? If so, an idealist or allegorical type of exegesis will not bring out their full meaning. The need is for a materialist exegesis that takes into account the fact that broad expanses of Palestine belonged to foreign land-owners, that they used stewards to supervise harvests, and that the wine produced in Israel was consumed in Egypt.

3) Another example shows how the lack of a materialist exegesis has had tragic consequences in the course of world history and church history. In the gospel of John the struggle in which Jesus is engaged is depicted as a struggle against "the Jews." In later centuries Jewish hatred of Christians and Christian hatred of Jews became ever more intense. In medieval theology there arose the totally unbiblical teaching of the rejection of Israel and the appointment of the Christian people as its successor.[1] This "succession theology," which clearly contradicts the texts of the New Testament, led to countless pogroms in all the countries of Europe and poisoned the souls of Christians. In fact, below the surface, the antisemitism of an Adolf Stöcker and an Adolf Hitler is connected with this Christian hatred of Jews.

A materialist exegesis could have preserved the churches from such horrors, for in the New Testament Jesus lives within a complex of social strata. The magistrates, the Herodians, Sadducees, Pharisees, and Zealots are all ranged against him. They represent the ruling powers. Jesus takes the side of "the weary and the heavily burdened," the ostracized "tax collectors and sinners."

Those who today fear a materialist exegesis have nothing to worry about. This approach, which concurs with the New Testament, will not turn the conflict between Jesus and the Pharisees into "a simple socio-ethical question." On the contrary: it brings to light the real problem with which the gospels are dealing: God's rule and God's people.

4) I take as a further example the resurrection of Jesus. The calling of the disciples was a calling to a life under the rule of God. Their experience of the resurrection of Jesus renewed that vocation after the master had died on the cross. The faith of the first disciples in the resurrection of Jesus was indivisible from their faith in the coming of God's reign. It was an expression of the same faith, but *under the signature of the cross.* By the third and fourth centuries, however, these two aspects of the one faith had become widely separated. The church took the place of the kingdom of God, and belief in the resurrection projected all the religious teachings of the New Testament to an otherworldly sphere, thus turning Christianity into a "Platonism for the people" (Nietzsche). Only an exposition of changing material conditions can shed light on this distortion of faith in the resurrection, correct it, and restore the "pure doctrine."

5) A materialist exegesis is no less important for the Old Testament than for the New. While the peoples prior to and contemporaneous with Israel were establishing vast kingdoms and building pyramids and ziggurats, while they were crafting paintings and splendid mosaics, building temples, and producing utensils of gold and silver, and cosmetic boxes and mirrors of lapis lazuli,

a small nomadic people scorned all those things. Yet its faith in God has outlived the more than four thousand gods and goddesses of Mesopotamia, as well as the gods of Greek and Roman antiquity. Its God transcends not only all geographical boundaries but even the boundaries of the cosmos.

We must raise the question of how Israel's faith was connected with its nomadic existence, and what similarities exist between our modern life and that of nomads, so that a modern atomic physicist can profess this faith, whereas all the other gods have come to grief on the millstone of history. Because this God was not an authoritarian despot sitting on a throne, but shares journey and camp and march, victory and suffering, with his people, is he alone the one, even today, to accompany human beings as they work out their destinies?

6) When it comes to the relative position of men and women in the Bible, again only a materialist investigation of their relationships provides a satisfactory starting point. At an earlier time, all agrarian peoples practiced a matriarchal religion, all nomadic peoples a patriarchal religion. Among nomads it is the man who determines the course and goal of the journeying, as well as the choice of pastures, the use of wells, springs, and the like. The woman, on the other hand, controls everything within the campsite. This is a necessary division of labor, and implies no contempt for women. In the Bible father and mother are usually set side by side: "Let your father and your mother find joy in you." The fourth commandment says: "You shall honor your father and your mother." Sometimes the mother alone is mentioned: "Neglect not the commandment of your mother!"; "A foolish son is an affliction to his mother"; "Despise not your mother when she grows old."

Contempt for women makes its way among the Jews only after the return from Babylonian captivity. Is it a result of the sojourn in Babylon? Is it a result of the uncertainty about salvation that seized upon those who could no longer harmonize their belief in being the chosen people of God with their political fate? This seems to be suggested by the Book of Ezra. "We have broken faith with our God and have married foreign women from the peoples of the land. . . . Therefore let us make a covenant with our God to put away all these wives and their children" (Ezra 10:2-3); and the community answered: "It is so; we must do as you have said" (10:12). This example shows how certain questions can be answered only in the context of a given situation, the intentions of the persons involved, and their material and conceptual interests and expectations.

7) Every form of idealist exegesis leads to abstractionism and global, undifferentiated views. To the mind that thinks in generalities, a king is a king; rule and power are always rule and power. As a result, rule is always repressive, power always evil, the "product of a male society," and so on. A materialist exegesis shrinks from this kind of undifferentiated judgments. It does not assume that it knows in advance what a "lord," a "commandment," a "kingdom," and so on, are. Rather it asks: What is Sumerian kingship?

Babylonian? Israelite? Prussian? Oriental kings were gods and embodied the will of the gods. Jewish kings were the servants of God. I still remember a Bible study meeting at which the participants—"good Prussians," all of them!—heaped a good deal of censure on King David for his "unkingly behavior." Those who do not guard against global judgments will not grasp the New Testament concept of the *basileia tou theou*, the kingdom of God. It is not to be identified with an oriental kingdom or with a Prussian.

8) The Psalms set many problems for a materialist exegesis. What is the significance of the psalms of complaint or the psalms of petition? Who are the accused? Who are the petitioners? Who are the enemies against whom God's help is sought? Is God's predilection for the poor—a theme that coursed the centuries and was resumed in the preaching of Jesus—perhaps an echo of nomadic life in which there had been no rich and no poor? Were distinctions between rich and poor taken as an insult to God by a people that regarded itself as God's people?

I have thrown out some questions that can be answered only if a materialist approach is taken; an idealist approach cannot even grasp them as questions. But it would be illogical for a theologian who searches out the "living context" (*Sitz im Leben*) of past histories, speeches, and narrations, not to also inquire into the place of the community in the contemporary world. For it is the world in its present state that the community must live in and with. Christians in the Second and Third Worlds have evidently discovered their own place in history. Things are more difficult for Christians in the First World. Due to religious traditionalism they have lost awareness of their proper task. Leonard Ragaz applied the term "fiction" to the idea of "believing but not living your belief."

I realize, dear friends, that a fool can ask more questions than ten wise men could answer. But just as the fertility of the land depends on the bacterial life in the topsoil, so the fruitfulness of a science depends on the questions put to it. A theology that asks no more questions is a dead theology. Theology has a great future, but most theologians do not realize that the future of their science has already begun. It began in 1903 when Hermann Kutter wrote in his essay "Sie müssen":

> The Spirit of God is at work in matter. Therefore the forces for a new world—all the changes, all the advances, all the transformations—are contained in the Spirit of God. . . . Spirit is the noblest thing there is. Spirit is the shaper of matter. . . . Abstract spirit is not really spirit but rather a corruption of spirit. If our Christianity is once again to be filled with spirit and life, it must turn once again to matter.[2]

Dear friends, I hope that in your undertaking you will have a vigilant sense of the loss of identity between modern Christianity and the spirit of the New

2

Materialist Readings of the Bible: Report on an Alternative Approach to Biblical Texts

KUNO FÜSSEL

Classics of the Materialist Reading of the Bible

Fernando Belo

The year 1974 saw the appearance of Fernando Belo's *Lecture matérialiste de l'évangile de Marc*.[1] With this book Belo, a Portuguese who was at that time living in French exile as a foreign worker and a laicized priest, set in motion a search for alternative readings of the Bible that has continued down to the present. His fascinating approach is marked by a certain inexorability; both qualities stem from his ability to bring almost the entire arsenal of Parisian theoretical productivity in the linguistic and social sciences to bear on a single basic question: What is the connection between political and radical Christian praxis? Or, to spell the question out in greater detail: How do economic, political, and ideological class struggles influence the composition and reception of biblical texts? What material presuppositions, interests, and needs lead to what concepts, ideas, and theories? What are the laws regulating not only the exchange of goods but also the circulation of signs in the systems of society formation that mediate meaning?

In the first part of his book Belo admittedly requires the reader to climb a whole mountain of methodological problems: the effort needed has certainly deterred many readers from continuing with the book or has forced them to approach it in a different way. But as early as the second part of the book the reader's perseverance receives its first reward when Belo comes to the conclusion that the Old Testament is shaped by two main opposed lines of thought. These are the expression not only of distinctive religious and theological traditions but, at a deeper level, of contrary socio-economic interests and power relationships. A system based on gift (a system that is Yahwist and concerned with equality and self-rule in the framework of tribal society) stands over against a system based on purity opposed to pollution (this system is priestly, centralizing, and bureaucratic with its focus on the exercise of sacral and royal power).

The struggle between these two approaches continues into the New Testament. At their point of intersection stands the cross of Jesus. Belo shows why this was inevitable, by means of a clear analysis of the function of the temple in Israelite religion. The proceedings against Jesus are really concerned with the role of the temple as the economic, political, and ideological focus of power. Jesus dies because he wishes to tear down this temple and build a new one distinct from the old temple and outside the holy city. This purpose distinguishes him from the Zealots, who die for and in the temple.

In Belo's view, the entire development of theology that follows on the death of Jesus (it begins in the Bible, although least of all in Mark, whose gospel Belo analyzes and comments on, sequence by sequence) must be described as an attempt to blunt and adapt the radical messianic praxis of Jesus. Perhaps Belo is here throwing out the infant (theology) with its idealist bath, but no one can dispute his claim that to follow Jesus without accepting his messianic praxis is simply to play games with labels.

Michel Clévenot

In 1976 Michel Clévenot published his *Approches matérialistes de la Bible*.[2] His study picks up the main points of Belo's book but puts them into a form better suited to group reading. Clévenot not only provides a simple methodological introduction to the interrelationships of historical materialism, linguistics, and scripture study, but also makes stimulating comments in explaining the Bible as a collection of literary texts and in interpreting the gospel of Mark as the story of the subversive praxis of Jesus. As for the main task, which is to ascertain and map the traces of Jesus' praxis at the level of the various societal influences, Clévenot seeks to accomplish this by reconstructing the class relationships current around A.D. 70 and by deciphering the codes used in Mark's literary production.

Georges Casalis

In 1977 Georges Casalis published his book *Les idées justes ne tombent pas du ciel* ("Correct Ideas Do Not Fall from the Skies"),[3] which describes numerous and varied approaches to a materialist *hermeneutic* that is valid not only for a materialist reading of the Bible but also for a theologico-political reading of Chrisitan revolutionary praxis in general. This brilliantly written account of the journey of a militant French professor of theology from a politically sensitive Barthian theology to a clear option for the oppressed classes may be regarded as the first contribution to a European theology of liberation. Casalis energetically continues the struggle, begun by Bello, against bourgeois logocentrism in theology—that is, the exorcism of rational thinking as a supposedly impartial grasp of objective thought-forms.

He shows that human alienation is not to be overcome by an ever new submission to ever new scientific considerations but only by liberation from what divides us from God, our neighbor, and ourself. In Casalis' view, theological thinking is primarily a trailblazing engagement in revolutionary practice; it is a risking of one's existence, and this usually means initially that one becomes an outcast in one's own church. Such an approach to theology means the end of theology as conceptual representation; it is a farewell to spectator theologians.

Another characteristic of this new kind of theologizing is a new manner of reading. It does not get entangled in abstract problems of understanding but uses book lore in order to experiment in behalf of life and thus to change one's own praxis. The world's structure of meaning, its intelligibility, "does not drop from heaven" as a gift, but must be created.

Who Engages in an Alternative Reading of the Bible and Why?

No one who is familiar with the professional scene will deny that, if the publication of technical studies be taken as a criterion, exegesis and the auxiliary biblical sciences have made great progress in the last thirty years. A decisive factor in this progress has been the acceptance of the historico-critical method by all scholars in these disciplines, almost without exception. It seems, however, that the undeniable multiplicity of exegetical results has not satisfied an equally great number of diverse interests and needs. In fact, there is reason for thinking that scholarly exegetical interest and the hermeneutic that guides it (rather than the formal method as such) have been directed unilaterally to the acquisition of authoritarian knowledge in the service of an elitist claim to dominance on the part of a few "reading experts" in the church. Their exegesis has thus become in large measure a legitimating science, and authentic exegesis has been distorted into an ideology.

When Belo, Casalis, Clévenot, and many others denounce this tendency as idealist, they are at least able to point out how surprisingly little of real history appears in the direct work done on the biblical text by outstanding representatives of the historico-critical method, such as Rudolf Bultmann. At the very time when Nazi Germany was attacking the Soviet Union and Jews were being murdered in concentration camps (1941), Bultmann, who was certainly not a fascist, published his book *Neues Testament und Mythologie*, in which he accepts the modern spirit as the criterion for interpreting the Bible. Yet Bultmann does not allow the pitiless consequences of this spirit, and of the technological mind to which it has given birth—as seen in war and the Holocaust—to exercise any influence on his exegetical principles.[4] It is clear that even in Bultmann "history" still means simply such residues of the past as can be reestablished and criticism is limited to the analysis of worldviews, forms, redactions, and traditions. Nothing is seen of history as the presently operative product of class struggle, or of a revolutionary "critique of the status quo" as a valid interpretive horizon for contemporary reading and for the discernment of spirits that is needed today.

In view of this observation, which is representative of many that might be made, we can understand the severity with which Belo criticizes this elimination of social contradictions and conflicts from the existential hermeneutic of the demythologization program:

> Bourgeois exegetes, working on the basis of anthropocentric logocentrism, have sought with varying success to undo the closure of the MYTH codes that plays in the New Testament texts. The name of Bultmann especially is connected with this attempt at demythologization. For a symptom of the fact that the attempt is being made on the basis of bourgeois logocentrism, I need point out only the appeal to "the modern consciousness," to scientific reason, and to advancing modernity that seems always to be the ultimate argument in texts aiming at demythologization. This effort at demythologization fails to understand the Scriptures and the narrative of power (the messianic narrative). This bourgeois form of the theological discourse ends up in *interiority* (even if it be called spiritual experience or a spiritual attitude), and it makes no difference whether or not the exegete be a "believer," as Bultmann is. These exegetes may talk about "the history of salvation," but in fact history has been dissolved into the timelessness of consciousness and interiority and its relation to the "eternity" of God.[5]

Ecclesiastical authorities and the dominant exegetes have reacted strongly to the charge of idealism. Catholic exegetes especially insist that in matters of scriptural exegesis they will allow no alien gods before them. Therefore any approach to the Bible that differs from theirs or represents a critical reaction to theirs is labeled unsound or unscientific or a passing fad (assuming that they do not join the bishops and reach for a stronger weapon, disqualifying other approaches as unecclesial or even unchristian).

It is evident, therefore, that attempts at a nonidealist approach to the Bible do not originate in the academic world of university theology but rather in the commitment of the leftist Christians who opt for the oppressed in the class struggles of our time and join them in the pursuit of liberation.

Revolutionary practice thus becomes the starting point for a comprehensive hermeneutic that not only makes possible a new interpretation of political and ideological reality in society but also becomes the basis for a new understanding of faith.

If a church of the oppressed is to be built and if the folly of the cross is to be taken seriously in political praxis, then there is need not only of bidding farewell to bourgeois religion and the church of the established classes, but also of forming a new identity. A materialist reading owes its existence to this need—springing from an altered praxis—for a Christian-socialist identity and for an appropriation of the tradition of faith and its sources that will make this identity secure.

Like every conversion, this new beginning has its problems. Two dangers must be avoided: that of an individualistic, spontaneous biblicism, and that of a completely functional approach to the Bible that looks upon it solely as a source of motivation for political action. A conscious and sustained materialist reading is therefore compelled to be clear about its own limitations, its procedural methods, and the fund of utilizable preliminary work. It is here that Belo and, following him, Clévenot and Casalis have made a valuable pioneering contribution.

Numerous groups throughout the world have adopted the program suggested by these pioneers and have made it the basis for their common study of the Bible. In addition, the groups have moved beyond the now prototypical gospel of Mark and have applied the method to other texts of scripture: in the Old Testament to the Books of Samuel and Kings, to Genesis and Jeremiah; in the New Testament, to 1 Thessalonians and 1 Corinthians, to the Gospel of John and the Acts of the Apostles. The Acts of the Apostles especially has attracted increasing interest, and this for two reasons. First, it provides a document in which the entire range of problems created by the entry of the church into the place left by Jesus ("Jesus went and the church came") may be studied. Secondly, it makes possible a closer examination of living conditions among the early Christians and especially of their common possession and sharing of goods.

In the Romance-language (and especially in the French- and Spanish-speaking) countries a materialist reading is practiced chiefly by groups made up of members from left-oriented church associations (in which an ecumenical composition is taken for granted), trade unions, and the Christians for Socialism movement. The important thing for them seems to be not the reading as such but rather the liberation and enlightenment it brings within the family, at work, and in political party activities. In terms of trade or profession, the members of the groups are quite varied; technicians, workers, elementary school teachers, nurses, housewives, students, retirees. There are few academic persons or professional theologians.

The composition of the groups is quite different, however, in the German-speaking countries (West Germany, East Germany, Austria, Switzerland). Here the universities and student associations provide the milieu for the groups devoted to the materialist reading of the Bible. As to methodology these groups frequently take their lead from the school of the Dutchman F. Breukelmann (thus, for example, T. Veerkamp and J. van Zwieten). Pastors, teachers, theology students, and church workers largely determine the manner in which these groups go about their work. The situation is similar in the Netherlands, where the phenomenon of the base-level communities and the general ecclesial climate of tolerance also provide a favorable atmosphere. In

both of these language areas, however, it can be said that Christians for Socialism play an important role in coordinating and giving guidance. This is
true of Belgium, England, Norway, Canada, Peru, Colombia, and Mauri-
tius.

The work of these groups derives the essentials of its structure from the
leftist Catholic periodical *Lettre*, which is published in Paris and has Michel
Clévenot as one of its editors.[6] Since the appearance of Belo's book, *Lettre*
has promoted the common cause in trailbreaking articles and has provided a
forum for supraregional and international discussion. The Supplement to
No. 237 (1978) may be regarded as a first comprehensive survey of the subject
of alternative readings. It contains reports of new groups, new exegetical
findings, and new tools of analysis.

With this Supplement as a basis and preparation, a first international meeting took place in Paris on November 11–12, 1978. There were over one hun-
dred participants from sixteen countries, among them, of course, Belo,
Clévenot, and Casalis, but it was the laity, not the professional textual ana-
lysts, who gave the event its stamp. The pentecostal power of Christian-
socialist internationalism supplied the normative guidelines: the primacy of
experience, the equal standing of all readers, unity in political commitment,
the impulse to ongoing personal work.

The Bible is, of course, not the only book these groups use in their often
discouraging struggle against the establishment in church and society. Perhaps it is not even the most important of the tools they use.

Christians who sum up in the term "socialism" their ideas and suggestions
for the improvement of the present social order realize that they cannot derive their views directly from the Bible. On the other hand, it would be at the
very least imprudent to take it for granted that militant Christians can in their
political involvement dispense with the rich treasures of the Bible and the
stimuli it affords. On the contrary, it is to be presupposed that the texts of the
Bible have something in common with the hope that keeps us going in political struggle—the hope, I mean, for a society without oppression and alienation. Consequently, the Bible is an indispensable aid to survival on the long
journey through the wilderness of capitalism.

Many of the groups mentioned above know from experience that a reading
of the Bible done in common not only brings new knowledge and helps eliminate old misapprehensions of the Bible as being a collection of pious statements for use on feast days, but also affords an authentic joy. Texts of the
Bible and the reading of them have contributed to the loosening of the
tongues of many in the groups. As a result, conflicts in the groups have found
their voice and a solution, whereas previously they had been unadmitted and
had unconsciously hindered practical action.

From this it can be seen that a materialist reading of the Bible has three
goals: (1) It aims at showing that the Bible does not simply contain scattered
expressions of the lives of the oppressed, but has the poor for its real subject.
(2) It aims therefore at rescuing the Bible from those who have wrongfully
appropriated it and put it in chains. (3) It aims at reading the Bible in such a

way that in its light our political praxis will receive a new clarification, and at the same time this practice and its clarification will help us find in the writings of the Old and New Testaments hitherto undiscovered paradigms of a subversive praxis.

What Does the Term "Materialist" Mean in this Context?

Inasmuch as the materialist reading of the Bible is carried on in groups that are at least socialist, if not Marxist, in their orientation, this kind of basic politico-practical direction must be made the starting point in interpreting the word "materialist."

The primary point of reference for a materialist reading is "revolutionary praxis"[7] as a concrete epistemological principle. In other words, transformative praxis determines in each instance the range of concepts and theories that are developed, and serves as criterion of truth for statements made with their help. This applies also to the hermeneutic for interpretation of the Bible.

The materialism in question here is therefore practical, not metaphysical. It begins with the concept of production, which, according to Karl Marx, is determinative of the human species. "The act by which they [living human individuals] distinguish themselves from animals is not the fact that they think but the fact that they begin to produce their means of subsistence."[8] Under the heading of productive activities Marx includes art and therefore literature as particular forms. "Religion, family, state, law, morality, science, art, etc., are only particular modes of production, and fall under its general law."[9]

There are, however, serious differences between the various productive activities just mentioned—between art and science, for example: "The whole as it appears in the mind as a conceptual totality [scientific investigation of social reality in its entirety] is a product of the thinking mind, which appropriates the world in the only way possible to it, a way that is distinct from the artistic, religious, or practical appropriation of the same world."[10] But in order to appraise correctly the place of writing, reading, and literature (the Bible belongs here), recourse must be had to a materialist theory of literature.[11]

In regard to such a theory careful heed must be paid to the guideline Marx sets down for any and every scientific materialism:

> It is, in reality, much easier to discover by analysis the earthly core of the misty creations of religion, than, conversely, it is, to develop from the actual relations of life the corresponding established forms of these relations. The latter method is the only materialistic, and therefore the only scientific one.[12]

By way of a rough and condensed formula, then, the following can be said with regard to a materialist theory of literature: applying Marx's maxim to the literary production of texts, we may assert that literature is to be understood as a product of social praxis and derives its character from the relationships at work in each instance.

Literary production is a form of ideological production. Like every other ideological production, literary production is determined by the relationship between basis and superstructure, and by class struggles. The production of texts is the privileged field of the conflict between the rival ideologies at work on the formation of a society. The basic structure of literary texts emerges from consideration of this primary contradiction. In itself, therefore, literature is always incomplete, incoherent, and open to new readings. What is called "the unity of a work of art" is simply a metaphor for the effort to resolve social conflicts in a symbolic way and achieve a fictive reconciliation by creating a secondary semiotic system (literary language).

A materialist theory of literature identifies types of texts and genres of texts as variations within a general social determination of literary form, and analyzes the religious, politicial, juridical, and other themes of a text in light of its function. This emphasis on the objective character of literature as a reflection of real life means the rejection of an attitude that regards literature as resulting from the genius or even the fully mysterious creativity of individuals.

Once literature is understood as a particular form of ideological praxis, it follows that it is not to be classified as an achievement of consciousness removed from reality, but that it is a material—that is, a practico-transformative—factor of social reality. Literary texts are not simply mental products of material life but rather themselves in their turn play a part in shaping this life. To produce and utilize literature is always at the same time to intervene and take sides in the struggle between the rival ideologies at work in societal formation, and it is therefore to make an active contribution to the shaping and differentiating of its contradictions.

A materialist reading (this applies not only to the Bible) must therefore strive to do justice, in dealing with a text, to the viewpoints of productivity and materiality. But productivity and materiality must themselves be seen from two points of view, lest we fall into the error of an esthetic of production, on the one hand, or an esthetic of reception, on the other.[13] Production and reception must be considered in relationship to the labor of the author, who makes the text out of the given material of his own language, but also in relationship to readers (interpreters), who make the text their own by their reading of it, implant it in their own speech, and so incorporate it into themselves.

As far as reading is concerned, this process means that the constitutive elements must be interrelated: (1) the given language; (2) the author who uses it, and the original addressees of the text; and (3) the present-day reader. At the same time, attention must be paid to the conditions in which the text was produced and those in which it now discloses itself, as these conditions are determined by the social situation of the author and that of the reader.

Clévenot therefore sets down the following minimal requirements for a materialist reading: it must lead the reader to the point at which (1) at least the basic syntactical structure of the text and the structure of its statements or actions is clear; (2) the manner in which the author says something to others, with the means that the author's language provides, likewise emerges; (3) the author-reader relationship and the influence of each on the other is clarified; and (4) enough information about the social situation of author and reader is brought to bear on the analysis of the text.[14]

What Method Is to Be Preferred?

The categories and methods that readers need and the degree of differentiation they claim for them will depend (1) on the field of practical needs and requirements in which they are taking their stand, and (2) on the degree of theory-development that they regard as obligatory and consider to be fruitful and helpful to them in their options. To the extent that the reading groups are made up of militants and not of university professionals, much less theoreticians of science, the first of these two criteria will be decisive for the choice of linguistic methods.

Texts for an initial understanding—which has not surveyed, and does not intend to survey, the entire discussion that goes on among modern theoreticians of texts—are to be regarded, in a quite general way, as linguistic entities that were produced under certain social conditions.[15] Materially speaking, texts are collections of signifiers (signs that convey meaning) connected with one another by precise relationships. The totality of these relationships reveals the structure of the text.

For a structural analysis of a text one particular relationship is especially important: the opposition between two elements (good/evil, stay/go, Jerusalem/Samaria, etc.).[16] The oppositions that occur in a text reveal the purpose of the text. This is also one of the most important formal bridges to historical materialism with its methodological emphasis on contradictions.

The ascertainment of the conditions of production and reception requires not only reliable information on the pertinent societal formation and its general indices—economy, politics, an ideology (consultation of the pertinent technical literature is indispensable here)—but also a clarification of the type of text. What is meant by "type of text"?

Most persons (this is something drilled into them in school) read texts (a newspaper, a book, a letter) either because they want to know what the author (a friend, a teacher, a politician) intended to say to them or others, or because they want to find out what happened, what it was really like then or now, who was involved, who did what.

Given these two basic interests, it seems plausible to divide the texts we meet in reading the Bible into two main groups: discourses or speeches, on the one hand (e.g., the letters of Paul), and stories or accounts, on the other (e.g., the Gospel of Mark).

A discourse is a text that establishes a relationship between a first person and a second person, an I and a you, and then fashions this relationship (developing it, intensifying it, weakening it). At the level of linguistic features, discourses are recognizable by the present tense of the verbs, the role of pronouns and adverbs, and the structure of the statements.

A story or narrative, on the other hand, eliminates references to the author's role in the process of expression. Events seem to narrate themselves, so that we do not know clearly who is speaking to whom. Consequently, the third person and the past tense are linguistic signposts of narrative. The change produced by the text is the change that takes place between the actants or agents who make their appearance in the text.

The distinction between discourse and narrative is usually made at the beginning of group work on the text.

According to R. Barthes (whom many study groups follow on this point in their reading), the mode of production peculiar to a text, and the structure that emerges from the text, are to be determined by deciphering the sequential codes used, whereas the insertion of the text into a particular situation can be known by the indicial or cultural codes.[17]

Sequential codes may be subdivided into three types: the actantial code, the analytic code, and the strategic code.[18] The working of these codes can be further specified depending on whether they are used in a discourse or in a narrative:

1) The actantial code enables us to see who the actors or actants are and what they do (Jesus, the Pharisees, the disciples).

2) The analytic code shows us how the actants read and analyze the events (the Pharisees and Jesus pass divergent judgments on cures worked on the Sabbath).

3) The strategic code permits us to evaluate the behavior of the actants in terms of the attitudes they adopt toward each other (e.g., the summoning of a sick person into the midst of the synagogue).

Once the overall plan of the text is known, the indicial or cultural codes tell us how the individual components of it are related (e.g., place names), in order that we may thus come to grasp the meaning of the whole. The most important thing here is the serial connections among the individual terms (e.g., whether they all have to do with health, sickness, healing, etc., or whether they deal with landed property, money, selling, contracts, etc.).

The most important cultural codes are the following:

1) The geographical code: it tells us the regions whence the information comes or where the action takes place.

2) The topographical code: it indicates locales, at least in a narrative: a house, the street, the sea, the temple.

3) The chronological code: it specifies the temporal sequence.

4) The mythological code: it establishes connections with the store of myths that were current throughout the entire East.

5) The symbolic code: it makes reference to the system of values and norms found in the Bible.

6) The social code: it indicates relationships to the economic and political aspects of society and to practical life generally.

Most groups begin their work by first investigating the way in which one particular code works and then adding code after code until the entire fabric has been reconstituted.

Why Has the Materialist Reading Undertaken to Link Historical Materialism and Structuralism?

A materialist reading of literary texts may be described, from the viewpoint of methodology, as an effort to draw profit from the socio-historical analysis of the production and reception of texts, on the one hand, and from the determination of their specific literary form, on the other, for an intensive reading.

In the process, the social background for the analysis is derived from historical materialism as a theory of the formation and history of societies. This is followed by a consideration of the text on the basis of linguistic structuralism. Is this combination of approaches accidental or necessary?

At least on historical grounds the claim that the conjunction is accidental can be dismissed. Ever since the beginning of Russian formalism in the 1920s,[19] which continues to exert an influence on French structuralism by way of R. Jacobson and T. Todorov, there has been a complementarity (often ignored) between the problems dealt with in the Marxist/materialist theory of literature and those in the formalist/structuralist theory:

1) Marxists insist on the need of showing how literary texts depend, even in their multiplicity of meanings, on the socio-historical context.

2) Formalists are interested primarily in the way in which a literary text manages to establish, between sign and reality, a relationship that is free from any utilitarian compulsion to represent reality. It is in this freedom that the autonomy of the work of art consists.

3) In concrete work on texts, each party gladly avoids the approach taken by the other or, by way of diversion, criticizes the other for neglecting its own (the criticizing party's) side of the investigation. There are only a few theories of literature that try to deal with both aspects at the same time and in a balanced way; some of the exceptions are W. Benjamin and T. W. Adorno, along with E. Balibar and P. Macherey.[20] Belo is very close to the last-named, even though he takes J. Kristeva as his explicit point of departure.[21]

The attempt to link historical materialism and structuralism in a dialectical way when working on a text is in keeping with an older aspiration, although one that is difficult to satisfy. In this context a dialectical approach implies the need of remaining aware that both the esthetic and the socio-functional aspects of a text are socially determined but are not on that account reducible to one another by any means. Theory of ideology and structural analysis of texts can therefore usefully complement one another when the goal is to explain how a literary work such as the Bible not only permits different and even contrary types of reading (one that confirms the dominant understanding of reality; another that shatters it), but is itself already the product of rival types of reading and represents their fictive reconciliation.

It is still possible, however, to argue about whether the alliance of methods and the practice of reading that are exhibited in this book are meaningful and helpful and carry us forward. It may be asked whether an equally fruitful or perhaps even more productive combination of the historico-critical method and the analysis of societal formation may not be possible. In my opinion, the likelihood of a positive answer to these questions has for the first time increased, now that L. Schottroff and Wolfgang Stegemann have published *Jesus von Nazareth: Hoffnung der Armen,*[22] which so brilliantly combines readableness, thorough information, and knowledge of the present state of scholarship with the concern for concrete socio-critical reading.

NOTES

1. *Lecture matérialiste de l'évangile de Marc: Récit—Pratique—Idéologie* (Paris, 1974; 2nd ed., 1975); M. J. O'Connell, trans., *A Materialist Reading of Mark* (Maryknoll, N.Y., 1981). I also refer the reader to the new exegetical journal *Texte und Kontexte*, which is published by Alektor Verlag (Stuttgart) and contains contributions from the area of alternative interpretations of the Bible.

2. Paris, 1976. In an appendix to the German translation of Clévenot's book—*So kennen wir die Bibel nicht* (Munich, 1978)—I have gone more fully into the theoretical background; I refer the reader to it for a more detailed discussion of the subject.

3. Paris, 1977; *Correct Ideas Don't Fall from the Skies* (Maryknoll, N.Y., 1984).

4. See also Casalis' critique in chap. 4 of his book.

5. Belo, *Materialist Reading*, p. 286.

6. *Lettre* is published by *Temps Présent*, Paris.

7. Marx's third thesis on Feuerbach, in L.S. Feuer, ed., *Karl Marx and Friedrich Engels: Basic Writings on Politics and Philosophy* (Garden City, N.Y., 1959), p. 244.

8. Karl Marx and Friedrich Engels, *The German Ideology*, Part 1, in *Basic Writings*, p. 409.

9. Karl Marx, *The Economic and Philosophical Manuscripts of 1844*, D. J. Spruik, ed., M. Milligan, trans. (New York, 1964), p. 136.

10. Karl Marx, *Einleitung zur Kritik der politischen Ökonomie*, in *Marx-Engels Werke*, 13:632–33.

11. I have indicated elsewhere the source on which Belo and Clévenot depend; see my essay, "Anknüpfungspunkte und methodisches Instrumentarium einer materialistischen Bibellektüre," in M. Clévenot, *So kennen wir die Bibel nicht*, pp. 145-70.

12. *Capital*, S. Moore and E. Aveling, trans., vol. 1, part 4, chap. 15, section 1 (New York, 1967 [1887]), p. 372, n. 3.

13. See P. V. Zima, *Kritik der Literatursoziologie* (Frankfurt, 1978), pp. 72-112.

14. See M. Clévenot, "Lectures matérialistes de la Bible," in *Introduction à la lecture matérialiste de la Bible* (Geneva, 1978).

15. There is an understandable difference in level between the reflections and researches of Belo and that which given groups can absorb of them.

16. There is a survey of the various methods in M. Titzmann, *Strukturale Textanalyse* (Munich, 1977).

17. See especially R. Barthes, *S/Z*, R. Miller, trans. (New York, 1974).

18. See Füssel, "Anknupfungspunkte," pp. 150-52.

19. See J. Striedter, ed., *Texte der russischen Formalisten*, 1 (Munich, 1968); V. Erlich, *Russischer Formalismus* (Munich, 1964); M. Bachtin, *Marxismus und die Philosophie der Sprache. Grundprobleme der soziologischen Methode in der Wissenschaft von der Sprache* (Leningrad, 1929; Frankfurt, 1976).

20. See E. Balibar and P. Macherey, "Thesen zum materialistischen Verfahren," *Alternative*, 98 (1974) 193-221.

21. See Füssel, "Anknupfungspunkte," pp. 152-54.

22. Stuttgart, 1978.

EXAMPLES

3

The Prophet Amos:
A Socio-Historical Assessment of His Ministry

WILLY SCHOTTROFF

Who Was Amos?

The prophetic book, nine chapters in length, that has come down to us under the name of "Amos,"[1] appears in the Old Testament as the third of the "twelve prophets"—that is, the third among the books of the twelve "minor" prophets that follow upon those of the three "major" prophets.[2] Contrary to the impression this order might give, it tells us nothing about the time when each prophet came on the scene or the temporal succession of the prophets.[3] As a matter of fact, Amos is the earliest representative of classical biblical prophecy in Israel.

Along with indications scattered through the Book of Amos (most notably the account in 7:10–17 of Amos's clash with Amaziah, priest of the royal sanctuary at Bethel), it is on the title of the book that we depend for clues to Amos's chronological place in the history of the Israelite monarchy, as well as to the facts about his geographical origin, his social position, and the context in which he carried on his prophetic ministry.

According to the title of the book, Amos exercised his prophetic ministry during the reigns of Kings (Azariah-)Uzziah of Judah (787–736 B.C.) and Jeroboam II of Israel (787–747 B.C.).[4] The period during which he was able to work as a prophet—that is, until the priest Amaziah put a sudden end to his activity at Bethel—is probably not to be regarded as very long. Amos 1:1 dates the prophet's ministry as "two years before the earthquake." The reference is clearly to the earthquake that Amos prophesies in 2:13; 3:15 (?); 9:1;[5] further reference to it occurs in Amos 8:8; 9:5; Zechariah 14:5; and

27

perhaps Isaiah 2:10, 21.[6] The formulation suggests that his prophetic activity lasted for a year at most. The evidence for the historical situation suggests that Amos's ministry dates, at the earliest, from about the middle of the 40-year reign of Jeroboam II of Israel. On the other hand, it probably begins no later than 760 B.C. For 759 (or, according to another calculation, 756) saw the beginning of the coregency of Jotham in place of his father (Azariah-) Uzziah, who had been stricken with leprosy (see 2 Kings 15:5; 2 Chron. 26:16–21). This historical datum would surely be mentioned in the title of the Book of Amos, as it is in Isaiah 1:1 and Hosea 1:1, if Amos had been active only after 760.

Amos functioned as a prophet in the northern kingdom, Israel: at its capital, Samaria (3:9; 4:1; 6:1; 8:14); at the sanctuary of Bethel (3:14; 4:4; 5:5–6; 7:10, 13); and probably also at the sanctuary of Gilgal (4:4; 5:5).[7] By birth, however, he was a Judean. His place of origin was the little village of Tekoa, which was seventeen kilometers south of Jerusalem in the Judean highlands, on the boundary between fertile farmland (to the west) and the arid region of the "wilderness of Judah" (in the east, toward the Dead Sea).

As Amos insists in the story of his clash with the priest Amaziah (7:14), he was not a professional prophet (*nabî*),[8] much less a cultic prophet,[9] nor was he a "prophet's disciple" (*ben-nabî*)—that is, a member of a guild of prophets, like the man who in the time of Joram (851–845 B.C.), the last member of the Omri dynasty to rule the northern kingdom, was bidden by Elisha to anoint Jehu, the "commander," as king of Israel (2 Kings 9:1–13) and thus to prepare the way for the latter's coup d'état. Finally, there are no grounds for the misunderstanding—under which Amaziah, the priest at Bethel, may have acted—that has taken Amos to be perhaps a seer (*hozeh*, Amos 7:12) who had institutional ties with the court at Jerusalem and went about the northern kingdom preaching rebellion against Jeroboam II in the interests of Judah (Amos 7:10).[10]

Contrary to all these hypotheses the story in Amos 7:10–17 attributes the ministry of Amos to an express and irreducible commission from Yahweh (7:15). It took Amos from his previous way of life and his trade and brought him to the northern kingdom.[11] In 3:3–8 Amos himself describes this commission as a compulsion originating outside himself; he found himself unable to resist it and compelled to follow it. We have no reason for doubting that the motivation for his prophetic ministry was primarily religious, although investigation is needed of the objective reasons that this motivation implied and that had as their background Amos's conception of God.

The trade that Amos originally followed in his Judean homeland seems to have been one that was natural for him in view of his rural origins. He was the owner of herds (or perhaps only a herdsman) and possessed (as a *noqed*, Amos 1:1) small livestock (7:15)—that is, sheep and goats—and (as a *bôqer*, 7:14), large livestock—that is, cattle (or else was simply the herdsman responsible for them).[12] In addition (as a *bôles*, or "slitter of mulberry figs," 7:14) he dealt with sycamores. It is true that sycamores do not thrive in the immediate vicinity of Tekoa in the Judean highlands, but they are to be found within a reasonable distance in the depressions of the Jordan valley and on the Mediterranean coastal plain. Either he picked the tasty figlike fruit in order to force its ripening or else—the point cannot be determined with certainty—he gathered the fruit and leaves of the sycamore as a supplementary food for his livestock.[13]

The indications given in 1:1 and 7:14, on Amos's trade, leave us uncertain about his social background. But we should not imagine it to have been very lowly. After all, he was able to acquire a high level of self-expression and a familiarity with the broad range of Israelite educational tradition, as the oracles preserved in the Book of Amos attest.

The Book of Amos and Its Problems

The fact that for the first time in the history of Israelite prophecy a book of oracles is transmitted to us under the name of an individual, Amos, signals a notable gain in authenticity as compared with the tradition regarding earlier prophets such as Elijah and Elisha. Our knowledge of them depends exclusively on stories that are told by others and are to be classed largely as sagas or legends.

At the same time, however, we should not set too high a value on this new type of prophetic tradition that links data about the person and ministry of the prophet (Amos 1:1; 7:10–17) with descriptions of visions (7:1–9; 8:1–3; 9:1–4) and with prophetic utterances that now become the main focus of attention. Especially must this new type of tradition not be misunderstood to imply that everything contained in the book transmitted under the name of Amos comes in fact from him or that he himself wrote the book.[14] The prophets did on occasion write down individual sayings (in all likelihood this is especially true of their visions; see Isa. 8:1–4; 30:8; Jer. 30:2–3; 51:59–64; Ezek. 43:10–11; Hab. 2:2–3) or dictate them to a secretary (Jer. 36:1–32). On the whole, however, such writing seems to have been rather limited or to have even been an exception due to unusual circumstances. By any accounting, the great preexilic prophets were primarily speakers, not writers.

The commitment of their utterances to writing was the work of later individuals, primarily their disciples and other supporters. Although the prophetic teacher was held in such high esteem by these individuals that they made it their acknowledged task to collect and preserve his utterances, this does not mean that this group of transmitters regarded the prophet's legacy as untouchable. They did not feel it wrong to freshen the inherited sayings by means of additions that applied the prophetic message to the new realities of changing times. On the contrary, this practice was so much the rule that when we deal with each prophetic book we must expressly ask to what extent the substance of the "authentic" tradition that goes back to the prophet himself has been infiltrated by subsequent additions.[15]

For the Book of Amos no clear and universally accepted answer has thus far been given to this question. The two most recent German commentaries on Amos by H. W. Wolff[16] and W. Rudolph[17] (to take but two examples) show how unsettled the situation is among scholars; Wolff and Rudolph take two wholly different approaches to the solution of the problems raised by the Book of Amos.

Rudolph conceives of the Book of Amos in its present form as resulting from the putting together of three originally separate partial collections of Amos material: Amos 1–2, 3–6, and 7–9. He also thinks that, apart from some transposition of verses, especially in the third part of the book, the substance of the original tradition going back to Amos himself can be reconstituted by eliminating a relatively small number of glosses.[18] Solutions of this type have been tried occasionally[19] since the days of J. Wellhausen.[20] But it is doubtful whether they really do justice to the probably much more complicated processes of transmission and redaction to which our prophetic books owe their origin.

Greater justice is likely to be done by conclusions such as those reached by Wolff in his analysis of the Book of Amos—although Wolff's attempt to reconstruct the development of the Amos tradition has met with criticism, and other suggested solutions have been offered in place of his.[21] Wolff sees the basic Amos tradition as consisting, on the one hand, in the basic content of the collection of "the words of Amos . . . of Tekoa" (1:1a* [the asterisk indicates a single word in a verse]) that is to be found in chapters 3 to 6, and, on the other hand, in the "literary fixation of the cycles," which Wolff attributes to the prophet himself and which he regards as comprising, along with the cycle of oracles against the nations (1:3–2:16*), the cycle of visions (7:1–9; 8:1–3; 9:1–4). In Wolff's view, these two blocks of tradition were linked by "the old school of Amos" that was active in Judah ca. 735 B.C., and were completed by the addition of 1:1b* ("which he saw concerning Israel . . . two years before the earthquake"); 5:5a, 13–15; 6:2, 6b; 7:9–17; 8:3–14*; 9:7, 8a, 9–10. Further additions and revisions, which brought the Book of Amos to its present form, are attributed by Wolff to a "Bethel-exposition of the Josianic age" (639–609 B.C.; specifically: Amos 1:2; 3:14b*; 4:6–13; 5:6, 8–9; 9:5–6), to a "deuteronomistic redaction" during the exile (Amos 1:1*, 9–12; 2:4–5, 10–12; 3:1b, 7; 5:25–26; 6:1*; 8:11–12?), and to a "postexilic eschatology of salvation" (Amos 5:22a*; 6:5*; 9:8b, 11–15).

In this essay I shall not make any new attempt at a literary analysis of the Amos tradition. Instead I shall presuppose the results of Wolff's analysis, which accepted and critically developed important work done earlier[22] and then formed a picture of the growth of the Amos tradition that probably represents fairly well the complex processes of reediting to which our present Book of Amos actually owes its origin. I refer the reader once and for all to H. W. Wolff's commentary on Amos for the reasons why, in the following pages, I regard certain passages of the Book of Amos as secondary and therefore leave them aside in dealing with the historical Amos.

The Era of Amos

We are not well informed about the events that accompanied the ministry of Amos.[23] Apart from the information given to us in the Book of Amos itself, we have for Jeroboam II and his reign (787–747 B.C.) only the few indications contained in the brief notice of him in 2 Kings 14:23–29.[24] In addition, there are a few epigraphical testimonies from the northern kingdom in the time of Jeroboam II, such as the seal of a royal high official that was found at Megiddo and bears the inscription: "[Belonging to] Shema' the servant of Jeroboam,"[25] and some of the Samaria ostraka, but neither of these sheds any light on the events of the time.[26] Somewhat more detailed are the accounts in 2 Kings 14:21–22, 15:1–7, and 2 Chronicles 26:1–23 of the reign of Jeroboam's contemporary, King (Azariah-)Uzziah of Judah (787–736 B.C.).[27] But these accounts give little further knowledge of the historical circumstances of Amos's ministry.

Despite these limitations, what the deuteronomistic history has to say in 2 Kings 14:25, 28 on the success of Jeroboam II has given rise to the widespread view that the reign of this king was a final age of domestic and foreign peace, political stability, and economic prosperity that was granted to the northern kingdom between its persistent and eventful disputes with its neighbors and especially with the Aramaeans in the second half of the ninth century B.C., and the increasing Assyrian threat to its very existence that began when Tiglath-pileser III (745–27 B.C.) took the throne.[28] But this picture is correct only with certain qualifications. What is true is that Kings Joash (802–787 B.C.) and Jeroboam II succeeded in recouping the territorial losses that the northern kingdom had suffered east of the Jordan from the middle of the ninth century on, and especially from the beginning of the Jehu dynasty (845 B.C.) to which both of these kings belonged (see 2 Kings 10:32–33). The territory of the northern kingdom was now once again approximately what it had been in the age of David and Solomon (see 2 Kings 13:24–25; 14:25, 28).[29]

The sources at our disposal do not tell us in detail of the events that led to these losses of territory, or of what it was that made their recovery possible. Apparently the reign of Ahab of Israel (871–852 B.C.) saw the first serious military conflicts between Israel and the Aramaean state of Damascus, even though in 853 this same Ahab fought at the side of Hadadezer (= Benhadad II) of Damascus near the North Syrian city of Karkar as part of an anti-Assyrian coalition of Suro-Palestinian forces against the Assyrian King Shalmaneser III (858–824 B.C.).[30]

The conflicts with Damascus continued under Jehoram (851–45 B.C.), the last king of the Omri dynasty (see 2 Kings 8:28–29; 9:14–15). It seems that from the time of Jehu of Israel (845–818 B.C.) and Hazael of Damascus (845–802 B.C.), who reached the throne at the same time and in equally violent ways (2 Kings 8:7–15), these conflicts were marked by special harshness and cruelty (2 Kings 8:13; Amos 1:3) and henceforth were less successful for Israel (2 Kings 10:32–33; 13:3, 7, 22). Initially the battles took place on the frontiers of Israelite territory—in the northern part of Transjordania at Aphek, east of the Lake of Gennesaret (1 Kings 20:26–30, 34; cf. 2 Kings 13:17), and at Ramoth in Gilead, southeast of there (1 Kings 22; 2 Kings 8:28–29; 9:1–16). But soon we hear of Aramaean attacks on the Ephraimite heartland west of the Jordan (2 Kings 6:8–23, where Dothan is named) and even of the Aramaeans besieging Samaria, the capital city (2 Kings 6:24–7:20).

Aided by the military conflicts with the Aramaeans which were absorbing Israel's energies, and perhaps even in direct alliance with the Aramaeans, Moab (probably in the time of Jehu) expanded its territory from the Arnon northward to the heights at the northern end of the Dead Sea (we learn of this from the inscription of Mesha the Moabite king).[31] In addition, at this time and probably into the subsequent period, Moabite (2 Kings 13:20–21) and Ammonite (Amos 1:13) raiding parties attacked the land of Gilead, east of the Jordan (there may even have been an attempt at a permanent Ammonite expansion in this region). It is clear that in the west, too, the Philistines also engaged in raids into Israelite territory (Amos 1:6).[32]

When Israel reversed the trend and, beginning with the accession of Joash in 802 B.C., succeeded in gradually regaining its territory, this was possibly connected in part with the continuous pressure that Assyria was bringing to bear on Damascus during the second half of the ninth century. We know of various expeditions that the Assyrian King Shalmaneser III (858–824 B.C.) led westward into Syro-Palestinian territory. Shalmaneser's grandson, Adad-nirāri III (810–783 B.C.), entered Syria twice more, in 805 and 802, and on these occasions received tribute from Damascus.[33]

But we should not exaggerate the effect of these Assyrian interventions into the destinies of the Syro-Palestinian area. They were limited measures and did not lead to any lasting Assyrian domination of the region. In addition, the reign of Adad-nirāri III saw a significant loss of Assyrian power, a half-century of weakness for this empire that lasted until the accession of Tiglath-pileser III (745 B.C.). The weakness of Assyria was conditioned by the growth of a new major power in the north, the empire of Urartu, which now advanced from its heartland in the East Anatolian mountains around Lake Van into northern Syria and Assyria.[34] The weakness of Assyria in the Syrian world allowed new rivalries to emerge among the Aramaean states, and these evidently favored Israel's recovery of territory more than did the previous Syrian expeditions of the Assyrian kings. Thus at the beginning of the eighth century we hear of military conflicts between a coalition of small Syrian states led by Ben-hadad III of Damascus (802–? B.C.) on the one side and Zaccur of Hamath and Lagash on the other.[35] Such a conflict probably absorbed the energies of those states to a great extent.

Israel's policy of restoration under Kings Joash and Jeroboam II was apparently successful, at least so long as the small Syrian states were occupied with military operations. During the reign of Jeroboam II, Amos alludes (in 6:13) to two victories (won probably in the first half of the reign) at Lo-debar and Karnaim, which contemporaries probably regarded as important stages in the carrying out of the recovery promised by Jonah son of Amittai, one of the prophets of salvation, of the lost regions east of the Jordan "from the entrance of Hamath as far as the Sea of the Arabah" (2 Kings 14:25) or "the Brook of the Arabah" (Amos 6:14)—that is, from a point in the north that is difficult to determine[36] as far as the northern end of the Dead Sea in the south.[37]

These victories, which in the eyes of contemporaries probably seemed to confirm Jonah's prophecy of salvation, led Israel, it seems, to widespread self-confidence (see Amos 6:1-7), national elation (Amos 6:8; 8:7), and hope of an imminent "Day of Yahweh" (Amos 5:18-19), with which the popular mind connected the expectation of still greater successes. But on the whole this was an apparently unrealistic assessment of the true situation.

As a matter of fact, perhaps from as early as the middle of Jeroboam II's reign, the situation was in reality once again increasingly shaped by difficulties originating abroad (chiefly among the Aramaeans and the Ammonites).[38] When Amos (6:6b) speaks of "the ruin of Joseph," which is already a fact but which causes no concern in responsible circles in the capital, Samaria (these being interested solely in a life of pleasure), the words—assuming they are not due to the disciples of Amos—refer to a clear deterioration of Israel's situation around 760 B.C., at least in the border regions of the northern kingdom.

The circumstances in which Israel found itself at this time must in any case have been such that Amos's bitterly ironical reversal of Jonah son of Amittai's prophecy of salvation (6:14) could seem quite plausible to his more soberminded contemporaries[39]—namely, that Yahweh intended to raise up a people that would press Israel hard "from the entrance of Hamath to the Brook of the Arabah"—that is, across the entire territory east of the Jordan. And Amos must certainly have seemed credible to some of his contemporaries when he intones a lamentation over Virgin Israel, "fallen, no more to rise" (5:1-3), as though the catastrophe that threatens the entire northern kingdom has already befallen it, or when, in explanation of his version of the basket of summer fruit, he has Yahweh speak words that sum up the only expectation left to Israel in Amos's view: "The end has come upon my people Israel."[40]

The Social Background of Amos's Message

The threat to the northern kingdom that was becoming increasingly visible on the frontiers of Israel at this time may have provided an external occasion and point of departure for Amos's pessimistic view of the future. The real basis for it, however, is to be sought not in the external circumstances of that particular moment but in the internal state of Israel itself.[41] The military successes won under Joash and Jeroboam II had evidently laid the basis for a period of relative peace and economic prosperity. These new conditions, however, seem to have benefited primarily, if not exclusively, the governing upper class in the northern kingdom of Israel. At any rate, it is the extravagant, luxurious lifestyle of "the notable men of the first of the nations" (6:11)—as Amos mockingly calls the members of the leading class among the Israelites in Samaria, the capital—that the prophet heavily emphasizes in his utterances.

An external, quite visible indication of the wealth of this stratum of society was its increased home-construction activity. The growing demand for comfort on the part of the Israelite upper class was no longer satisfied, it seems, by a house that would adequately lodge a family. Rather, the well-off wanted separate homes for each of the two main seasons, each residence in its appropriate climatic surroundings—a "winter house" and a "summer house" (3:15a).[42] These houses were carefully built of hewn stones (5:11a). The special type of dwellings built by the Israelite upper class can now be seen from archaeological findings—for example, at Tirzah (Tell el-Far'a), a city near Shechem and capital of the northern kingdom for a time (see 1 Kings 14:17; 15:21, 33; 16:6, 8, 9, 15, 17, 23–24).[43] These were quite different from the family dwellings of the early monarchy (tenth to ninth century B.C.), which were all of the same size and similar in layout and construction. At Tirzah the larger houses of the rich, easily recognizable by their more careful and expensive construction, were all located in a separate quarter and divided by a wall from the rest of the city, where the smaller and more poorly built houses of the remainder of the population were to be found.

Luxury also marked the interior furnishings of the homes of the rich: the use of ivory and costly ebony (or: many-colored hangings or tapestries? Amos 3:15b).[44] The expensive decor of these homes of the upper class was matched by the costliness of the appointments and furniture. Thus Amos (3:12; 6:4) mentions upholstered couches decorated with artistically carved ivory panels.[45]

It was on these couches that the wealthy reclined for the numerous banquets that they held (Amos 3:12; 6:4–6; cf. Isa. 28:1–4; for Judah or Jerusalem, see Isa. 5:22; 28:7–13; Mic. 2:11). They often began drinking wine early in the day, as Isaiah tells us when speaking of Jerusalem (Isa. 5:11–12), but the same may probably be taken as applying to the upper class in Samaria. The women of the leading circles of Samaria, whom Amos mockingly compares to the cows of Bashan across the Jordan, were no exception. Perhaps his comparison refers to their ample figures, but it is more likely that he is thinking of their pretensions and inconsiderateness.[46] The boisterous high spirits that reigned at the feasts found expression in music and song (Amos 6:5; see also 6:7; 8:3a; for Jerusalem, Isa. 5:12).

The luxury of this upper class is also seen in the fact that not only was meat taken for granted at the banquets—although the masses could only rarely afford it and therefore only rarely saw it on their tables—but the meats were of the choicest kinds: the flesh of calves that were kept in herds in the fields[47] and the flesh of calves that were fattened in stalls (Amos 6:4b).[48]

It was also taken for granted that the banqueters should apply only the best olive oil to their bodies (6:6a), and in all likelihood it is only an accident that Amos gives no detailed description of the expenditures that this upper class made for other cosmetics and for clothing, adornment, and other accessories. We probably need have no great scruple about filling in the lacuna here with the aid of the picture that the somewhat later prophet Isaiah gives of the elegant women of Jerusalem in his day (Isa. 3:16-24). The picture surely applies as well to Samaria in the time of Amos.

Amos's critical description of the life and doings of the leading class in the northern kingdom in the time of Jeroboam II is not meant as a critique of luxury as such nor is it inspired by the concerns of a critic of culture (of whatever school). Nor does his criticism imply an ideal of the simple life or ascetical zeal.[49] Amos was opposed to the luxury and expensive lifestyle of the upper class in the northern kingdom because he regarded the price paid for this wealth as being too high: the impoverishment, even destitution, of other strata of the population. Moreover, the means by which this wealth was gained—the unscrupulous exploitation of the masses by those in a position to oppress them—seemed to him impermissible, at least when judged by norms that he regarded as alone compatible with the basic experience of Israel. This basic experience of Israel past and present told the nation (as the few passages show in which Amos describes the relationship between Yahweh and Israel in positive terms) that Yahweh scorns what is mighty (*gbh*, Amos 2:9a) and strong (*hason*, 2:9a) and takes his place at the side of the weak and the small (*qaton*, 7:2, 5) in order to provide them with living space (2:9) and the necessities of life (7:1-3, 4-6).[50]

Social reality in Israel in the time of Jeroboam II was, of course, in striking contrast to this ideal. The Book of Amos paints a picture of a society in which many preferential distinctions were observed and in which a comprehensive solidarity was replaced by a system of social violence that ran from top to bottom through all classes of society. The fact that in Samaria many forms of "intimidation" (*mehûmot rabbôt*) and "oppression" (*'asûîm*) were the order of the day and that "violence and repression" (*hamas wasod*) marked social relationships, as Amos 4:9-10 points out (see also 2:7a; 8:4), is confirmed for the northern kingdom by the somewhat later prophet Hosea (Hos. 4:2). In Judah, too, at least from the second half of the eighth century on, similar phenomena must have been widespread, as we can see from passages such as Isaiah 10:1-2 (cf. 5:8, 20); Micah 2:1-2; Jeremiah 5:26-28; 22:13-17; Ezekiel 34:2-6.[51]

The most conspicuous means used by those in positions of economic and social power to promote their own interests was the manipulation of the law, which only too readily opened the door wide to a perverted and corrupt administration of justice. Especially the poor, the widow, the orphan, and the foreigner—in other words, those groups among the people that were in a weak position both socially and legally—and, generally speaking, those low on the social scale were the victims of this biased interpretation of the law in favor of the mighty and the socially influential (see Amos 5:7, 10; 6:12; also 1 Kings 21; Isa. 1:21–23; 5:20; 10:1–2; Mic. 3:1–3, 9–11). The upper class, insatiably hungry for land and bent on building up great landed estates (for Judah see Isa. 5:8; Mic. 2:1–2) robbed the people of house and land on a scale that reminds us of the repression of the peasantry in the history of East German territories.[52]

But the social and economic pressure on the socially weak in Israelite society at that time did not cease when they had been driven from their ancestral land. In fact, Amos's reproaches and his concrete images of the typical situations of injustice that were evidently characteristic of the time show us that oppression and exploitation took many forms and ran right through the various strata of society. It seems that the upper class was not alone in practicing these injustices.

Amos's accusations make especially clear the unmerciful fate of a debtor at the hands of his creditors (whoever they might be) if he defaulted or perhaps even became completely insolvent. They endeavored without pity to extract everything they could from him in payment of rent due or taxes still owed, in the form of grain (Amos 5:11).[53] They ruthlessly impounded a debtor's vintage in order to collect a fine (*'anôs*) that may have been set arbitrarily high to begin with (Amos 2:8b; see Exod. 21:22; Deut. 22:19; also Exod. 21:19, 30, 33–34).

Just as unfeelingly, and often for no good reason (see Mic. 2:10), they kept pledges, even a man's garments (Amos 2:8a), if he seemed to possess nothing else that could serve as a pledge—despite the express prohibitions in the ethical and legal tradition of Israel (Exod. 22:25; Deut. 24:10–13, 17; Job 22:6; 24:9).[54] A trifling debt—the price of a pair of sandals, for example—was enough to bring the insolvent debtor into slavery for debt and to be sold (Amos 2:6) and bought (8:6) as a serf.

The worst instance of this reduction of human beings to the level of things in the context of the creditor-debtor relationship is probably the one described in Amos 2:7: the slave girl kept in a dwelling in order to satisfy the lust of both father and son (contrast Exod. 21:7–11).

The widespread indigence of the people was, finally, a source of gain even for the merchants, in whom the Canaanite spirit lived on. As Amos tells us (8:5–6), these men could not even wait for the completion of the days of the new moon and the Sabbaths (on which they were not to do business) but were eager to use their false grain-scales and money-scales (see Mic. 6:10–11; Hos. 12:8) in order to sell at a profit the lowest grade of wheat to the poor.

Summing up the impression given by the accusations Amos makes in his prophetic reproaches, we may say that in the first half of the eighth century

Israel had reached the climax of a development that had begun at the latest in the period when the monarchy came into existence and that had now brought the traditional economic and social system into a condition of profound crisis. The real problem here was not that a quondam purely agricultural society had been overwhelmed by the transition (reminiscent of developments in the early capitalist period) to more intensive industrial activity, trade, and urban living.[55] Rather, these changes were themselves connected with a development that a society still basically agricultural was to some extent compelled to accept as part of the shift from a tribal constitution to statehood.

Both Israel's original tribal constitution (a democratic union of families, its members being in principle free and equal villagers with full civil rights) and its special approach to the possession of land (the concept of inherited possession [*nahᵃlā*] of land that was, as far as possible, allotted in equal measure to each clan and family—though account was taken of variations in the number of members, Num. 26:52–56; 33:54—and was never to be sold but passed on only through hereditary succession) had their roots in the settlement of the national territory and in the processes by which it was accomplished.[56] The basic rights of the free Israelite citizen were connected with the possession of property that had been distributed by lot at the time of the settlement: his right to take part in the judicial assembly that convened at the gate of each village; his right to participate in public worship; and, especially in the earlier period, his right and duty to accept military conscription (Neh. 2:20).

It is true, of course, that even in that initial period the vicissitudes of nature and history as well as good or bad fortune in the management of the land, and differences in the fertility of the soil all helped start a process of social differentiation. Among the factors that played a part were, in particular, variations in weather, which led to different levels of crop yield from region to region; droughts, which affected the human members and the livestock of different families in varying degrees; the contrasting consequences that the duty of military service and the accompanying obligation of the soldier to provide his own equipment had on the cultivation of each family's land, especially because the men in service were unavailable for work in the fields as long as the campaign lasted. Then, too, it was possible only within limits to make provision for the slowly increasing population by clearing new land (Josh. 17:14–18), because it was soon used up. The result was that a part of the population did not have an adequate portion of land.

Thus even before the monarchy was instituted, there existed, on the one hand, a small group of rich and prestigious families (1 Sam. 25:2–3) and, on the other, a numerically much larger stratum of poorer families. It seems that there were already a great many persons "in distress" and "in debt" (1 Sam. 22:2), who were forced to hire out as soldiers, or as day laborers, or were, even at that early period, so hard pressed as to have no choice but to accept serfdom because of the debts they had run up. The existence of this last option is suggested by the fact that the basic provisions of the "Book of the

Covenant'' (Exod. 20:22-23:33*) begin with a law about Hebrews enslaved because of debt (Exod. 21:2-11).

The monarchy, which began in Israel under Saul as a defense against the Philistine threat, was originally a response to the need of the moment. The king was the head of the army, and the monarchy was intended primarily to ensure a united military leadership in defensive warfare. But it became in its turn the decisive factor in the evolution of society.[57] This was due to the new demands that this new institution in Israel brought with it, at least from the time of David and Solomon on, and which required extensive resources for their satisfaction.

In addition to the expenses of the royal household and the royal building program, we must mention here the shift from the old ungainly levy of farmer-warriors to an efficient army of mercenaries (with their war chariots) that developments in the art of war required. Also to be mentioned is the establishment of a complex bureaucracy whose growth in numbers and whose constant amplification through division of responsibilities we can still follow with the help of the information supplied to us by the Old Testament for the period of Saul (1 Sam. 14:47-52), David (2 Sam. 8:15-18; 20:23-26), and Solomon (1 Kings 4).[58] Last, but not least, there were the expenditures required for the worship of Yahweh, which the monarchy had taken under its charge.

The consequences for the individual of this constitutional change brought by the formation of a state are forcefully explained in the speech that is put into the mouth of Samuel in 1 Samuel 8:10-18.[59] First, there was the general loss of status that free Israelite citizens suffered and that turned them into subjects, with limited rights, of an oriental despot. Then, in addition to the obligations of compulsory labor and taxes, there were in particular the king's encroachments on the land system in the interests of the newly established crown lands,[60] which were used especially for bestowing fiefs on officials. The nucleus of the crown lands, which provided the primary means of defraying the many and increasing expenses of the monarchy, consisted of the lands of the family to which the king himself belonged. Only in a limited degree was it possible to increase those holdings through conquest or through the purchase of land (such purchases were possible, in the main, only in formerly Canaanite areas where there were fewer laws regarding property rights; (see 2 Sam. 24:18-25; 1 Kings 16:24). The crown lands were extended chiefly by the acquisition of property that lacked an owner because the family had died out or the owner had gone abroad (2 Kings 8:1-6) or had been executed for a capital crime (1 Kings 21:1-19). The monarchy now took over the right of succession from the clans and families, which formerly had the right to dispose anew of such ownerless property.

Even more than the monarchy and its expansion of the crown lands, the establishment by the kings of a new aristocracy—an upper class of administrators—affected the life of the free peasantry throughout the country.[61] This aristocracy of civil servants resided in the capital but exercised administrative functions in the various districts of the country. These functionaries were recruited—in the early days of the monarchy at any rate, but surely later on as well—at least in part from the educated upper class of the old Canaanite city-states and other territorial enclaves that since the time of Saul and David had been ever more fully integrated into Israel. These officials brought into Israel a different conception of property and of the acceptability of striving to acquire property than the peasantry of Israel had. This new outlook probably soon became that of Israelites who had made their way into the upper class. Unlike the Israelites, the Canaanites regarded land as a commodity that could be freely transferred. Moreover riches and pursuit of gain were, in their view, unqualifiedly positive values.

With their own lands and those bestowed on them by the king as a base, the officials of Canaanite background, but probably also such Israelites as belonged to the administrative upper class, sought to increase their holdings at whatever cost and therefore without heed to the restraints, highly esteemed in Israel, imposed by solidarity and an adequate livelihood—restraints that set strict limits on the striving for further property. In the process these officials did not always act within the law but all too often made unscrupulous use of the power given them by the king in order to enrich themselves at the expense of the rural population of Israel dependent on them.

Another factor in the worsening of the situation of rural Israel was the transition under the monarchy from the old barter economy to a money economy.[62] To the extent that the latter took over in Israel, it became more and more difficult to meet deficits, and especially taxes due, by means of what one produced. On each occasion money, the medium of exchange (originally silver in the form of bullion that was weighed), had to be acquired first. This led to numerous debts, which in the course of time the debtor became increasingly incapable of paying off. A small farmer, for example, could get into a hopeless situation because, after a year of drought, he could obtain the seed he needed only at a high price, whereas the return on a subsequent, even very good, harvest was exceptionally small. The result was that a rural family could no longer pay off its debts but instead, if this up-and-down chain of events was repeated, worked itself into an ever worse predicament. Such quandaries were a source of profit to all creditors (e.g., to the tax collectors who could either grant a delay in the payment or else advance the date of payment) but especially to the local Canaanite merchants who provided the population with the necessities of daily life (whereas international trade was a royal monopoly).

Amos predicted a brutal downfall for Israel, which was experiencing its final period of prosperity in the time of Jeroboam II. No boastful appeal to the divine favor shown by God's choice of Israel (Amos 3:1-2; 9:7-8; see also 5:14-15), no cultic performance (Amos 5:21-27; see also 5:4-6), could change its destiny or bring security (Amos 5:18-20). In his prophecy Amos had in mind chiefly the Israel that had achieved eminence, and the mighty ones of the nation: the influential representatives of society who had profited, and were still profiting, most from developments in Israel. But he also had in view those others who had gone along with the trends of the times in order to get whatever might be left over for themselves.

The God of Amos is not the defender of the political and social system, as the Israel of that age thought him to be, or of its questionable "achievements." Rather he refuses it any permanence and even any right to permanence. The God of Amos is the God of the lowly, the victims who were crushed without pity in the economic machinery of the Israel of that age. Amos sees Yahweh as the God of much more than Israel; he makes him the God of the entire world (1:3-16; 9:7-8). We might almost say that he does so because his God no longer has a home in Israel, any more than do the victims driven from home and land with whom he identifies himself. But perhaps we ought rather to say that Amos universalizes this God in order that he may be able all the more effectively to resist the Israel that has abandoned the conception of life and values that Yahweh requires and guarantees.

Amos regarded the victims of the Israel in which he carried out his ministry simply as victims; he did not promise them a future. But he did, like his younger prophetic contemporaries, name the values that were important to his God. He regards as desirable the "good" (*tôb*, Amos 5:14-15; cf. Mic. 6:8), the "right" (*nᵉkohā*, Amos 3:10), and, above all, "justice and righteousness" (*mispat ûsᵉdaqā*, Amos 5:24; cf. Isa. 1:16-17, 27). These he failed to find elsewhere, and therefore in his eyes the "needy" man (*ᵉbyôn*) is at the same time the "righteous" man (*saddîq*, Amos 2:6b).[63] It is not competitiveness and the ruthless pursuit of gain that should be taken as a model, but rather solidarity and the provision of adequate living conditions for all. Not long after Amos, Micah will sum up this social model in a terse principle: "A man and his house, a man and his inheritance" (Mic. 2:2),[64] and in so doing will make an ideal out of a principle followed among the small farmers in the early period of the old clan system. Now, in changed social conditions, this principle acquires a wholly new character as a vision of a just social order.

With his emphasis especially on "justice and righteousness" as the fundamental values to be realized in the common life of human beings (precisely because they had been lost in contemporary society), Amos is the first to enunciate a basic theme of the history of Western society. Isaiah and Micah especially will follow him in this. After them it will be repeated in similar terms by Hesiod in Greece (ca. 700 B.C.).[65]

NOTES

1. On what follows, see what I have already written in my "Amos—Das Porträt eines Propheten," *Stimme der Gemeinde*, 24 (1972) 113-15, 145-46, 193-96, 225-27, 289-92. This sketch is expanded and developed in the present essay.

2. This is the order of the prophetic books in the Hebrew Bible. The order in English versions of the Bible is somewhat different.

3. On this point, see O. Kaiser, *Einleitung in das Alte Testament* (Gütersloh, 3rd

ed., 1975), pp. 196ff., where he discusses questions concerning the date when each prophet began his ministry.

4. The dates given here are from the chronological table drawn up by A. Jepsen in the commentary by W. Rudolph, "Joel-Amos-Obadja-Jona," KAT, 13/2 (Gütersloh, 1967).

5. This earthquake is perhaps the same one that has been archaeologically established at Stratum VI of the upper city at Hazor and that destroyed Hazor during the reign of Jeroboam II. See Y. Yadin in M. Avi-Yonah, ed., *Encyclopedia of Archaeological Excavations in the Holy Land*, 2 (London, 1974), pp. 485 and 495.

6. See J. Milgrim, "Did Isaiah Prophesy During the Reign of Uzziah?," VT, 14 (1964) 178ff.: "Excursus B. II 10ff. and the Earthquake."

7. In the tradition regarding the activity (and grave) of a man of God from Judah in 1 Kings 13 (2 Kings 23:15-18) there is perhaps a popular echo of Amos's ministry at Bethel. See J. Wellhausen, *Die Composition des Hexateuchs und der historischen Bücher des Alten Testaments* (Berlin, 4th ed., 1963), pp. 277-78; O. Eissfeldt, "Amos und Jona in volkstümlicher Überlieferung" (1964) in his *Kleine Schriften*, 4 (Tübingen, 1968), pp. 138-39.

8. On this point, see especially R. Smend, "Das Nein des Amos," EvTh, 23 (1963) 416ff.

9. This interpretation has been proposed very energetically by E. Würthwein: "Amos-Studien," in his *Wort und Existenz: Studien zum Alten Testament* (Göttingen, 1970), pp. 68-110; see also H. Graf Reventlow, "Das Amt des Propheten bei Amos," FRLANT, 80 (Göttingen, 1962).

10. See Z. Zevit, "A Misunderstanding at Bethel, Amos VII 12-17," VT 25 (1975) 783-90; but see too the critical reaction to Zevit's theses in Y. Hoffman, "Did Amos Regard Himself as a Nābî?," VT, 27 (1977) 209-12. The tense relationship between Judah and Israel in the first half of the eighth century can be seen by the military conflict between Amaziah of Judah and Joash of Israel that began in 788 B.C. and ended in defeat for Israel (2 Kings 13:12; 14:8-15).

11. On this point, see H. Schult, "Amos 7, 15a und die Legitimation des Aussenseiters," in H. W. Wolff, ed., *Probleme biblischer Theologie. Gerhard von Rad zum 70. Geburtstag* (Munich, 1971), pp. 462-78; but Schult's thesis—that the motif in 7:15a of the "call of the shepherd or countryman at his work" is to be understood "not biographically but 'ideologically' . . . as a means of 'legitimating the outsider' "—is hardly convincing.

12. Less convincing is the thesis of A. S. Kapelrud, *Central Ideas in Amos* (Oslo, 2nd ed., 1961), pp. 5-8, who sees Amos as exercising administrative tasks in connection with the flocks and the sycamores belonging to the Jerusalem temple. For other attempts to interpret him as a religious functionary, see S. Segert, "Zur Bedeutung des Wortes NOQED," in *Hebräische Wortforschung. Festschrift zum 80. Geburtstag von Walter Baumgartner*, VT Suppl., 16 (Leiden, 1967), pp. 279-83.

13. See T. J. Wright, "Amos and the 'Sycamore Fig,' " VT, 26 (1976) 362-68.

14. On the questions of prophetic tradition that are discussed briefly here, see the more detailed treatment in H. Gunkel, "Die Propheten als Schriftsteller und Dichter," in H. Schmidt, *Die grossen Propheten und ihre Zeit*, SAT, 2/2 (Göttingen, 1915), pp. xxxvi-lxxi; A. H. J. Gunneweg, *Mündliche und schriftliche Tradition der vorexilischen Prophetenbücher als Problem der neuren Prophetenforschung*, FRLANT, 73 (Göttingen, 1959), and the more recent summary in Kaiser, *Einleitung*, pp. 272-78.

15. For the problems this raises in the effort to reconstruct the "authentic" ele-

ments of tradition in the prophetic literature, see W. Schottroff, "Jeremia 2, 1-3. Erwägungen zur Methode der Prophetenexegese," ZThK, 67 (1970) 263-94, esp. 293-94.

16. *Joel and Amos*, W. Janzen, S. Dean McBride, Jr., and C. A. Muenchow, trans. (Hermeneia Series, Philadelphia, 1977), esp. pp. 106-13. This volume is a translation of Wolff's Dodekapropheton 2. *Joel und Amos*, BK, 14/2 (Neukirchen-Vluyn, 1969).

17. "Joel–Amos," esp. pp. 100-103.

18. According to Rudolph these secondary parts of the text include the following verses, or parts of a verse, or even single words (indicated by an asterisk): Amos 1: 11*; 2:4b*, 12; 3:1b*, 7, 13; 4:10a*; 5:13, 26b; 6:2b*; 8:3a*, 8b (?), 13-14; 9:6b*, 9a*.

19. See, e.g., B. W. Nowack, *Die kleinen Propheten*, HK, 3/4 (Göttingen, 2nd ed., 1903), pp. 121-23; K. Marti, *Das Dodekapropheton*, KHC, 13 (Tübingen, 1904), pp. 150-53; B. Duhm, *Die Zwölf Propheten. In den Versmassen der Urschrift übersetzt* (Tübingen, 1910), pp. 1-20; idem, "Anmerkungen zu den Zwölf Propheten. I. Buch Amos," ZAW, 31 (1911) 1-18.

20. *Die kleinen Propheten übersetzt und erklärt* (Berlin, 4th ed., 1963), pp. 1-10, 67-96. Wellhausen regards the following verses as spurious: Amos 1:9-12; 2:4-5; 4:12-13; 5:8-9, 26; 6:2, 9-10; 8:6, 8, 11; 9:5, 8-15.

21. See, e.g., J. Willi-Plein, *Vorformen der Schriftexegese innerhalb des Alten Testaments. Untersuchungen zum literarischen Werden der auf Amos, Hosea und Micha zurückgehenden Bücher im Zwölfprophetenbuch*, BZAW, 123 (Berlin-New York, 1971), pp. 15-69, 254-68.

22. For example, for the assumption of a thorough deuteronomistic redaction of the Book of Amos: W. H. Schmidt, "Die deuteronomistische Redaktion des Amosbuches," ZAW, 77 (1965) 168-93. For Wolff's "Bethel exposition of the Josianic age" and the role played in this by the hymnic passages in Amos 4:13; 5:8-9; 9:5-6; E. Sellin, *Das Zwölfprophetenbuch*, KAT, 12 (Leipzig, 2nd ed., 1929), p. 193; F. Horst, "Die Doxologien im Amosbuch," in his *Gottes Recht*, ThB, 12 (Munich, 1961), pp. 155-66.

23. For what follows, see especially the detailed description of the historical events by R. Labat and O. Eissfeldt, *Die altorientalischen Reiche*, 3 (Fischer Weltgeschichte 4, Frankfurt, 1967), pp. 25-51, 169-80. Also: M. Noth, *The History of Israel*, P.R. Ackroyd, trans. (New York, 2nd ed., 1960), pp. 238-50; A. H. J. Gunneweg, *Geschichte Israels bis Bar Kochba*, ThW, 2 (Stuttgart, 1972), pp. 96-101; S. Herrmann, *A History of Israel in Old Testament Times*, J. Bowden, trans. (Philadelphia, 1975), pp. 227-42.

24. On the literary problems of this passage, see M. Noth, *Überlieferungsgeschichtliche Studien* (Darmstadt, 2nd ed., 1957), p. 75; A. Jepsen, *Die Quellen des Königsbuches* (Halle, 2nd ed., 1956), appendix "Übersicht über Quellen und Redaktionen." For the interpretation of 2 Kings 14:27 as a deuteronomistic attack on Amos (against Amos 8:26), see F. Crüsemann, "Kritik an Amos im deuteronomistichen Geschichtswerk," in Wolff, *Probleme*, pp. 57-63.

25. See, e.g., A. Jepsen, ed., *Von Sinuhe bis Nebukadnezar. Dokumente aus der Umwelt des Alten Testaments* (Stuttgart-Munich, 1975), p. 161 and plate 75. But see also S. Yeivin, "The Date of the Seal 'Belonging to Shema' (the) Servant (of) Jeroboam,' " JNES 19 (1960) 205-12; he dates the seal to the time of Jeroboam I (927/6-907 B.C.).

26. See, e.g., Jepsen, *Von Sinuhe*, pp. 161-63. For the interpretation and dating of

this group of texts, see M. Noth, "Das Krongut der israelitischen Könige und seine Verwaltung," in this *Aufsätze zur biblischen Landes- und Altertumskunde,* 1 (Neukirchen-Vluyn, 1971), pp. 159–82, and Y. Aharoni, *The Land of the Bible. A Historical Geography* (London, 1968), pp. 315–27.

27. For the historical problems connected with the passage in Chronicles, see, e.g., M. Noth, *Überlieferungsgechichtliche Studien,* pp. 141–43, and the discussion in P. Welten, *Geschichte und Geschichtsdarstellungen in den Chronikbüchern,* WMANT, 42 (Neukirchen-Vluyn, 1973), index of biblical passages.

28. This is the view of, for example, Noth, *History of Israel,* p. 250, and Gunneweg, *Geschichte Israels,* pp. 100–101.

29. On this point, see Noth, *History of Israel.*

30. On this battle, which is known to us from Assyrian sources, see W. W. Hallo, "From Qarqar to Carchemish. Assyria and Israel in the Light of New Discoveries," BA, 23 (1960) 39–40; Jepsen, *Von Sinuhe,* pp. 152–55.

31. See the account given of the events in the inscription on the stele of King Mesha of Moab in Jepsen, *Von Sinuhe,* pp. 148–52.

32. The date of the events to which allusion is made in the undoubtedly genuine stanzas of the poem on the nations at the beginning of the Book of Amos (1:3–8, 13–15; 2:1–3, 6–9, 13–16) is disputed. But probably "they need not refer to new clashes in Amos's own time, but may cover the whole period of the dynasty of Jehu" (Herrmann, *History of Israel,* p. 234).

33. See Hallo, "From Qarqar," pp. 40–43; Jepsen, *Von Sinuhe,* pp. 155–59.

34. See Hallo, "From Qarqar," pp. 43–46; on the effect that the decline of Assyria and the expansion of Urartu had on Israel and its neighbors, see S. Cohen, "The Political Background of the Words of Amos," HUCA, 36 (1965) 153–60.

35. See Jepsen, *Von Sinuhe,* pp. 159–61.

36. According to Noth, *History of Israel,* p. 228, the reference is to "the frontier as it was in the age of David and Solomon, which included a strip of the city-state territory in the northern land east of the Jordan with Ramoth in Gilead"; for a more detailed discussion, see Noth, *Aufsätze,* 1:271–75, 2:158–60. But most scholars are of the opinion that the "entrance of Hamath" was much farther north—namely at Riblah about halfway between Damascus and Hamath; for a summary of the discussion, see W. Zimmerli, *Ezechiel,* BK, 13/2 (Neukirchen, 1969), pp. 1213–16. In this connection the view is sometimes defended that, as 2 Kings 14:28 seems to suggest, Jeroboam II succeeded in winning control of Damascus and Hamath; see A. Malamat "Aspects of the Foreign Policies of David and Solomon," JNES, 22 (1963) 6–8; M. Haran, "The Rise and Decline of the Empire of Jeroboam Ben Joash," VT, 17 (1967) 278–84; also O. Eissfeldt, " 'Juda' in 2. Könige 14, 28 and 'Judäa' in Apostelgeschichte 2, 9," in his *Kleine Schriften,* 4 (Tübingen, 1968), pp. 99–120, and " 'Juda' und 'Judäa' als Bezeichnung nordsyrischer Bereiche," pp. 121–31.

37. The "brook of the Arabah" (Amos 6:14) is probably identical with the wādi kefrēn on the eastern side of the Jordan; see A. H. van Zyl, *The Moabites* (Pretoria Oriental Studies 3, Leiden, 1960), pp. 147–48.

38. Thus Cohen, in his "Political Background," who regards especially the attacks of Aramaeans and Ammonites on Israel that are mentioned in Amos 1:3, 13, as occurring during the second half of the reign of Jeroboam II. According to Haran, ("Rise and Decline"), however, the expansionist policy of Israel under Jeroboam II reached the high point of its success precisely during this period with the subjection of Damascus and Hamath.

39. For another view, see, e.g., W. H. Schmidt, *Zukunftsgewissheit und Ge-*

genwartskritik, BSt, 60 (Neukirchen-Vluyn, 1973), pp. 15-23, esp. 22-23. Schmidt maintains that the point of departure for the prophets was "the presentiment of a general future that would affect the entire people and was already making its mark on the present"—in other words, the prophetic "certainty about the future" (p. 18)—and that this future "could not be inferred simply from the present historical situation" (p. 22) in which the prophets were exercising their ministry. Thus the period of Amos's ministry, for example, gave no basis for fear of a coming catastrophe.

40. The initial picturing of the earthquake (Amos 2:13; 3:15?; 9:1), which depicts the end awaiting Israel, is increasingly supplemented, or possibly replaced, by pictures of a military catastrophe (Amos 2:14-16; 9:1-4; etc.).

41. On what follows, see the following works that explain the general background of the social criticism of the prophets: A. Alt, "Der Anteil des Königtums an der sozialen Entwicklung in den Reichen Israel und Juda," in his *Kleine Schriften zur Geschichte des Volkes Israels*, 3 (Munich, 1959), pp. 348-72; H. Donner, "Die soziale Botschaft der Propheten im Lichte des Gesellschaftsordnung in Israel," OrAnt, 12 (1963) 229-45; K. Koch, "Die Entstehung der sozialen Kritik bei den Propheten," in Wolff, *Probleme*, pp. 236-57; G. Wanke "Zu Grundlagen und Absicht prophetischer Sozialkritik," KuD, 18 (1972) 2-17. On Amos in particular, see G. Botterweck, " 'Sie verkauften den Unschuldigen um Geld,' " BuL, 12 (1971) 215-31; M. Krause, "Das Verhältnis von sozialer Kritik und kommender Katastrophe in den Unheilsprophezeiungen des Amos" (dissertation, Hamburg, 1972); M. Fendler, "Zur Sozialkritik des Amos. Versuch einer wirtschafts- und sozialgeschichtlichen Interpretation alttestamentlicher Texte," EvTh, 33 (1973) 32-53. See also S. Hom-Nielson, "Die Sozialkritik der Propheten," in *Denkender Glaube. Festschrift C. H. Ratschow* (Berlin-New York, 1976), pp. 7-23.

42. But according to S. Mittmann, "Amos 3, 12-15 und das Bett der Samarier," ZDPV, 92 (1976) 166-67, the reference is to "the two palaces or palace quarters of the royal residence; suitably furnished, each was used for one of the seasons. They represented a luxury that only a king, and sometimes not even a king, could afford." See Jer. 36:22 and the inscription of King Barrākib of Sam'al from Zincirli in H. Donner and W. Rölling, *Kanaanäische und aramäische Inschriften*, 2 (Wiesbaden, 1964), pp. 232-34, No. 216.

43. See R. de Vaux, "Tell El-Far'a (North)," in M. Avi-Yonah, ed., *Encyclopedia of Archaeological Excavations in the Holy Land*, 6, 2:400ff.

44. The traditional Hebrew text at the end of Amos 3:15— "many houses come to an end—oracle of Yahweh"—seems to be a corruption, but the emendations differ according to the passages chosen as parallels for restoring the original reading: Ezek. 27:15 (Marti, *Dodekapropheton*, p. 178); or Ezek. 27:24 (Donner, "Die soziale Botschaft," p. 237, n. 19); or Prov. 7:16 (Mittmann, "Amos," p. 150).

45. See H. Gese, "Kleine Beiträge zum Verständnis des Amosbuches," VT, 12 (1962) 438; Mittmann, "Amos," pp. 149-67.

46. Thus G. Dalman, *Arbeit und Sitte in Palästina*, 6 (1939; reprint: Hildesheim, 1964), p. 176. There is no basis for the supposition of H. M. Barstal, "Die Basanskühe in Amos IV, 1, " VT, 25 (1975) 286-97, that what we have here is an attack on a fertility cult.

47. See Dalman, *Arbeit und Sitte*, and, by way of complement, the following statement on modern Turkey in K. and L. Barisch, *Istanbul* (Cologne, 1977), p. 178: "The flavor of veal depends largely on the feeding habits and age of the animal. The best flavor is found in animals that have grazed on thyme. They should not be over

eighteen months old, or they will already be too tough for a gourmet. Lamb's flesh that still has a good deal of fat and iron from the mother's milk is, despite the usual opinion, much harder to digest than sheep's flesh, which is often preferred to veal because it looks more appetizing and cooks more quickly. Veal, on the other hand, is much tastier.''

48. See Dalman, *Arbeit und Sitte*, pp. 178–79, 285–86.

49. A "nomad ideal" supposedly stands behind the critical attitude of the preexilic prophets to social trends in contemporary Israel, according to S. Nyström, *Beduinentum und Jahwismus. Eine soziologisch-religions-geschichtliche Untersuchung zum Alten Testament* (Lund, 1946), pp. 122–58. But see also W. Schottroff, "Soziologie und Altes Testament," VF, 19 / 2 (1974), pp. 51 and 56–60.

50. On Amos's acceptance and treatment of Israel's historical traditions, see J. Rieger, *Die Bedeutung der Geschichte in der Verkündung des Amos und Hosea* (Giessen, 1929), pp. 2–44; J. Vollmer, *Geschichtliche Rückblicke und Motive in der Prophetie des Amos, Hosea und Jesaja*, BZAW, 119 (Berlin, 1971), pp. 8–54.

51. It is unlikely that a development in Judah similar to that in Israel began only after 733 and 722 B.C., due to the flight of rich northerners who at this time supposedly bought up a good deal of land in Judah, as H. Bardtkle tries to show in his "Die Latifundien in Juda während der zweiten Hälfte des achten Jahrhunderts v. Chr.," in *Hommages à A. Dupont-Sommer* (Paris, 1971), pp. 235–54. See also W. Dietrich, *Jesaja und die Politik*, BEvTh, 74 (Munich, 1976), pp. 12–55, esp. p. 15, n. 5.

52. See H. Bechtel, *Wirtschafts- und Sozialgeschichte Deutschlands. Wirtschaftstile und Lebensformen von der Vorzeit bis zum Gegenwart* (Munich, 1967), pp. 127–28, 264–65; H. Mottek, *Wirtschaftsgeschichte Deutschlands. Ein Grundriss. 1. Von den Anfängen bis zur Zeit der Französischen Revolution* (Berlin, 5th ed., 1974), pp. 339–53.

53. H. Torczyner suggests that the difficult hapazlegomenon *bôsas̀kaem* be read as *sabs̀kaem* (see W. Baumgartner, *Hebräisches und aramäisches Lexikon zum Alten Testament*, 1 [Leiden, 1967], p. 158) and connected with the Accadian *sibsa sabāsu(m)*, "to collect taxes of grain" (see F. R. Kraus, "Ein Edikt des Königs Ammisaduqa von Babylon," in *Studia et Documenta ad iura orientis antiqui pertinentia*, 5 [Leiden, 1958], pp. 126–32). See also G. Prenzel, *Über die Pacht im antiken hebräischen Recht*, Studia Delitzschiana, 13 (Stuttgart, 1971).

54. See also the seventh-century "Plea of a Judean Reaper" that has been preserved on an ostrakon; the man's clothing has been taken as a pledge by an overseer. Text in K. Galling, ed., *Textbuch zur Geschichte Israels* (Tübingen, 2nd ed., 1968), pp. 70–71, No. 42.

55. Thus—but without justification—for example E. Neufeld, "The Emergence of a Royal-Urban Society in Ancient Israel," HUCA, 31 (1960) 31–53.

56. See F. Horst, "Das Eigentum nach dem Alten Testament," in his *Gottes Recht. Gesammelte Studien zum Recht im Alten Testament*, ThB 12 (Munich, 1961), pp. 203–21.

57. In addition to the studies of A. Alt and H. Donner (listed in note 41, above), see F. Crüsemann, *Der Widerstand gegen das Königtum. Die antiköniglichen Texte des Alten Testaments und der Kampf um den frühen israelitischen Staat*, WMANT, 49 (Neukirchen-Vluyn, 1978).

58. See T. N. D. Mettinger, *Solomonic State Officials. A Study of the Civil Government Officials of the Israelite Monarchy*, Collectanea Biblica, Old Testament Series, 5 (Lund, 1971).

59. See Crüsemann, *Der Widerstand*, pp. 60–73.

60. In addition to the works of A. Alt mentioned in note 41, above, see M. Noth, "Das Krongut der israelitischen Könige und seine Verwaltung," in his *Aufsätze zur biblischen Landes- und Altertumskunde*, 1 (Neukirchen-Vluyn, 1971), pp. 159-82; Y. Aharoni, *The Land of the Bible*, pp. 315–27; P. Welten, *Die Königs-Stempel. Ein Beitrag zur Militärpolitik Judas unter Hiskia und Josia*, Abhandlungen des Deutschen Palästinavereins (Wiesbaden, 1969).

61. See especially the work of H. Donner, "Die soziale Botschaft."

62. See H. Weippert, "Geld," BRL, 2nd ed., pp. 88–90.

63. See H. H. Schmid, *Gerechtigkeit als Weltordnung*, BHTh, 40 (Tübingen, 1968), pp. 111–13.

64. See A. Alt, "Micha 2, 1-5. *Gēs anadasmos* in Juda," in his *Kleine Schriften zur Geschichte des Volkes Israels*, 3 (Munich, 1959), pp. 373–81.

65. See Hesiod, *Works and Days*; H. Bengtson, "Griechische Geschichte von den Anfängen bis in die römische Kaiserzeit," *Handbuch der Altertumswissenschaft*, 3/4 (Munich, 4th ed., 1969), pp. 102-27; V. Ehrenberg, *Die Rechtsidee im frühen Griechentum. Untersuchungen zur Geschichte der werdenen Polis* (Leipzig, 1921); and, for the comparison with Old Testament prophecy, O. Kaiser, "Gerechtigkeit und Heil bei den israelitischen Propheten und griechischen Denkern des 8.-6. Jahrhunderts," NZST, II (1969) 312-28; but especially (and also for the similar socio-economic development in Israel and in Greece), H. G. Kippenberg, "Die Typik antiker Entwicklung," in Kippenberg, ed., *Seminar: Die Entstehung der antiken Klassengesellschaft*, stw 130 (Frankfurt, 1977), pp. 9–61.

4

The Prophetic Discourse and Political Praxis of Jeremiah: Observations on Jeremiah 26 and 36

JÜRGEN KEGLER

Recent years have seen an increasing interest in those aspects of prophetic preaching that have to do with criticism of society and social life. Politically involved communities of students and politically oriented student groups that are inspired by Christian motives have formulated their analysis and critique of society in the light of the critique offered by a Hosea, an Amos, or an Isaiah. In ecumenical dialogue the indictment of social and political injustice is playing an increasingly prominent role, and the connection with similar indictments in the judgment oracles of the prophets is implicitly or explicitly made. "Political theology" justifies its claim to criticize church and society not least by a conscious appeal to the radicalism of the prophets. The "theology of revolution" derives its revolutionary attitude to society from Marxism *and*—among others—the Old Testament prophets.

This growing awareness of a *political* dimension of Christian existence (I shall not discuss here the reasons for this awareness) has not failed to have an influence on the scholarly study of the prophets. There has been a greater interest in the relationship of the prophets to politics and a more careful study both of their indictments of society and of the theological and historico-traditional (more rarely, the economic) background of those indictments.[1] The main concentration in all this has been on the intention of prophetic preaching and, insofar as this preaching has political implications, on its political message. On the other hand, the problem of the political praxis of the prophets has been largely ignored,[2] despite the present-day call for a political praxis on the part of theologians and despite the appeal to the political

47

dimension of prophetic existence. Meanwhile, there has also been a continuation of the type of study of the prophets that pays no attention at all to the political aspects of prophecy.[3]

At this point the concept of political praxis must be defined. I am deliberately limiting the term "political praxis" to mean here the exercise of influence on the decisions of persons or institutions that have authority to decide and the power to back up their decisions. This limitation is necessary because at the present time there is a tendency in various quarters to regard every aspect of life as being in principle political. But such a broad concept is useless for describing social processes in which decisions are made that apply to a state in its entirety. In their own lives the prophets were affected by the decisions of rulers—decisions that, according to their preaching, meant the end of the nation and therefore their own end as well. The question of the prophet's political praxis is thus the question of their concrete activity and attitude in regard to those who exercised real power in their society.

That the question of the political activity of a given prophet is not out of place is clear from the simple fact that the Old Testament contains traditions that undoubtedly report very concrete political activities of prophets and prophetic groups. A very striking instance of political activity by a group of prophets is the anointing of Jehu by a disciple of Elisha, who thus incited and legitimized the rebellion against *Jehoram*, the reigning king (2 Kings 9). Unfortunately, we do not know what significance the writer-prophets assigned to such a tradition of political action by groups of prophets; the only thing sure is that they dealt extensively with traditions, accepted them, critically revised them, and gave them current application. But there are also indications in the writer-prophets that show that they exercised an influence on political developments and that their activity can therefore be described as political.

Political praxis calls for allies: political praxis that is intent on influencing those who make decisions requires access to those individuals or to others who can act as go-betweens. The function of such allies is to help in the carrying out of political aims and to ensure protection for the agent; it has therefore both an objective and a personal aspect.

These two aspects—protection and support in the accomplishment of political purposes from allies, at the political level, who are men of power and decision-makers—are to be found in the prophetic tradition, though little attention has been paid to them to date. Most instructive in this regard are certain data contained in the Book of Jeremiah. I shall study these by way of example and ask what they can tell us about the political praxis of this prophet.

Background

Let us begin by looking for a moment at the domestic and foreign political situation. In 609 B.C., the year when Josiah, king of Judah, died, Pharaoh

Neco, who had just returned from a successful expedition to Haran, deposed the reigning king, Jehoahaz, and replaced him with a son of Josiah, Eliakim by name. This appointment carried with it an obligation to pay tribute and be a faithful vassal. Eliakim, who was henceforth known as Jehoiakim, quickly adapted to the new power situation: "And Jehoiakim gave the silver and the gold to Pharaoh, but he taxed the land to give the money according to the command of Pharaoh. He exacted the silver and the gold of the people of the land, from every one according to his assessment, to give it to Pharaoh Neco" (2 Kings 23:35).

This short notice in the Old Testament makes it clear that the people had to bear the burden of the tribute; the amount (determined by royal officials) of the assessment on the land or on the produce to be expected from it determined the amount of the contribution. It is not said, however, that the palace treasures must also be used for the payment of the tribute. On the contrary, Jeremiah 22:13–19, the date of which is disputed, but which is aimed directly at Jehoiakim, makes it clear that Jehoiakim shamelessly exploited his subjects:

> Woe to him who builds his house by unrighteousness,
>   and his upper rooms by injustice;
> who makes his neighbor serve him for nothing,
>   and does not give him his wages;
> who says, "I will build myself a great house
>   with spacious upper rooms,"
> and cuts out windows for it,
>   paneling it with cedar,
>   and painting it with vermilion. . . .
> But you have eyes and heart
>   only for your dishonest gain,
> for shedding innocent blood,
>   and for practicing oppression and violence [vv. 13–14, 17].

These words are an open declaration of war on the king. They also show that Jeremiah takes sides. A king who does not support the cause of the wretched and the poor but instead creates wretchedness and poverty by his manner of government violates the express will of God. This kind of public criticism, which calls into question the entire way in which the king exercised power, could not but meet with resistance from the king.

The short passage in Jeremiah 26:20–24 shows how Jehoiakim dealt with opposition. It is an originally independent literary entity that reports the fate of a prophet of Yahweh.[4] Uriah, son of Shemaiah ('Urijjahû ben-sᵉma'jahû), from Kiriath-jearim, spoke with prophetic authority and foretold disaster for Jerusalem and Judah, just as Jeremiah did (as the text makes explicitly clear). The text thus asserts an identity of intention and function, of authority and fulfillment of mission in the two prophets. In so doing it presupposes a knowledge of Jeremiah's predictions of disaster. The writer is thus relying on a prior contextual knowledge on the part of the reader, in which the emphasis is on Jeremiah's prophecy of disaster for Jerusalem and Judah. This is a legitimate way of characterizing Jeremiah's prophetic activity, as reference to his prophecies of disaster for Jerusalem and Judah will show—for example, 1:15–16; 4:5–8, 11, 27–28; 5:14, 17; 6:1, 11–12; 9:16–21; 10:21; 13:12–13; 15:2, 13–14 (= 17:3–4); 18:15–17. These texts announce total destruction and do so with unalleviated harshness. In the intention of the writer it is against this background that the action of Uriah is to be understood.

Jehoiakim attempted to do away with the troublesome Uriah—a solution that was evidently not untypical of his manner of governing.[5] Uriah learned of Jehoiakim's intention (which suggests that Uriah had sympathizers at court) and fled to Egypt. The text explains Uriah's flight by reference to his understandable fear. Jehoiakim then sent an agent, Elnathan, son of Achbor, and some accomplices to Egypt, the country to which he owed his power (2 Kings 23:34). They kidnaped Uriah and handed him over to the king (Jer. 26:33). The prophet was put to death, and his body was buried in a clearly dishonorable manner.[6]

The passage is a short one, but it permits some instructive observations:

1) The murder of the prophet is, in my opinion, an undoubtedly political act on the part of the king. This is shown by the way in which the murder is carried out: the sending of emissaries to kidnap subjects in a foreign country is the mark of a despot and a still common way of eliminating opponents.

2) The manner of burial shows that a dramatic act of intimidation is intended: the mistreatment of corpses or their treatment in ways clearly meant to dishonor them symbolizes victory over the slain person and at the same time serves to intimidate his sympathizers (cf. 1 Sam. 31:10; 2 Sam. 4:12). We are probably not overshooting the mark when we suspect that by his actions Jehoiakim was attempting to deter potential or present supporters of the prophet. This in turn allows us to conclude that there existed a wider movement of opposition to the king; this inference is confirmed by the fact that Uriah was warned of the king's plot to kill him (v. 21b).

3) The fact that Jehoiakim pursued a prophet who had already fled shows that he judged the prophet's activity to be *political* and, concretely, a danger to his rule. But power is endangered only when a contrary power begins to take shape. Such a buildup can start when the public utterances of an individual find widespread agreement that is in oposition to the official views of those in authority, or when an individual dares to say openly what others venture only to think. In any event, such occurrences make it plain that the ruler and his policies are at odds with the people and their interests. Jehoiakim clearly regarded the effects of Uriah's actions as dangerous.

Against this background, verse 24 shows in a new light: "But[7] the hand[8] of Ahikam the son of Shaphan was with Jeremiah so that he was not given over to the people to be put to death." This somewhat roundabout sentence may be intended to indicate that Jeremiah would have been put to death, as Uriah had been, if Ahikam had not protected him; only this protection prevented his death. The writer would then be saying that Jeremiah's role was to be regarded as identical with Uriah's, but that, in contrast *('ak)* to Uriah, Jeremiah had a powerful helper to rescue him. What are we to make of this statement?

Almost all commentators are content to point out that Jeremiah evidently had a powerful friend at court, who kept him from the clutches of the king.[9] Only Nötscher has some further reflections on the political importance of Ahikam:

> Against these plots [i.e., the attempts to eliminate him] Jeremiah had a protector in an influential man named Ahikam, whose father, Shaphan, was probably the secretary (or minister) under Josiah, of whom 2 Kings 22:8 and 22:12 speak and whose son was Gedaliah, the governor appointed later on by the Babylonians (Jer. 40:5ff). Another son of Ahikam was Gemariah (36:10ff). Ahikam had held a responsible position at the court of Josiah and was one of those who, after the Book of the Law had been discovered in the temple, were sent by the king to Huldah the prophetess to receive her advice (2 Kings 22:12). Ahikam continued to show good will to Jeremiah, as did his son Gedaliah after him. This favor was a very important factor in the prophet's freedom to carry on his ministry.[10]

Ahikam was a member of the delegation sent to Huldah the prophetess, after the finding of the Book of the Law (*seper habbᵉrît*) in the temple, in order to ask her about the discovery. Ahikam's father, Shaphan, had the office of a *sopher* in the reign of Josiah.[11] Mettinger defines this office as follows: "The royal *swfr* was 'writer' par excellence and from the beginning responsible for the royal correspondence."[12] Begrich adds that the task of a *sopher* was to compose ordinances and regulations.[13] The office had extraordinary political importance and brought great power with it. Under Josiah, Shaphan evidently had the crucial task of carrying out the royal reforms to which the finding of the book led. The story in 2 Kings 22:12, 14 shows that at that time Shaphan's son Ahikam was likewise among the highly placed confidants of the king. It is thus clear that he was one of the persons who carried out the Josian policy of reform.

Jeremiah adopted a positive attitude to Josiah and his reform.[14] A common attitude to a politics of reform seems to have united the two men. May we think, then, that even in Josiah's time Jeremiah had contacts among the politicians who were implementing the reform? In any case, we grasp the full *political* significance of Ahikam's support of Jeremiah during the reign of Jehoiakim only when we bear in mind that Jeremiah was an opponent of the king and was the object of political persecution (Jer. 11:18–23; 20:1–6). Support for him meant great danger for the supporter. Now, such a commitment might well be explained by personal friendship or by attachment to the truth of the prophetic preaching, were it not that clear indications in Jeremiah 36 show the existence of a whole faction that was closely associated with Jeremiah.

If we look into the functions of the men named in Jeremiah 36, a surprisingly varied picture emerges. To begin with, it is in the chamber of Gemariah, son of Shaphan the secretary (the text uses the title *sopher*), that Baruch reads the scroll that Jeremiah had composed (v. 10). In other words, Jeremiah was on intimate terms not only with Ahikam but also with the latter's brother, Gemariah. Gemariah's son, Micaiah, acts as the messenger who keeps the secretary informed; Jeremiah's preaching is so explosive that those at the head of the government must be kept au courant.

There is a meeting going on in the chamber of Elishama, the secretary (v. 12). Present at it are the king's chief advisers. Those named are: Delaiah son of Shemaiah, Elnathan son of Achbor, Gemariah son of Shaphan, and Zedekiah son of Hananiah (v. 12). After Micaiah has given his report Baruch is summoned and asked to read the scroll again. The reaction of the assembled advisers is very interesting: "We must report all these words to the king" (v.16). This is the language of duty: as the king's foremost subjects they must keep him informed of all politically relevant happenings. But these men also give Baruch a bit of advice: "Go and hide, you and Jeremiah, and let no one know where you are" (v. 19). This is the language of conspiracy; this is how sympathizers speak to someone under political persecution.

The list of names in the text as we have it is intended to highlight the fact that these men, the chief administrators of the king, are supporting Jeremiah and helping him to escape the king's anger. Elnathan, Delaiah, and Gemariah are named again as men who vainly protest Jehoiakim's burning of the scroll (v. 24). These princes are accurate in their anticipation of the king's reaction: he orders the arrest of Baruch and Jeremiah (v. 26); "but the Lord hid them," and the sympathizers closed ranks.

From all this the following picture emerges:

• Sure allies of Jeremiah who play a leading role at the royal court are Ahikam, son of Shaphan,[15] Gemariah, son of Shaphan,[16] and Delaiah, son of Shemaiah.[17]

• The role played by Elnathan, son of Achbor, is somewhat unclear: he is one of those who stand up for Jeremiah,[18] but in Jeremiah 26:22 he is the one responsible for bringing the prophet Uriah back from Egypt. He is presumably the son of the Achbor who with others implemented the reform policies ordered by Josiah.[19]

• The role played by Micaiah, son of Gemariah, son of Shaphan, is unclear; the text mentions him only as a conveyer of information.[20]

• Elishama the *sopher*, who is evidently Shaphan's successor, is one of those who advise Baruch to hide. The fact, explicitly mentioned, that he initially kept the scroll in his chamber (vv. 20–21) and did not immediately bring it to the king seems to suggest that he first attempted to suppress the corpus delicti and make a verbal report. Unless, of course, the delay is simply a literary device to heighten tension, for the text shows an obvious interest in the fate of the written prophetic word.[21]

• Zedekiah, son of Hananiah, is mentioned only once;[22] it is therefore not possible to say anything about his functions.

Nötscher's reference[23] to the fact that Gedaliah,[24] one of Ahikam's sons who was appointed governor at Mizpah (Jer. 40:10) after the Babylonian capture of Jerusalem under Nebuchadnezzar, permits a very important political inference: the group that supported Jeremiah pursued a pro-Babylonian policy. The victorious Babylonians rewarded them for it by advancing Gedaliah. The policy was opposed to Jehoiakim's efforts to rid himself of his Babylonian overlords (2 Kings 24:1).

It was Jeremiah who voiced the most pointed criticism of Jehoiakim's policy, a criticism that culminated in the demand that the king bend his neck to "the yoke of Babylon" (Jer. 27). This was not the least of the reasons why the prophet was arrested as a traitor to his country (Jer. 37:11–16). The Babylonians honored Jeremiah for his attitude by making him promises of personal protection (Jer. 39:11ff.). But this amounts to saying that the Babylonians regarded Jeremiah's activity as *political*.

This activity was political from several points of view. To the group at court that more or less openly pursued a pro-Babylonian policy, Jeremiah was a figure of key importance. Supported by the authority of his prophetic office, he dared to bring the criticism of Jehoiakim and his policies out into the open. This same group at court was able by its secret protection to ward off from Jeremiah the danger he was incurring of being liquidated by the king. From a political standpoint Jeremiah's public function was to show that Jehoiakim's pursuit of autonomy was a rebellion against God's will and, in the last analysis, a deadly danger to the state, and to create an understanding of the need of accepting Babylonian supremacy. Objectively speaking, Jeremiah was the public spokesman of a faction opposed to the king.

From the viewpoint of Jeremiah himself and his mission, the association with the reform politicians under Josiah made his public ministry possible. Without their protection he would have suffered the fate of Uriah, as we are told in Jeremiah 26:24. I think we may even go a step further, although this is very much a matter of speculation. For Jeremiah this association was also a key condition for the accomplishment of the goals of his prophetic preaching. The fact that Baruch could use Gemariah's chambers as the place for reading the scroll shows clearly that Jeremiah was using his connection with the antiroyal faction in order to be able to carry on his own work. And this work was not limited simply to proclaiming what was unchangeable, but also included the dimension of concrete political change. This was what linked Jeremiah with the group at the court. Instead of rebellion against Babylon he called for submission (chap. 27), and this was precisely the aim of this group's policy. In other words, the two parties had reason for collaborating.

Prophecy and Politics

Insofar as Jeremiah's life was that of a prophet it was also political. His political praxis consisted in his public activity as a radical critic of the royal policy and its agents. He articulated his critique orally, in symbolic actions (chap. 19, 27, 28), and in writing. He was not content simply to call attention to the unchangeable. His intention was to cause a policy of autonomy to be changed into a pro-Babylonian policy—with the dependence this involved— as being the only way of ensuring the continuation of the nation's existence. The proclamation of this need for a new policy was one of his prophetic tasks, and he could carry it out only with the help of a group of influential politicians. This he found among the reform politicians under Josiah. Thus Jeremiah's political praxis also involved maintaining relations with this leading group of pro-Babylonian statesmen. It was a connection that ensured his survival. Precisely because Jeremiah thus linked his prophetic preaching with political praxis in such a striking way, he had to put up with periods of withdrawal from the public eye and, under Zedekiah, even of arrest. These are always symptoms of a political existence that includes opposition to the ruling power.

In saying all this I have already implied that Jeremiah's political praxis was not limited to the time of Jehoiakim. The biblical tradition enables us to see even now that there was an astonishing continuity in Jeremiah's political activity. After the death of Jehoiakim, his son Jehoiachin continued for a short time to resist Babylon. Jeremiah sharply criticized him for this: "As I live, says the Lord, though Coniah the son of Jehoiakim, king of Judah, were the signet ring on my right hand, yet I would tear you off" (22:24). With these words Jeremiah was renewing his radical criticism of an anti-Babylonian policy; the severity of the rejection was underscored by attributing it to God himself.

Jehoiachin's resistance soon collapsed. Nebuchadnezzar captured the city (597 B.C.), took Jehoiachin prisoner, and deported him along with the upper class and seven thousand soldiers. He placed Mattaniah, a brother of Jehoiachin, on the throne and renamed him Zedekiah.

M. Noth[25] has shown that the rule of Zedekiah, who was after all king by favor of the Babylonians, was resisted by many Jerusalemites. They continued to regard the deported Jehoiachin as their rightful king. The prophet Hananiah especially was the spokesman for this group, which was counting on the proximate return of Jehoiachin and the collapse of Babylonian supremacy (Jer. 28). Jeremiah continued to resist this movement. It was in his own interest to support Zedekiah in the latter's pro-Babylonian stance. But Zedekiah allowed himself in the end to be forced to adopt, like his predecessors, a policy of emancipation from Babylonian domination; he was hoping to receive military aid from Egypt.

It is not possible in the present short essay to analyze the conflicts between various interest groups among the Jews that led to Zedekiah's change of policy; the beginnings of such an analysis can be found in an article of A. Malamat.[26] In any case, Jeremiah once again began to criticize this return to an anti-Babylonian policy, although he did not adopt an attitude of complete rejection toward King Zedekiah himself (this mildness is perhaps an indication that Jeremiah realized the king had been forced into this policy). The prophet's attitude to the king emerges clearly in his conversation with Zedekiah during his imprisonment (Jer 38:14–28); the radical critique of royal policy did not preclude conspiratorial tactics.

Even after the second deportation (587 B.C.) Jeremiah continued his pro-Babylonian policy. He took a positive attitude to Gedaliah, the governor appointed by the Babylonians (chap. 41).[27] This kind of consistency in political outlook is proof enough that the prophet understood himself in *political* terms. His preaching of the word was accompanied by political praxis.

NOTES

1. For example, H. W. Wolff, *Joel and Amos*, W. Janzen, S. Dean McBride, Jr., and C. A. Muenchow, trans. (Philadelphia, 1977), introduction to the commentary on Amos; S. Cohen, "The Political Background of the Words of Amos," HUCA, 36 (1965) 153–60; H. Donner, "Die soziale Botschaft der Propheten im Lichte der Gesellschaftsordnung in Israel," OrAnt, 12 (1963) 229–45. The present chapter is the revised version of an essay that appeared under the title "Prophetie und politische Praxis—Beobachtungen zu Jer 26, 20–24," in *Festgabe für Hartwig Thyen zum 50 Geburtstag* (privately printed, 1977).

2. This can be seen from the terminology used. Thus the popular genre known as "symbolic action" (G. Fohrer, *History of Israelite Religion*, D. E. Green, trans. [Nashville, 1972], pp. 233ff.) suggests a priori a nonpolitical event; but in fact many of these actions (e.g., Isa. 20; Jer. 19; 27; 28; Ezek. 4; 5; 12) are striking and stirring political provocations.

3. This lacuna is especially notable in quite recent publications. This question of the political elements in the preaching of the prophets (to say nothing of a possible political praxis) is not raised either in G. Münderlein, *Kriterien wahrer und falscher Prophetie—Entstehung und Bedeutung im Alten Testament*, Europäische Hochschulschriften, 33 (Bern and Frankfurt, 1974), or in R. E. Clements, *Prophecy and Tradition*, Growing Points in Theology Series (Richmond, 1975). Even in S. Herrmann, *Ursprung und Funktion der Prophetie im alten Israel* (Opladen, 1976), there is no reference to any *political* functions of the prophets.

4. I follow here F. L. Hossfeld and I. Meyer, "Der Prophet vor dem Tribunal. Neuer Auslegungsversuch von Jer. 26," ZAW, 86 (1974) 30–50. G. Wanke has given a detailed analysis of chapter 26 in his *Untersuchungen zur sogenannten Baruchschrift*, BZAW, 122 (Berlin, 1971). He too regards the story of Uriah as originally an independent entity; v. 24 is a concluding observation. C. Rietzschel, *Das Problem der Urrolle. Ein Beitrag zur Redaktionsgeschichte des Jeremiabuches* (Gütersloh, 1966), p. 99,

considers v. 24 to be a tendentious addition in which the previous exoneration of the citizens of guilt in the fall of the state is altered to make them appear now as enemies of Jeremiah.

5. To the extent that one regards 2 Kings 24:4 as substantially historical.

6. This seems to be the meaning of *qibrê b'nê ha 'am*. It presupposes that Uriah belonged to an upper stratum of society that was accustomed to showing off its unique social position by a special place and manner of burial (see Isa. 22:15-19).

7. See KBL, 1:44.

8. *Yad* here means the power Ahikam had by reason of his office, and especially his power to protect.

9. W. Rudolph, *Jeremia*, HAT, 1/12 (Tübingen, 3rd ed., 1968), p. 171. A. Weiser, *Das Buch des Propheten Jeremia*, ATD, 20-21 (Göttingen, 1951-55) speaks of a "patron," which suggests someone playing the Maecenas.

10. F. Nötscher, *Das Buch Jeremia*, HSAT, 7/2 (Freiburg, 1934), p. 200.

11. 2 Kings 22:3, 8, 9, 10, 12, 14 = 2 Chron. 34:8, 15, 16, 18, 20.

12. T. N. D. Mettinger, *Solomonic State Officials: A Study of the Civil Government Officials of the Israelite Monarchy* (Lund, 1971), p. 42.

13. J. Begrich, "Sōfēr und Mazkīr," ZAW, 58 (1940-41) 1-29.

14. See 22:15, and Rudolph, *Jeremia*, p. iv.

15. Jer. 26:24.

16. Jer. 36:10, 12, 25.

17. Jer. 36:12, 25.

18. Ibid.

19. 2 Kings 22:12, 14. 2 Kings 24:8 mentions the daughter of an Elnathan as the mother of Jehoiachin; no connection with the Elnathan of Jer. 36 has been shown.

20. Jer. 36:11-13.

21. Jer. 36:12, 20, 21.

22. Jer. 36:12.

23. See above, pp. 50-51, and n. 10.

24. Jer. 39:14ff. = 2 Kings 25:22.

25. M. Noth, "Die Katastrophe von Jerusalem im Jahre 587 v. Chr. und ihre Bedeutung für Israel," in his *Gesammelte Studien*, 1, ThB, 6 (Munich, 3rd ed., 1966), pp. 354ff.

26. A. Malamat, "Jeremiah and the Last Two Kings of Judah," PEQ, 83 (1951) 81-87.

27. This point had been developed especially by K. Baltzer, "Das Ende des Staates Juda und die Messias-Frage," in *Studien zur Theologie der alttestamentlichen Überlieferungen. Festschrift G. v. Rad* (Neukirchen-Vluyn, 1961), pp. 33-43. On the various parties active ca. 587 B.C., see especially M. Smith, *Palestinian Parties and Politics That Shaped the Old Testament* (New York and London, 1971).

5

The Unchangeable World:
The "Crisis of Wisdom" in Koheleth

FRANK CRÜSEMANN

I am fascinated by the relevance of Koheleth. Unlike any other book of the Bible we can read him without intermediaries and think that we understand him.[1] Key sentences and insights can be directly translated into our everyday phraseology of resignation, although admittedly they lose something in the process. His summation, "all is vanity" or emptiness, a stirring of the air (*hebel*; 1:2; 12:8), is really not so different from our modern "everything is shit."

Koheleth is unable to find either meaning or reason for hope in the realities of his experience; wherever he turns he encounters sameness, unchangeable power structures, and, in the last analysis, randomness: do what you will, nothing changes. The resultant retreat into an individualistic enjoyment of life, even though with full awareness that it really does not bring much enjoyment and leaves a stale taste behind it, is something unparalleled in the Bible and seems to have a specifically modern ring to it. Critical-minded intellectuals, with their hidden or open despair and their feeling of being trapped in the "iron cage" of capitalism feel quite at home with Koheleth.[2]

In Koheleth keen rational observation and analysis turn into a resigned and often cynical acceptance of things as they are. With a bluntness greater even than that of the prophets, he acknowledges the universality of suffering as well of the power that causes suffering. At the same time, however, he insists that both of these are unchangeable. Any rebellion brings incalculable risks and is in any case pointless. And all this comes from the pen of a man who is evidently not badly off and doubtless has the means of enjoying life in the fashion he recommends.

Up to now, however, the question of what Koheleth's place in society has to do with his thinking has hardly been raised. And yet for me that is what is really interesting about him. Especially because my approach to exegesis bears the impress of, among other things, a church that on really important issues takes political positions that are often identical with those of Koheleth. Being rich and conservative, it renounces in principle the struggle for a more just world; like Koheleth it cannot harmonize God's action with the socio-political realities of our experience. The fear of becoming involved in conflicts and of losing its privileges is obviously connected with its tendency to take given reality as unchangeable. As long as the world lasts, there will be nothing new under the sun. This theological resignation in the face of so-called reality is often sold as the truly radical Christian attitude, and it seems reasonable. The attitude, in effect, of our churches in the conflicts of the present age—as we compare these churches, let us say, across the ecumenical spectrum—is uncannily close to that of Koheleth. But, as I remarked earlier, how many of us can say that we are far removed from the same attitude?

Here then, stated briefly and in broad terms, are some of the present-day concerns and areas of conflict that call for historical study. The linking of apparently radical rational criticism with a resigned withdrawal into individualism and with what is effectively a cynicism in the face of concrete suffering must be regarded as a challenge to the exegete. The effort to determine how the link came about, how indeed it could possibly have come about, must keep in mind the alternatives available then and now. The aim is to uncover one of the wellsprings of theological resignation and to enquire into its presuppositions and consequences.

We can expect only limited help from past and present studies on Koheleth. As early as 1932 Kurt Galling saw the scholars concentrating on four main questions, and not much has changed since then.[3] The study of Koheleth has focused on (1) the theme of the book, its organization, and the isolation of the units that make it up[4]; (2) the question of the I-statements and the "historical" allusions; (3) the connections with Near Eastern wisdom literature, and (4) with Greek philosophy. Thorough investigation of the geographical origin of Koheleth's ideas—Greece,[5] Egypt,[6] Mesopotamia,[7] as well as conceivable combinations of them,[8] are all possibilities—has not led to any fully convincing results. I shall not touch on this problem at all, inasmuch as the decisive question is of the basis and conditions for the possibility that at a particular time foreign elements exercised an influence in Israel. As regards the date and provenance of the book, I accept the broad consensus that Koheleth was active in Jerusalem around the middle of the third century.[9]

German Old Testament scholarship has almost unanimously avoided making any attempt to determine Koheleth's socio-historical context.[10] But in 1943/44 Robert Gordis had already shown that Koheleth unquestionably belonged to a rich and aristocratic upper class.[11] In Germany Hengel is the one who has most clearly come out for this view.[12] But no real connection has been established between this fact and the contents of the book. However, Hengel's reference to connections with somewhat later confrontations in the time of the Maccabean uprising is important and helpful in this context.[13] Perhaps the most concrete attempt to understand the man and his book comes from Bickerman: "Koheleth is a sage who in an age of investment teaches not dissipation but the enjoyment of wealth. Addressing affluent hearers his theme is the meaning of toil for the rich man."[14]

Many questions of method and content, then, have thus far received almost no attention from the scholars. Postexilic social history, which has been little studied—not least because of a dearth of sources—raises further important problems. Consequently, many of the considerations I shall propose can be regarded only as tentative; to some extent, even, I shall be simply raising questions and outlining tasks.

The basic methodological principle I shall be applying is the effort to relate all statements in the text to the concrete "social whole" of the time from which the text comes and to which it speaks. As Lukacs wrote in his *History and Class Consciousness*, "concrete analysis means . . . the relation to society as a whole."[15] Yet the isolation of individual phenomena—be they concepts, texts, genres, traditions, vital situations (*Sitze im Leben*), or responsible groups—from all the other phenomena of the same period seems often to be taken as the basis for exegetical work. Consequently, the reconstruction of the spiritual conflicts of the time, and especially of their relationship to social conflicts and their roots in production relationships, is avoided in principle. As a result, Old Testament scholarship often gives the impression that the various observable strands of tradition stand side by side in an apparently empty space. The connection with society as a whole can, in my opinion, be translated into a series of heuristic approaches and practico-pragmatic procedures, and thus linked up with classical exegetical methods.

It is perhaps not unnecessary for me to point out that I shall not be beginning with specialized kinds of textual analysis, with the relationship between speaker and hearers, and so on, or, concretely, with the question of the "schools" of that time, the role of the wisdom teachers, and so on. I do not regard that kind of ultimately textual approach as an alternative to the one I am taking here, but rather as a necessary completion or specification of mine.[16] But that other kind of approach can, in my estimation, be only the second step, not the first. Otherwise there is a danger of ending up with findings that are too abstract. I do not see that kind of detailed analysis as my task here.

In this essay I shall (1) investigate the fundamental breakdown of the act-consequence connection; (2) make a concrete application of my findings to some major themes of Koheleth; and (3) turn to the political and social statements of the book.

The Collapse of the Act-Consequence Connection

A basic presupposition of Koheleth's thinking is that there is no connection between what human beings do and how they fare. This means, of course, that the world and the God who acts in it are completely impenetrable, unpredictable, and unjust. Koheleth finds this state of affairs to be constantly confirmed by experience:

> 8:14 There is a vanity which takes place on earth,
>   that there are righteous men to whom it happens
>   according to the deeds of the wicked,
>   and there are wicked men to whom it happens
>   according to the deeds of the righteous.
> 9.2 One fate comes to all,
>   to the righteous and the wicked . . . ,[17]
>   to the clean and the unclean,
>   to him who sacrifices and him who does not sacrifice.
>   As is the good man, so is the sinner;
>   and he who swears is as he who shuns on oath.
> 9:3 This is an evil in all that is done under the sun,
>   that one fate comes to all.
> 9:11 Again I saw that under the sun
>   the race is not to the swift,
>   nor the battle to the strong,
>   nor bread to the wise,
>   nor riches to the intelligent,
>   nor favor to the men of skill;
>   but time and chance happen to them all.

This experience of the world is conceptualized in theological terms in 3:11:

> 3:11 He [God] has made everything beautiful in its time . . .[18]
>   yet so that he [man] cannot find out what God has done
>   from the beginning to the end.

God may, therefore, have assigned a meaning to what happens in the world, but human beings cannot discover any such meaning. "That which is, is far off, and deep, very deep; who can find it out?," Koheleth says in 7:24, speaking of the happenings of everyday life.

At the same time, it is impossible to influence or change the mysterious course of the world. The same is true of the God who stands behind everything and with whom the human person cannot debate because God is stronger (6:10):

> 7:13 Consider the work of God;
>   who can make straight what he has made crooked?

In this view of reality Koheleth differs completely from older Israelite wisdom as it finds expression above all in Proverbs 10ff. This older wisdom speaks consistently of an intrinsic connection between what human beings do and how they fare. "I have been young, and now am old; yet I have not seen the righteous forsaken or his children begging bread" (Ps. 37:25). This assertion can be taken as typifying the older wisdom in its entirety.[19] But the loss of the experience of living in a justly ordered world is something that preceded Koheleth and had already found expression in the Book of Job.[20] Koheleth brings Job to its logical conclusion.[21] This radical difference from the older wisdom has rightly been taken as marking a "crisis of wisdom" and has been described as consisting in the lack of any relationship between persons and either their actions or their fate.[22] God thus becomes an opaque, impersonal power of destiny that nothing can influence.

This difference between Koheleth and his predecessors must be taken as the starting point for understanding Koheleth. The exegetical literature has consistently described the difference as a break with tradition and thus as a landmark in the history of human thought. Correspondingly, the entire approach to it becomes a matter of looking for the roots of the change in the history of ideas and of theology.[23] As a result, the question of the reasons for the change is a priori excluded. Nor can a simple reference to the "spirit of the time" or the new "feeling about life" of the Hellenistic age suffice here.[24]

Inasmuch as the old wisdom in its reflection on experience saw everywhere an orderly connection between human behavior and human destiny (saw, that is, a just world), and inasmuch as this attitude changed so radically in the postexilic period, we must ask first of all whether a change of reality did not precede the change in thinking. Did the older wisdom and with it by far the greater part of Israel's preexilic literature—to say nothing of the corresponding texts from surrounding cultures—simply ignore reality?[25] Or, on the contrary, was it, in the last analysis, that Koheleth and with him—for example—postexilic prophetic literature simply overlooked what was in fact there to be seen? It is true, of course, that an existing tradition plays an important role in the shaping of experience generally and that in large measure it provides the categories for interpreting experience. Furthermore, each person's manner of life also plays an important role.[26] But when texts explicitly appeal to experience, it is not possible simply to prescind from the reality being experienced. On this key point, which plays a determining role in the entire feeling about life, I should like to try to give the change of tradition a basis in reality.

What lies behind the old principle, based on experience, that act and consequence are connected?[27] This question immediately calls up another: that of the connection of this thinking with a social class. A slave, or an Israelite who lost his land and became a slave to pay his debts, would hardly have seen their fate as wholly the result of their own wickedness. The prophets do not pass such a judgment, nor do, for example, the miracle stories about help given to the poor. One need only think, for example, of the miracles in the Elisha tradition. The older wisdom in Proverbs, and indeed wisdom generally, must, however, be regarded as expressing the outlook of a rich landed upper class. Gordis was the first to provide an irrefutable, even if somewhat unspecific, demonstration of this,[28] and the same view has since then been frequently repeated, although usually in even vaguer terms than Gordis used.[29]

Whether the outlook in question be rooted in the family or due to education or to a combination of the two,[30] in any case it sums up the experience of a class of free landowners who were influential in the state. During the later monarchy, it shared to a large extent the interests of the court and its school.[31] The Israel of this period was a society largely molded by segmentary—that is, kinship—structures; we may speak of a segmentary state.[32] Below the level of the state, and to some extent incorporated into the very structure of the state, kinship marked social relationships and created relationships of solidarity that afforded security, just as it left its mark on many of Israel's laws.[33] Ownership of land, which was a family matter, ensured a large measure of economic self-sufficiency.

Now, where ownership of land is uncontested and at the same time a segmentary solidarity reigns, it will be normal to expect a correspondence between what one does and how one fares. The problem of chance and contingency is not thereby eliminated, however, and in fact it forms a secondary but almost equally important theme in the earlier wisdom.[34] The basic human types found in Proverbs are the diligent and the slothful, the just and the wicked, the wise and the foolish. And experience is said to show that a due measure of sloth, stupidity, or behavior deviating from the social norm is usually at work when a person falls into distress and decline. This view is not to be thought of as evidence of an unrealistic contrast between traditional categories of thought and social reality. For in fact the man who is upright (*tsaddîq*) is one who meets the requirements set by his fellows and thus lives in accordance with the customs and norms of his group;[35] he can therefore depend on the solidarity of the group and will receive help from his kindred, just as he in turn gives the same kind of help.

I do not think, therefore, that we can deny the validity of the act-consequence relationship for the social stratum from which the earlier wisdom came, or deny that it was based on experience. It would be worthwhile to pursue this idea and to ask, for example, how tradition, experience, and ideology were interrelated here. It is clear, for example, that this kind of wisdom thinking could not comprehend a social crisis like that of the eighth century and would in fact be forced rather to gloss it over.

What were the changes that occurred in the time of Koheleth and of the composition of Job? Once again, I am attempting only to elucidate the basic content of experience, and for this I rely especially on the results of Kippenberg's work.[36] The determining factor in the new situation is, of course, the national disaster suffered by Israel, even if the wisdom literature does not reflect on it explicitly.[37] Israel and thus the landowning classes are now among the immensely rich and thus in a quite different degree the object of history. The social and political balance between the free peasantry and the monarchy that was characteristic of preexilic Judah has ceased to exist. Taxes and duties are levied by outside forces, bringing heavy burdens and serious causes of insecurity.[38] The pressure is intensified by the fact that the economy is increasingly based on money and then on coinage,[39] and the self-sufficiency of the individual farm and village is significantly undermined. Increasing pressure for productivity leads to the conversion of farmland to olive orchards and vineyards, which are geared to export.[40] Because the productive forces remain essentially unchanged, the inevitable result is a reduction in the number of units (families) that are productive.[41] The great and rapid economic changes, especially of the Hellenistic age, cause insecurity; they cannot be understood or controlled.[42]

It was indeed possible, especially through the reform of Nehemiah, to maintain a class of free small farmers,[43] but a rich class of aristocrats becomes at the same time an ever more clearly distinct entity.[44] Especially for the aristocratic class, a segmentary solidarity with poorer relations becomes a chancy matter.[45] In the Ptolemaic period the state begins to intervene much more fully and even directly in the economy[46] and seeks an enormous increase in its revenues.[47]

To some extent at least, the idea now becomes current, even in Judah, that all land belongs in the final analysis to the crown.[48] The Zeno correspondence "gives the picture of a very active, almost hectic commercial life, originated by that host of Greek officials, agents, and merchants who flooded the land in the truest sense of the word and 'penetrated into the last village of the countryside.' "[49] It was primarily the urban aristocracy that shared in this economic prosperity.[50] But the decisive factor was that this aristocracy became involved in the state system of taxes and imposts as a lessee of the state.[51] In so doing it came to represent objectively the interests of foreign rulers. This meant in turn its inevitable alienation from the other groups in Judah and, finally, the open conflict that broke out under Antiochus IV.

These few indications must suffice here. In point of fact, little Judah, a province ruled by foreigners and located on the periphery of history, could no longer understand the world and the way in which it was ordered, any more than it could the reasons for the economic fate of individuals. The decisive factors were probably the developing monetary economy, the decline in rural self-sufficiency and thus in the importance of land ownership, and the heavy burden of taxes and duties about which nothing could be done. All this was at the expense of segmentary structures and of the ethic of solidarity that was grounded in those structures. The growing economic inequality within kinship groups undermined both the structures and the ethic. The result—and this is all that concerns us here—was that the traditional norms of thought and action were no longer in harmony with social reality. Tradition and experience were diverging.

These basic facts are handled in different ways in postexilic Israel. Job and Koheleth adopt the pessimistic traditions of surrounding cultures (in which, we must think, similar processes had occurred at an earlier time),[52] because these were a help in giving expression to their own basic experiences. Later eschatological prophecy and early apocalyptic bear witness in their own way to a comparable experience of this world, but they look for an intervention of God that will change everything and restore justice.[53]

Major Themes

In the light of this first rough description of the experiential basis of Koheleth's thinking, I should like now to consider some principal aspects, questions, and themes of this book by relating them to the society of his day as a whole. If the collapse of the act-consequence relationship and thus the gap between experience and tradition is Koheleth's starting point, then it is here that his personal thinking will surface.

Break with the Yahwist Tradition

I begin with 1:9–11.

1:9   What has been is what will be,
         and what has been done is what will be done;
         and there is nothing new under the sun.
1:10 Is there a thing of which it is said,
         "See, this is new"?
      It has been already,
         in the ages before us.
1:11 There is no remembrance of former things,
         nor will there be any remembrance
      of later things yet to happen
         among those who come after.

It is utterly astonishing that in Israel, with its obsession with history, this kind of statement could be offered as a conclusion to be drawn from processes in the world of nature (vv. 4–8). Nor should we set this astonishment aside too quickly. After all, Koheleth's contemporaries did remember things from the past! Families preserved the genealogies that are such a characteristic part of, for example, the almost contemporaneous Books of Chronicles. More importantly, the Pentateuch, which was by now canonical, is full of genealogies; it is full of the past and of profound changes: Abraham, the exodus, Sinai, the settlement of the promised land.

I regard it as methodologically unacceptable to proceed as though Koheleth, a third-century intellectual, could possibly not have known the Torah. Disputes about whether or not, for example, it can be shown from verbal echoes that he made use of the creation accounts in Genesis[54] certainly have their place, but I am speaking here of something much more elementary. Basic elements in the self-understanding of Israel and even of the official Judah of his day are simply denied or ignored in Koheleth. This is a fact that is entirely independent of how good a knowledge he himself had of these texts and of whether or not he explicitly comes to grips with them.[55] In the earlier wisdom, for all its peculiarities, this is not the case in the same way. In its ethics, that wisdom is not only not very far removed from the laws of Israel,[56] but, as is being recognized more and more, it also has close connections with important literary products of the preexilic period: the succession narrative, the Joseph narrative, prophets such as Amos and Isaiah, and Deuteronomy.[57] Koheleth, on the other hand, challenges—and does so almost explicitly—the prophetic expectations of his day, which make use of the same word and speak frequently of the "new" (*hadash*) that is coming: the new covenant and the new heart, a new heaven and a new earth.[58]

Moreover, Koheleth is completely untouched by the religious conflicts with Hellenism that have begun in his century and that find expression in the legends about Daniel and in the Book of Esther.[59] In regard to the national God in the temple of Jerusalem, Koheleth advises only caution; the best thing is to have nothing to do with him (5:1ff). In his eyes God has been reduced to an incomprehensible power of destiny. Even his own ethical principles cannot be positively grounded in God.[60] In view of this entire attitude it can be regarded only as consistency on Koheleth's part that, unlike the earlier wisdom, he avoids the name of Yahweh in principle.

There is thus an unbridgeable distance from all the basic Yahwist traditions. The same distance separates him from the groups who maintain these traditions: the families in which genealogies are preserved, the priests and Levites who serve in the temple, those who want life to go on being regulated by the ancient laws of Israel, those who expect Yahweh to produce a radical change in the world.

Though we have thus far been unable really to situate all these persons in the Judean society of Koheleth's day, there is no overlooking the contrast between them and the group that thinks as Koheleth does: the aristocracy. We should not dissociate the increasing alienation of the aristocracy and its interests from those of almost all the rest of the people (as manifested, for example, in the absorption of the aristocracy into the system of state monopoly, which makes them agents of foreign overlords) from the ideological alienation represented by Koheleth. A few decades after Koheleth, a decisive part of this aristocracy will definitively separate itself from all that was of fundamental importance to Israel, and will attempt to embrace Hellenistic norms without reservation. Opposition to these norms will come from other circles and have its ideological basis in the Torah and the prophets.[61]

Materialization of Thought

"The protection of wisdom is like the protection of money," says Koheleth in 7:12. In order to characterize the relative value of wisdom he harks back here, as in other passages, to statements that sound traditional.[62] What is new here is, first of all, the special place assigned to money, or silver, in relation to the other forms of wealth. He is living in an age in which, as he says, everything can be had for money (10:19). Moreover, the "protection of money" has left a profound mark on his personal thinking.

More important, even, than the explicit value set on wealth[63] is the fact that Koheleth's really basic question, from a methodological point of view—or, if you will, the measure that he applies to everything—is related to wealth. In every situation he asks what is to be "gained." *Jitrôn* probably means "the net gain from an economic transaction," to use Galling's definition.[64] "What does a man gain by all the toil at which he toils under the sun?," Koheleth asks in 1:3, 3:9, and 5:15 (cf. 10:12). But, if one applies this commercial category to life as a whole, then, given the fact of death, the answer can only be: no gain (2:11). Nonetheless, Koheleth is able to assign wisdom a relative "gain" (as in 2:13; 7:12; 10:10). He is certainly not unjustified in doing so, we may say; he lives by it. The same is true of the king (5:8)—a point I must go into later on.

The basically "calculative" character of Koheleth's thinking is thus pervasive.[65] The result of applying so fundamentally impersonal a criterion as "net profit" is that the things that enrich life lose their savor. Life is reduced to enjoyment, and this in turn to eating, drinking, and sex. In the only passage (quite beautiful in itself) in which solidarity is mentioned, the notion remains completely abstract: "Two are better than one . . . " (4:9ff.). We are not even told what it is that binds the two together. Community is reduced to a matter of utility. No attention is paid to the multiplicity of human relationships that are to be found in, for example, the earlier wisdom. Parents and neighbors—to take but two instances—do not appear at all; children are not a positive value;[66] for women Koheleth has only contempt (7:26ff). He can even say: "Man does not know what love is, or hate" (9:1, JB).

We need only look for a moment at the Song of Songs with its talk of the love that is stronger than death and cannot be bought with money (Song 8:6-7), and we will see how alien from this Koheleth is. (Yet the compilation of this collection of songs was perhaps not far removed from Koheleth in time.) At every point Koheleth shows himself an isolated individual who stands alone before the world and undertakes to study it.[67]

It can hardly be denied that there is a correlation between this kind of thinking and the orientation of all activity in the Ptolemaic state (of which the aristocratic class in Judah was now a part) toward purely economic profit and productivity. The quest for gain undermines all traditional human relations. Koheleth's thinking, taking gain as its criterion, perceives everything as *hebel*, a stirring of the air.

Death

The meaninglessness and opaqueness of the world finds its climactic expression in death. In Koheleth's eyes death makes all human efforts antecedently useless. And he regards death as final and insuperable. Here is a representative passage:

3:19 For the fate of the sons of men
>   and the fate of beasts is the same;
>   as one dies so dies the other.
>   They all have the same breath,
>   and man has no advantage over the beasts;
>   for all is vanity.

3:20 All go to one place;
>   all are from the dust,
>   and all turn to dust again.

3:21 Who knows whether the spirit of man
>   goes upward
>   and the spirit of the beasts goes down to the earth?

3:22 So I saw that there is nothing better under the sun
>   than that a man should enjoy his work,
>   for that is his lot;
>   who can bring him to see
>   what will be after him?

In this view of death Koheleth is, at first glance, simply repeating ideas long cultivated in Israel.[68] At this point he is apparently conservative in regard to tradition. His rhetorical questions—"Who knows . . . ? " and "Who can bring him . . . ? "—suggest that he is rejecting other views.[69] If we agree that Koheleth was influenced by Greek thinking, this point becomes important methodologically. Why does he accept Hellenistic pessimism but not, for example, the Greek idea of immortality? This question makes it clear that nothing is to be gained by looking for the provenance of ideas unless one has first determined the principle that guides the selection of ideas.

On this very question of death, other circles in the Israel of Koheleth's day moved in the opposite direction. Some late psalms, such as Psalm 49 (v. 16) and Psalm 73 (vv. 24–25), but especially the early apocalyptic writing found in Isaiah chapters 24 to 27 (note esp. 25:8; 26:19), mark the first appearance in the Old Testament of hope in an action of Yahweh that will have the dead for its object. And in all these texts the hope is related to the very same problems that are at the center of Koheleth's thinking, for it is an answer to situations of injustice, to the uselessness of human effort, and to the lack of any recognizable divine intervention.

The early Israelite idea of death as an insuperable barrier is accepted by Koheleth in a seemingly conservative way, but in fact the idea has an entirely different function in his thinking. In him, for the first and last time, it serves to demonstrate the vanity of life. In an earlier day the conclusion drawn was entirely different. Not death in itself but only an early and untimely death was regarded as reason for despair; in itself death made life shine more brightly and inspired human beings to live it more intensely.[70]

In this context it seems to me important that Koheleth links the problem of death to the problem of one's heirs:

2:18   I hated all my toil
         in which I had toiled under the sun,
         seeing that I must leave it to the man
         who will come after me. . . .
2:21   Sometimes a man who has toiled
         with wisdom and knowledge and skill
         must leave all to be enjoyed by a man
         who did not toil for it.

Clearly, it is envy of his successor that turns life bitter for him. As a matter of fact, envy is for Koheleth one of the principal motives of human action, as he says in 4:4 (an insight that even in our century has been able to provide the basis for an entire theory of society!).[71] Moreover, it is evidently a matter of indifference to him whether the successor be a son or a stranger. The fact that he has an heir is no consolation to him; in fact, it is even a cause for resignation. We should recall at this point what Koheleth says in 6:3, that an abundance of children means nothing. Once again we see the rejection of segmentary categories and values. The name that is continued by an heir, protected by laws such as that of the levirate (Deut. 25:5ff.), and closely connected with the manner of ownership is no longer anything real to him.[72]

The role played by death in Koheleth has parallels in the history of religion: "Degree of individualization and experience of death are correlative."[73] It is the breakdown of supportive group identity in the class to which Koheleth belongs and the focusing of attention on the isolated individual and his or her "gain" that give death a fascination that eclipses everything else. Consequently we must agree with Leszek Kolakowski on the inverse genesis of the logical connection that Koheleth establishes between life and death:

> The abstract fear of death is a secondary phenomenon, a result of the feeling that life is meaningless, a product of the alienation of the individual consciousness from the historical reality of the human race, a consequence of the uneasiness experienced when facing the external world. The meaninglessness of life is not the consequence of the tormenting thought of death but rather its cause.[74]

In the society of which Koheleth was a member, the continued assertion of life as meaningful, the preservation of Yahwist traditions, and the call for righteousness meant, at least for certain groups, that persons looked to God for an intervention that would affect the dead.[75] Contrary to appearances, such an outlook represented adherence to the real tradition of faith and thus also to the ethic of solidarity and the ancient traditions of freedom. In societal terms the rebellion against Antiochus IV came, as Kippenberg has shown, from those strata in which segmentary structures had been preserved and had given persons the strength to resist.[76] In this rebellion hope in resurrection played a part that should not be underestimated (e.g., Dan. 12), but I cannot undertake here to draw more precise distinctions. Aristocratic circles did not share this hope; their interests lay elsewhere. At a later time the Sadducees (whose possible influence by Koheleth has long been debated, although a lack of sources probably makes the question impossible to answer successfully)[77] were evidently still unable to share this hope.

Ethics and Politics

Koheleth sees himself as living in an inexplicable world and faced with death as his inevitable fate. God he experiences only as an incomprehensible power of destiny. Adherence to traditional ethical norms proves to be senseless. In the ethical demands that he himself makes and in their political consequences the viewpoint dictated by his class probably emerges most clearly. From the viewpoint of methodology I am interested here primarily in placing a stronger emphasis on the political and social aspect of his statements than is usually done, and in locating them in the context of the society of his time.

When all is said and done, the only thing that Koheleth can recommend is, as everyone knows, the enjoyment of life, the *carpe diem:* eating, drinking, and sex:

9:7 Go, eat your bread with enjoyment,
  and drink your wine with a merry heart;
  for God has already approved what you do.
9:8 Let your garments be always white;
  let not oil be lacking on your head.
9:9 Enjoy life with the wife whom you love,
  all the days of your vain life . . .[78]
  because that is your portion in life and in your toil
  at which you toil under the sun
  [See also 3:12, 22; 5:17ff.; 8:15; 11:9–10].

But Koheleth is also aware that this course of action provides no real fulfillment; it brings no gain and has no meaning (see esp. 2:1ff.; 7:1ff.). This kind of enjoyment of life is not possible for everyone, and it requires certain conditions. Most of Koheleth's ethical and political assertions reveal their meaning when we pursue this line of thought.

We might begin with the fact that the enjoyment of life is possible chiefly for the young. The deterioration of old age and the picture of its obnoxiousness that is given in 12:1–8 represent a typical reversal of segmentary thinking, according to which the elderly embody the human ideal.

Above all, of course, a certain level of prosperity is one of the conditions for enjoying life. Riches alone are admittedly not enough, as Koheleth shows in a detailed critique in 5:9ff.: others want a share in this wealth; it can be lost in a surprisingly short time; it brings cares and insomnia. Here Bickerman's attempt to show in Koheleth a philosophy for a prosperous class that is to be

trained to withdraw from the stress and strain and to enjoy life is fully justified.[79] But the decisive point is that for Koheleth even the internal possibility
of enjoyment is a free gift of God, which means a gift that comes by chance:

> 5:19 Every man also to whom God has given wealth and possessions
> and power to enjoy them,
> and to accept his lot
> and find enjoyment in his toil—
> this is the gift of God.

We may say, in fact, that in this combination Koheleth sees the sole but quite
crucial action of God in this world.[80]

But this action is the exception, and the world that Koheleth sees is by no
means determined by it. The thing that characterizes this world is rather
domination. The statement that one person dominates another comes from
him: he sees himself living in a time when "man lords it over man to his hurt"
(8:9), a statement in which the word *lô* has, probably not accidentally, a
double reference. This lordship takes concrete form in a vast hierarchy and is
the cause of oppression and suffering:

> 5:8 If you see in a province the poor oppressed
> and justice and right violently taken away,
> do not be amazed at the matter;
> for the high official is watched by a higher,
> and there are yet higher ones over them.[81]
> 5:9 But in all, a king is an advantage
> to a land with cultivated fields.

Noteworthy here is the straightforward attribution of ubiquitous oppression and injustice to the hierarchic organization of the state. But Koheleth's
purpose is to advise his reader to accept this situation as inevitable and not be
upset by it. The disputed sense of verse 9 is probably that Koheleth wishes to
exempt the supreme member of the system—namely, the king—from his
criticism and to present his existence as a relative "gain." As thus interpreted
the Masoretic text does not have to be altered, and the verse is in clear agreement with other passages, especially 10:20. In Koheleth's conception of
things, God is not included as supreme guarantor, although he is to be found
in principle behind all that happens, even this.

Any criticism of this oppressive system, but especially of the king as its
representative, brings dangers that must be avoided. Koheleth's repeated ex-
hortations to obedience to the king are based on the consequences of disobedience:

> 8:2 . . .[82] Observe the precept of the king,
> and in view of your oath to God,

8:3 be not hasty to withdraw from the king;
  do not join in with a base plot,
  for he does whatever he pleases,
8:4 because his word is sovereign,
  and who can say to him, "What are you doing?"
8:5 He who keeps the commandment experiences no evil [NAB].

Whether "base plot" (literally, "evil thing," *dabar ra'*) refers to specific historical occurrences is, in my opinion, less important than the way in which subordination to a foreign power is justified here.[83] The key point in verses 3b–4 is the reference to a de facto power that must be approached with caution. On the other hand, we should not overlook the fact that at least in verse 2, but possibly in verse 5 as well, religious categories are used *(sh^eb\u00fb 'at 'eloh\u00eem, mitswa)*, though I cannot here discuss the possible interpretations of these terms.[84] However, inasmuch as such categories have no central importance elsewhere in Koheleth, their ideological function of lending support to authority is unmistakable.

In a few passages Koheleth does admit the real possibility of blunders by rulers (10:5) and of weak kings and the evil consequences their reigns bring (10:16ff.). But even, and in fact especially, in these cases the rule holds:

10:20 Even in your thought, do not curse the king,
  nor in your bedchamber curse the rich;
  for a bird of the air will carry your voice,
  or some winged creature tell of the matter.

These words show with definitive clarity the fear that dominates Koheleth's society and even lurks beneath his apparently so radical thinking. One had to reckon everywhere with eavesdropping and the presence of spies. The king and the wealthy, whose incorporation into the apparatus of the state is shown here more clearly than anywhere else, must be exempted from any criticism. One must always be ready to side with the ruling order.

But if prosperity and the avoidance of conflict are conditions for being able to enjoy life in peace, then many individuals will find the conditions impossible. Nothing shows more clearly the gulf dividing Koheleth from these disadvantaged persons than the still unmistakable cynicism of 5:2: "Sweet is the sleep of a laborer, whether he eats little or much." Even clearer is the following passage:

4:1 Again I saw all the oppressions
  that are practiced under the sun.
  And behold, the tears of the oppressed,
  and they had no one to comfort them!
  On the side of their oppressors there was power,
  and there was no one to comfort them.

4:2 And I thought the dead who were already dead
    more fortunate than the living who are still alive;
4:3 but better than both is he who has not yet been,
    and has not seen the evil deeds
    that are done under the sun.

When confronted with the concrete suffering in society Koheleth knows of
no comforter. He is sure that he himself is not called upon to fill this role—a
possibility that had been viewed far differently in the earlier caritative wisdom (see Prov. 24:11ff.!). Despite his negative view of death elsewhere—"a
living dog is better than a dead lion" (9:4)—death is the best and only thing he
can wish for the oppressed. A strange consolation! What would the individuals in question have thought of it?

Koheleth's social position and the cynicism that accompanied it (a cynicism of which he himself was, in all probability, hardly conscious) are again
manifest in 7:21:

Do not give heed to all the things that men say,
lest you hear your servant cursing you.

In the light of verse 22 the intended meaning here is probably: Do not
listen, lest you have to take steps against him, although knowing that you
yourself have occasionally uttered curses. All the more significant, then, is
what the verse reveals incidentally, as it were. First, that "men"—he himself
and his hearers and readers—have servants; secondly, that these servants
obviously have reason to curse their masters at least occasionally (without, of
course, having to fear any real punishment on this account—a dialectical
result of enlightenment); finally, that there is no need of inquiring into the
reason for the servant's curse and of trying to remedy the situation. The
acceptance of universal domination holds even here.

The last and clearest consequence of Koheleth's ethic of enjoyment is to be
seen in 7:16ff.:

7:16 Be not righteous overmuch, and do not make yourself overwise;
    why should you destroy yourself?
7:17 Be not wicked overmuch, neither be a fool;
    why should you die before your time?
7:18 It is good that you should take hold of this,
    and from that withhold not your hand;
    for he who fears God shall come forth from them all.

Here we see the radical thinker traveling the middle of the road. Surprisingly enough, one is to have equal amounts of righteousness and wickedness, but not overdo either, lest one incur risks! And this attitude is even
called "fear of God"[85]—a response that is born of weakness and resignation

and proves here to be "fear" in the full sense of the term.[86] Nowhere is the break with Israelite tradition so clear: one is not to be too much of a *tsaddîq!* The *tsaddîq* was a person who satisfied the claims of both God and human beings.[87] Now the only goal is to avoid all dangers, because God has long since approved whatever a person does (9:7). The only thing to watch for is not to get really involved in anything, not to get caught up in conflicts. Wisdom and righteousness, like sin and wickedness, are measured solely by how much danger they may entail. Pessimism here shows its lack of backbone.

Once we see clearly these ethical and political consequences of Koheleth's thinking, the attack made in the Book of Wisdom on a closely related type of thinking will not appear to be so wide of the mark. The attack is hardly directed against Koheleth himself; but the persons described in the attack have evidently emphasized in their practice only certain aspects of his thought. Here the comment is valid: "he created a school and made enemies."[88] In Wisdom 2 the godless and the wicked are initially described entirely after the manner of Koheleth:

2:1 For they reasoned unsoundly, saying to themselves,
  "Short and sorrowful is our life,
  and there is no remedy when a man comes to his end,
  and no one has been known to return from Hades."
2:6 "Come, therefore, let us enjoy the good things that exist,
  and make use of creation to the full as in youth."

But then the passage continues:

2:10 "Let us oppress the righteous poor man;
  let us not spare the widow
  nor regard the grey hairs of the aged.
2:11 But let our might be our law of right,
  for what is weak proves itself to be useless."

My starting point in this essay was the relevance, the topicality, of Koheleth. This certainly has a further basis in his poetic power. And we must also apply to him what Ernst Bloch has said of Schopenhauer, Koheleth's modern cousin: without him "it is impossible to conceive of hope, for otherwise 'hope' would be just a word or a kind of wretched trustfulness, which is the last thing that hope really is."[89] At the same time, however, Koheleth is not so much giving expression to something universally human as he is drawing the conclusions from a social development and expressing therein the interests of a particular class. In an age when traditional faith and inherited ethics had come into conflict with the world of experience, Koheleth thinks in terms of "the protection of money" and of a class whose interests clash with those of the oppressed strata of society. He is not, of course, a spokesman for this class nor yet merely an example of it;[90] on the other hand, his rejection of the

Yahwist tradition and ethic does reflect the isolation of this class from the rest of Israel.

A few decades after Koheleth the two opposing sides that are recognizable in his writing will be at the barricades. The resistance arose in circles that had preserved the remnants of peasant freedom and segmentary ways of life and in which some persons had held fast to temple, law, and prophecy and thus to ancient traditions of freedom and had in any case acquired some measure of Israel's still uncorrupted faith in an intervention of God on behalf of the dead. This alone made it possible "to grasp the objective possibilities present in reality and to fight for their fulfillment"[91] and thus for a real change in a seemingly so unchangeable world.

NOTES

1. On this point, see Gerhard von Rad's warning on method in his *Wisdom in Israel*, J. D. Martin, trans. (Nashville, 1972), pp. 297-98.

2. Max Weber, *The Protestant Ethic and the Spirit of Capitalism*, T. Parsons, trans. (New York, 1958 [1930]), p. 181.

3. "Kohelet-Studien," ZAW, 50 (1932) 276.

4. On this point, see W. Zimmerli, "Das Buch Kohelet—Traktat oder Sentenzen-Sammlung?," VT, 24 (1974) 221-30.

5. See the detailed discussion in R. Braun, *Kohelet und die frühhellenistische Popularphilosophie*, BZAW, 130 (Berlin, 1973); also M. Hengel, *Judaism and Hellenism*, J. Bowden, trans. (Philadelphia, 1974), 1:107-30.

6. P. Humbert, *Recherches sur les sources égyptiennes de la littérature sapientiale d'Israël*, Mémoires de l'Université de Neuchâtel, 7 (Neuchâtel, 1929); W. Rudolph, *Vom Buch Kohelet* (Münster, 1959), p. 17.

7. Especially O. Loretz, *Qohelet und der alte Orient* (Freiburg, 1964).

8. See H.-P. Müller, "Neige der alttestamentlichen 'Weisheit.' Zum Denken Qohäläts," ZAW, 90 (1978) 254-55.

9. See H. W. Hertzberg, *Der Prediger*, KAT, 17/4 (Gütersloh, 1963); K. Galling, *Der Prediger*, HAT, 1/18 (Tübingen, 2nd ed., 1969); Hengel, *Judaism*.

10. Thus the more recent commentaries of Hertzberg, Galling, and W. Zimmerli, *Das Buch des Predigers Salomo*, ATD, 16/1 (Göttingen, 1962). See H. Gese, "Die Krisis der Weisheit bei Kohelet," now in his *Von Sinai zum Zion* (Munich, 1974), pp. 168-79; A. Lauha, "Die Krise des religiösen Glaubens bei Qohelet," VTSuppl, 3 (Leiden, 1955), pp. 183-91; Loretz, *Qohelet*; F. Ellermeier, *Qohelet*, 1/1 (Herzberg/ Harz, 1967); E. Wölfel, *Luther und die Skepsis* (Munich, 1958); H. H. Schmid, *Wesen und Geschichte der Weisheit*, BZAW, 101 (Berlin, 1966), esp. pp. 186ff. The picture is quite vague in Braun, *Kohelet*, p. 178, and in von Rad (*Old Testament Theology* and *Wisdom in Israel*), although von Rad does at least describe this wisdom as connected on the whole with "the middle classes" (*Wisdom in Israel*, p. 17).

11. "The Social Background of Wisdom-Literature," HUCA, 18 (1943-44) 77-118; idem, *Koheleth—The Man and His World*, Texts and Studies, 19 (New York, 1955). See also H. L. Ginsberg, "The Structure and Contents of the Book of Kohelet," VTSuppl, 3 (Leiden, 1955) 138-49, and in a number of other works; E. Biker-

man, "Koheleth (Ecclesiastes) or The Philosophy of an Acquisitive Society," in his *Four Strange Books of the Bible* (New York, 1967).

12. *Judaism*, pp. 126-27. See also R. Kroeber, *Der Prediger*, Schriften und Quellen der alten Welt, 13 (Berlin, 1963), p. 24 and passim; Müller, "Neige," pp. 256ff.

13. *Judaism*, pp. 228-29.

14. "Koheleth," p. 165; see pp. 158-67.

15. *History and Class Consciousness: Studies in Marxist Dialectics*, R. Livingston, trans. (Cambridge, Mass., 1971), p. 50.

16. See esp. Hardmeier, *Texttheorie und biblische Exegese. Zur rhetorischen Funktion der Trauermetaphorik in der Prophetie*, BEvTh, 79 (Munich, 1978).

17. Deletion; see the commentaries.

18. I leave aside here the difficult and debated interpretation of 'ôlam.

19. On the act-consequence relationship, see, e.g., von Rad, *Wisdom in Israel*, pp. 124-37.

20. Thus Galling, "Kohelet-Studien," p. 291.

21. On this point, see F. Crüsemann, "Hiob und Kohelet. Ein Beitrag zum Verständnis des Hiobbuches," in *Werden und Wirken des Alten Testaments. Festschrift C. Westermann* (1979).

22. Especially Gese, "Die Krisis." But I cannot agree with his interpretation of the "fear of the Lord" (pp. 178ff.); on this, see Schmid, *Wesen und Geschichte*, p. 193, and n. 86, below.

23. I have not found a single attempt to relate the change in wisdom thinking to a change in reality that does more than make some very general references to the drift of early Hellenism, etc. But see Müller, "Neige," pp. 258-59.

24. Thus Hengel, *Judaism*, p. 121.

25. There can be no question here of ascertaining the reality content of texts from the surrounding cultures.

26. See the important remarks of von Rad on this point in *Wisdom in Israel*, pp. 303-4.

27. On what follows, see esp. C.-A. Keller, "Zum sogenannten Vergeltungsglauben im Proverbienbuch," in *Beiträge zur alttestamentlichen Theologie. Festschrift W. Zimmerli* (Göttingen, 1977), pp. 223-38.

28. "The Social Background of Wisdom-Literature," esp. pp. 105ff.

29. See above, nn. 11 and 12.

30. See, e.g., on the one side, H. W. Wolff, *Amos the Prophet: The Man and His Background*, F. R. McCurley, trans. (Philadelphia, 1973), and, on the other, H.-J. Hermisson, *Studien zur israelitischen Spruchweisheit*, WMANT, 28 (Neukirchen-Vluyn, 1968).

31. It will be enough here to refer to the connection between wisdom and Deuteronomy; see M. Weinfeld, *Deuteronomy and the Deuteronomic School* (Oxford, 1972), pp. 244ff.

32. On the concept and the reality, see F. Crüsemann, *Der Widerstand gegen das Königtum*, WMANT, 49 (Neukirchen-Vluyn, 1978), pp. 203ff., 215-16.

33. See esp. H. G. Kippenberg, *Religion und Klassenbildung im antiken Judäa*, SUNT, 14 (Göttingen, 1978), pp. 25ff. and passim.

34. See von Rad, *Wisdom in Israel*, pp. 97ff.

35. Thus, e.g., G. von Rad, " 'Gerechtigkeit' und 'Leben' in der Kultsprache der Psalmen," in his *Gesammelte Studien zum Alten Testament*, ThB, 8 (Munich, 3rd ed., 1965), pp. 225ff.

36. See n. 33, above.

37. It is not surprising that the first and basic disputes over this thinking should have come during the exile; see, e.g., Ezek.18.

38. Kippenberg, *Religion,* esp. pp. 50ff., 78ff.

39. Ibid., pp. 49ff.

40. Ibid., pp. 45ff.

41. Ibid., esp. p. 82

42. See, e.g., F. Heichelheim, *Wirtschaftsgeschichte des Altertums,* 2 (Leiden, 1961), pp. 438ff.

43. Kippenberg, *Religion,* pp. 55ff.

44. Ibid., passim but esp. pp. 82ff.

45. Ibid., pp. 36ff.

46. Ibid., pp. 78ff.

47. See M. Rostovtsev, *The Social and Economic History of the Hellenistic World* (3 vols., Oxford, 1941), 1:278ff.

48. Kippenberg, *Religion,* p. 79.

49. M. Hengel, *Judaism,* p. 43; the words Hengel quotes are from M. Smith in *Fischer-Weltgeschichte,* 6 (Frankfurt, 1965), p. 255.

50. See, e.g., Rostovtsev, *Social and Economic History,* p. 277.

51. Kippenberg, *Religion,* pp. 78ff.

52. See what Hengel says in his *Judaism,* p. 121.

53. How the optimistic type of wisdom, esp. Prov. 8, fits in here with its image of a world "in which he [man] does not need to be afraid" (von Rad, *Wisdom in Israel,* p. 193) must remain an open question; see the indications in Schmid, *Wesen und Geschichte,* pp. 149ff. and 189 on the structural similarities between optimistic wisdom and pessimistic wisdom.

54. See, e.g., Hertzberg's commentary, pp. 227ff.

55. Whether or not Nietzsche actually read Marx is unimportant in comparison with the undeniable fact that he writes as he does of a vast movement of workers (this, quite independently of whether or not he explicitly reflects on the subject). For a man of his position in society, the mere juxtaposition is significant.

56. See, e.g., E. Gerstenberger, *Wesen und Herkunft des apodiktischen Rechts,* WMANT, 20 (Neukirchen-Vluyn, 1965), pp. 110ff. and elsewhere.

57. See G. von Rad "Josephsgeschichte und ältere Chokma," in his *Gesammelte Studien zum Alten Testament,* ThB, 8 (Munich, 3rd ed., 1965), pp. 272-80; idem, *Wisdom in Israel,* pp. 46-47, 291; R. N. Whybray, *The Succession Narrative* (London, 1968), pp. 56ff.; H.-J. Hermisson, "Weisheit und Geschichte," in H. W. Wolff, ed., *Probleme biblischer Theologie. Gerhard von Rad zum 70. Geburtstag* (Munich, 1971), pp. 136-54; J. Fichtner, "Jesaja unter den Weisen," in his *Gottes Weisheit* (Stuttgart, 1965), pp. 18-26; Wolff, *Amos the Prophet*; M. Weinfeld, *Deuteronomy and the Deuteronomic School* (Oxford, 1972). These names are offered simply as providing presentations of a wide-ranging discussion.

58. Jer. 31:31ff.; Ezek. 36:26-27; Isa. 65:17.

59. Both achieved their final form during this third century; see the commentaries. On Hellenistic political philosophy, with which conflicts must have quickly arisen, see E. R. Goodenough, "The Political Philosophy of Hellenistic Kingship," YCS, 1 (1928) 55-104; Kippenberg, *Religion,* pp. 122ff.

60. On this point, see pp.69 and 72-73 of this volume.

61. See Kippenberg, *Religion,* pp. 87ff.

62. See, on the one hand, 2:12-14; 4:5-6; 9:17; 10:1-4, 12-15, and, on the other,

7:23ff.; 8:6–7, 17. I cannot provide here a presentation of the meaning of wisdom in Koheleth.

63. See p. 69 of this volume.

64. In his commentary, *Der Prediger,* p. 84.

65. Hertzberg, in his commentary, *Der Prediger,* p. 69.

66. On this point, see pp. 67–68 of this volume.

67. See Bikerman, "Koheleth," p. 154.

68. On this point, see O. Kaiser, in O. Kaiser and E. Lohse, *Tod und Leben,* Biblische Konfrontationen (Stuttgart, 1977), esp. pp. 15ff.

69. Thus Hengel, *Judaism,* p. 124. See also U. Kellermann, "Überwindung des Todesgeschicks in der alttestamentlichen Frömmigkeit vor und neben dem Auferstehungsglauben," ZThK, 73 (1976) 279ff.

70. See C. Barth, *Die Errettung vom Tode in den individuellen Klage- und Dankliedern des Alten Testaments* (Zurich, 1947), pp. 54–55.

71. H. Schoeck, *Der Neid. Eine Theorie der Gesellschaft* (Freiburg and Munich, 1966); as far as I can determine, Eccles. 4:4 is not taken up.

72. See Loretz, *Qohelet,* pp. 225ff.

73. E. Fuchs, *Todesbilder in der modernen Gesellschaft* (Frankfurt, 1969), p. 30, where he is accepting the results of the work of Lévy-Bruhl, Malinowski, and others. I cannot here go beyond this brief allusion to the point.

74. L. Kolakowski, *Der Mensch ohne Alternative* (Munich, 1964), p. 214.

75. I cannot here undertake to make the needed distinctions, for which there have until now been few items of concrete evidence as a working basis.

76. Kippenberg, *Religion,* pp. 87ff.

77. See, e.g., Bikerman, "Koheleth," p. 157.

78. Deletion; see, e.g., Galling's commentary on this passage.

79. Bikerman, "Koheleth," esp. pp. 158ff.

80. See, e.g., Galling's commentary on the passage.

81. In my opinion the text need not be changed (see, e.g., Hertzberg's commentary, pp. 119–21, and Galling's, p. 100). Only in v. 9 is mention made of the apex of the hierarchy, which is exempted from criticism.

82. See the Kittel and the Stuttgart editions of the *Biblia Hebraica,* and the commentaries.

83. Thus Hertzberg, in his commentary, pp. 50–51.

84. See Galling's commentary, p. 110; Hertzberg's commentary, pp. 164ff.

85. For a different but quite tortuous interpretation, see, e.g., Hertzberg's commentary, p. 154.

86. On the fear of God in Koheleth, see S. Plath, *Furcht Gottes,* AThANT, 2/2 (Stuttgart, 1962), pp. 80ff.: "It [this attitude] can only culminate in a fear that is born of weakness and resignation and that under dint of necessity accepts this only possible way of dealing with the ruler" (p. 82); cf. 5:6; 7:18; 12:13–14. Although the term is not used in 6:10–12, the statements there give precise expression to what, in my opinion, "fear of God" means in Koheleth.

87. See above, n. 35.

88. Hertzberg in his commentary, p. 237.

89. A. Münster, ed., *Tagträume vom aufrechten Gang. Sechs Interviews mit Ernst Bloch,* Edition Suhrkamp, 920 (Frankfurt, 1977), pp. 96–97.

90. The optimistic wisdom of Prov. 1–9 must come from approximately the same period and the same social class.

91. Ernst Bloch, in Münster, *Tagträume,* p. 117.

Part Two

New Testament

Introduction to Part Two

WOLFGANG STEGEMANN

When poor peasants in Solentiname (Nicaragua) read the Bible, they learn something about themselves. To them, unlike us, many of the gospel stories about Jesus of Nazareth do not seem at all foreign. They see reflected in these stories the same poverty and hunger, the same powerlessness in the face of oppression and violence, that marks their own lives. No ugly historical gulf seems to divide the world of the lowly of present-day Nicaragua from that of their counterparts in Palestine in the time of Jesus.

Moreover, those who read Ernesto Cardenal's excellent book *The Gospel in Solentiname*[1] will themselves gain a new access to the life of Jesus and his disciples in Palestine. They will feel that the God of Jesus Christ is utterly different—different, that is, from the God we have learned. He is not the relationless "Wholly Other," to use the strange formula under which he has become familiar to us. Rather this God is very much related to us affluent Christians, for he confronts us as indeed a "Wholly Other"—namely, as the God of the lowly of Palestine, Nicaragua, and elsewhere. This God of the poor and oppressed has become visible in a unique way in Jesus himself.

In this context we think immediately of Jesus' defending the tax collectors and sinners, healing the possessed and the sick, and leveling such unusually sharp criticism against the rich. This aspect of Jesus' life has led Friedrich Naumann to call him the great "man of the people": the man who, as one of the people, led a struggle on behalf of the people. So too in modern presentations of Jesus a certain amount of attention is paid to his sympathy for outcasts. But we seem able to think of Jesus' solidarity with the poor and the despised only as being a "downward movement" (Ernst Bloch), only as a case of a person in a higher social position becoming an advocate for the lowest social strata of his or her people. Was Jesus, however, really a radical outsider who took sides with the lowly? This conception directs Gerd Theissen's researches (in many respects convincing) into the Jesus movement in Palestine.

In the present book Theissen's picture of the ethical radicalism of the Jesus movement is subjected to a critical examination in terms of its textual basis in

81

the Bible. In the light of this criticism, it is doubtful that before the year 70 there really existed in Palestine a voluntary "vagabond radicalism" practiced by desperately poor followers of Jesus. Voluntary renunciation of possessions, the abandonment of family and home, and other ethical renunciations on the part of the disciples of Jesus are probably the product of a later interpretation of the Jesus movement by Mark and especially by Luke.

Jesus and his followers seem to have themselves belonged to the lowly of Palestine and to have shared the lot of the poor and the weak by force of circumstance rather than by a voluntary acceptance of such a life. The socio-historical interpretation of Mark 2:23–28 in part 2 of the present work points to this real experiential background of the earliest Jesus movement. It was not a rigorist ethos but radical personal suffering under, and because of, the condition of their people that led Jesus and his followers to a solidarity with their fellow Israelites and a confrontation with the cautious guardians of the status quo (and the rich). Jesus and his followers did not want a new religion; they remained Jews. They were not looking for a new God, but preached the Merciful One. This God—so they believed—had no interest in a Stoic observance of the Sabbath rest so long as the majority of his people were hungry and wretchedly poor. Our usual interpretation of the ancient story about Jesus and the plucking of the ears of grain on the Sabbath has not only robbed the story of its point but also the early Jesus movement of its object and us of the hope it brings.

The narrow-minded "casuistry" that we unjustly attribute to the Pharisees in this story is probably our own. We have turned an intra-Judaic debate about the central religious task of Israel in the face of the cruel living conditions of the majority of the people, into a religious opposition between Christians and Jews. But there is no question of such an opposition in the oldest form of this story. It is only the experiential horizon of the redactor of the Markan gospel that suggests such an interpretation. The analysis given here of Mark 2:1–3:6 makes it clear that Mark has systematically shifted this conflict over the Sabbath into a larger context. An intra-Judaic critique of the Sabbath observance becomes an irreconcilable conflict between Jews and Christians. The sovereignty of the "Son of man" is contrasted with the decision of Jewish groups to have Jesus killed (3:6). Behind this interpretation there may be quite real experiences of Jewish hostility to the Christians of the Markan community. In any case, their situation is no longer ours. We are now reaching the end of a murderous reversal of this history of hostility and suffering. This reversal no longer permits an isolated theological appeal to Mark, but demands rather a historical clarification of the roots of anti-Judaism.

Chapters 7, 8, and 9 in the present volume make it clear that the connection between the critico-historical interpretation of biblical texts and our present theological statements about these texts is different from what traditional theoretical hermeneutical models would suggest. The attempt, initiated especially by Rudolf Bultmann, to actualize the "kerygma" by a return to the constant "self-understanding" that underlies it, inevitably reduces diverse and even contradictory experiences to formal patterns of human existence. And yet at every stage of the tradition about Jesus of Nazareth in the New Testament, the "kerygma" was always concrete; at every point it was already a "kerygma that reflects a particular situation and task" (J. Schniewind). Fidelity to the tradition about Jesus, on the one hand, and the actual following of Jesus, on the other, can be made coextensive only in concrete practice, not at the hermeneutical and theological levels.

In this regard the evangelist Matthew might well be taken as a "doctor of the church." For in his particular situation he retained the original goal of the following of Jesus, even though he and his community were no longer in the same situation as the earliest followers of Jesus. Those who no longer suffer the hunger of the poor should, according to Matthew, share their bread with them. Solidarity *among* the poor is replaced by solidarity *with* the poor and with all who are "little."

The story of the workers in the vineyard (Matt. 20:1-16) does not make use of just any image in order to bring home the goodness of God. The socio-historical dimension of the story, which is described in the present volume, clarifies the theological intention as well. Until just before its end, the parable depicts a real-life experience. And its surprising conclusion is not meant to open up an infinite gulf between human reality and God's majesty. On the contrary. In the context of Matthew's gospel the parable proves to be part of a broad theological effort to intensify human solidarity by offering the example of God's goodness. Matthew's theology does not isolate the experience of faith in Jesus Christ from the experience of human beings in their dealings with one another.

Such a separation between the experience of faith and the realities of life is simply a variation on the age-old idealist tradition of the separation of body and soul, corporeal reality and spirit. In Paul, matter and spirit are, of course, still thought of as forming a unity in the human "corporeality" that embraces them both. As chapter 6 of this present volume shows, a new attitude to this dimension of our life is more than a philosophical or theological problem—in fact, it is not a theoretical problem at all, but a problem of social practice. But then theology becomes a source of discomfort; it becomes political and passes from the study to the public scene.

The essays in part 2 of this book, like those in part 1, originated in the "Study Group for a Materialist Exegesis of the Bible." This group comprises pastors and teachers of religion as well as university professors—Evangelical, Catholic, and Jewish—of theology and the religious sciences. By comparison with the exegesis that is usual in the history of ideas and religion in Germany, the term "materialist" is intended to assert that an investigation of the economic, social, political, and ideological situation of the writers and addressees of biblical texts is indispensable for an understanding of these texts.

"There can be no legitimate interpretation that ignores the concrete situation established by social forces. An interpretation that denies this is neces-

REFLECTIONS

6

Between Matter and Spirit:
Why and in What Sense Must
Theology Be Materialist?

DOROTHEE SÖLLE

I am made of earth

I am made of earth, of dust and muck. More than 90 percent of me is fluid. Soap can be made from my bones and lampshades from my skin. I am made of earth.

That the human person stands "between" matter and spirit is an often-repeated but somewhat vague statement. It sounds as though it were a donkey placed between two bundles of hay, drawn to both yet independent of them, so that it may freely turn now to the one, now to the other. As though it may make a choice. The "between" entices us into the assumption of freedom, but the very assumption is already a step into idealism, because it represents an overvaluation of freedom and decision, and a disregard for human dependence on material—that is, biological and economic—conditions. I am made of earth, and I want to know what it means, what it implies, to say that I am made of earth.

I am appealing here for a rapprochement with materialism, and I am doing so from a biblical and theological standpoint. My interest in this is not systematic and theoretical; it is heuristic, not dogmatic. I am making use only of the materialist thesis that understands reality as matter in motion. In explaining this thesis other principles of a higher order need not be brought into discussion. In my view the important thing here is to communicate the spirit and atmosphere of materialism as well as its power to unlock the mystery of the world. I want to bring out the sensuous element in materialism, to convey its beauty and intensity. It is not the abstract "that" of materialism that interests me but the concrete "what." Therefore: what difference will it make if I stop looking at matter with contempt, as in the Western idealist tradition? What difference will it make in my perception, my feelings, my understanding?

The Bible says of the human person that God made him and her from earth. The expression "created by God" means: willed, needed, planned, and formed by God. At the end of the story of the world's origin stands the remarkable assertion that everything was "very good" in the eyes of the creator. In other words, the whole story culminates in the notion that we are loved, willed, and welcomed by God. Moreover, all that is said has to do not with my life as something situated "between" spirit and matter but with me as a material, sense-endowed, mortal being. I am made of earth, and it is precisely this sensuous, transient, cancer-prone flesh that is to be regarded as "very good."

I am made of earth, and I want to be able to accept myself as made of earth. We can perhaps better understand the difficulties that this simple and wholly normal desire entails if we belong to that sector of the human race that has for thousands of years been oppressed, humiliated, and insulted because of its material and biological peculiarities. To say that I personally "am made of earth" means concretely, for example, that I menstruate. To mention only one ordinary experience that most women have: I see a spot of blood on my clothes, I am ashamed, I am compelled to feel ashamed. If I have sexual intercourse with someone, I do not go away merely a stronger and happier person; instead I worry that I may have conceived a child. I am not located between spirit and matter in such a way that I can determine for myself the kind of materiality, the kind of biologico-economic existence that is to be mine. I do not simply have a body, I *am* my body. I—and not just my body—experience hunger and exhaustion. If I become ill with cancer, it is *I* who have the cancer, and it makes no sense to say "my body has contracted cancer," as though there were something intermediate between me and my body that remains free of the cancer and untouched by it.

I am my material body, this matter in motion. The Middle High German word for body, *lip,* meant first of all "life," a meaning that can still be more or less clearly discerned in such expressions as *beileibe nicht!,* "not on your life!," or that someone should *mir vom Leibe bleiben,* "keep their distance" (that is, not attack my body, my life). Fritz Zorn writes:

> I repeatedly endure two bodily sensations in particular: I often feel as though someone were slowly pushing a sword down through my spine to the last vertebra; and frequently my entire body is shaken by pain. It is not a chill, not the heat or the cold, not the weather or an early rising on Monday morning that agitates me. It is the unveiled, unmasked suffering of the soul that makes the body toss and turn in helpless, hopeless despair.[1]

What we are talking about is not a machine that becomes rusty and breaks down, but a human being who falls ill in his or her material body, becomes ill in body and soul as an indivisible unity.

To use another literary example: a hospital is not a place where broken-down machines are repaired or maintained. A cancer ward is a social unit that reflects what is happening in society at large; the ward and its nurses and doctors are the victims of cancer. Solzhenitsyn is indebted to a materialist theory of literature to the extent that unlike Fritz Zorn, who does not confront us with the ward, he does not bracket or forget the very important dimensions of materiality, corporeality, and society. As a great writer in the realist tradition he makes it clear that it is not only the cancer-stricken who have cancer.

We like to talk today of body-soul unity, but our habits of language and thought are certainly not shaped by a consciousness of this unity; we must set about learning it, we must master its alphabet. The better way to do this, it seems to me, is not by a more profound observation and analysis of the soul, but by an observation and analysis of the body to which the soul belongs. The aim must be to explore the spiritual relevance of the body. To become more sensuous, to think more sensuously, to express ourselves more sensuously, to differentiate sensuous experiences and thus to develop them more fully: such would be the goals of a materialist and esthetic education. If we were successful in this, we would be able to say "I am made of earth" without meaning it as a complaint or wishing it were not so; we would be able to say it in such a way as to make our own the remarkable statement that God saw everything to be very good. We would thus be attuned to God and would see things as God saw them on the evening of the sixth day.

Materialist thinking represents an effort to overcome the separation of spirit and matter that has been accepted in the West, and to do so by taking material existence seriously in both of its dimensions: corporeality and society. Simone Weil says of unhappiness that it reaches the point of feeling abandoned by God—that is, the point at which a radical denial of any resolution becomes possible—only when it destroys the physical and social existence of the sufferer and not simply his or her psychic reality. Happiness, on the other hand, comes closer to perfection when it liberates our corporeality and sociality as well as our psyche, and does not bracket any of these dimensions or pass them over in silence.

Zorn calls cancer "the bodily manifestation of my soul's condition." The metaphor of a "manifestation" of a condition of soul is perhaps too weak; a manifestation can disappear. The cancer that is destroying Fritz Zorn is in fact a luxuriation of pseudo life; its unhindered, irresponsible, exponential growth cannot disappear. Spirit and matter alike are affected. Psychic impoverishment, a lack of emotional development, an inability to face conflict—that is, the desire to pass through life without suffering and to avoid any contact with suffering, or, in other words, to live the life of the upper class on Zurich's Gold Coast—is a sickness that affects soul, spirit, and body.

The statement "I am made of earth" presupposes a holistic or all-embracing view of things. Such a view finds expression in the Bible inasmuch as such basic anthropological concepts as soul, life, breath, kidneys ("reins"), heart, spirit, nerve (courage), and sense are more or less interchangeable, because they do not refer to organs or a special part of the human being but in each case embrace the totality of the person as an entity that is at once biological, spiritual, and social. To rearticulate this holistic outlook was the goal of the existentialist philosophy of the 1930s (to which many are returning today). In this sense, Zorn's *Mars,* a report on an illness, is an existentially relevant book. But I have doubts about its author's ability to write in a realistic way. Without the materialist dimension, existentialism degenerates into a form of abstraction.

If, on the contrary, one takes the sensuous and concrete as the starting point for a holistic view of things—if, that is, the "existence" of the existentialists is anchored in the corporeal and economic—then one comes close to the holistic materialism of the Bible. Materialism here does not imply a one-sided concentration on the material, which is then abstracted and turned into the purely quantifiable. The materialism, on the other hand, that developed in the framework of the natural sciences and that Goethe and Blake attacked, understands matter as something that can be possessed and used and mastered. This frivolous kind of practical materialism, as we know it in our everyday linguistic usage, is ahistorical and undialectical. Its deepest concern is possession and mastery. Accordingly, it thinks of everything as quantifiable, because quantified matter can be dominated, possessed, bought and sold. The sensuous and social aspects of biblical materialism, as they find expression in, for example, the basic sensuous and social term "body," are denied here.

Precisely because of its bleakness this superficial bourgeois materialism looks for superimposed "higher values," for an ineffective idealism that is not mediated by history and existence. This kind of materialism must, above all, deny the basic experiences reflected in biblical materialism; it has no concern for either the earth or the body. And yet—to use the language of the Bible—we are made of earth, of this contaminated, pitted, looted earth. Its cancer is ours. We are made of this earth that cannot be sold or possessed, and is—when all is said and done—habitable.

"Brethren, be faithful to the earth" (Nietzsche)

The claim that traditional theology betrayed the earth has been a commonplace since Nietzsche's time, but it is still worth reflecting on. This theology denied the earth by taking the human person seriously only insofar as it is a spiritual entity and by neglecting its bodily and social needs and requirements in favor of those that are intellectual, spiritual, and individual. It rejected a culture focused on the earth and dismissed and suppressed its divinities. It accepted and adored a lord whose most important relationship to the earth is one of ruling and dominating: the Lord God, the God of the hunter, the God of males.

The traditional God has exactly the same relationship to the earth as the traditional male has to woman. To dominate and conquer, to hunt and take booty, to command and subjugate: these are his primary activities. The most important attribute of this God is power, even total power or omnipotence, as theological language (shaped and applied by males) puts it. This God is sought and honored and emulated. According to Western tradition the power in question has its seat in a creative immaterial principle: spirit. Spirit asserts itself against others and against matter; it subjugates matter—which is "mother"—and forces form upon it.

When the human person is located between spirit and matter, woman usually comes to grief because the dichotomy is blamed on her and used against her. She is thought of as matter, as formable material, and feared as being chaotic and formless. Ever since Christianity was hellenized, traditional theology has been idealist in outlook: friendly to spirit and hostile to body, individualistic and inimical to the masses, and masculine (that is, formed and used by males). From the time of the church fathers down to Karl Barth, who was clearly sexist, a misogynist theology has repeatedly been turned into an instrument of subjugation, in opposition to the interests of others: the poor, those of other races, women. A religion of the people was replaced by a religion of the ruling classes. The material hopes of the Bible for an earth on which justice and therefore peace is possible were replaced by a "Platonism for the people," which locates all hopes in the framework of here versus there, now versus someday, earth versus heaven.

In consequence, theologians came to look upon materialist thinking as hostile to God. Materialist hopes of food for the hungry, healing for the sick, and leisure for the uneducated were increasingly weakened in this process of creeping Platonism. Material desires, sexual and economic needs, were in this same process cut down to size and distorted. God was increasingly expelled from the world of the flesh; the incarnation—taking-flesh—was reversed.

Brethren, be faithful to the earth.

A Christian understanding of the incarnation contradicts any purely idealist interpretation of it. For incarnation means that God has entered precisely into sensuous and social reality and that therefore he cannot be experienced apart from corporeality and society.

Many religions and quasi-religious worldviews promise their followers an experience of God in other media and other realms of existence: in nature, in timeless eternity, or in the depths of the human soul. These various possible ways of forging a link with the totality of things and of achieving meaning are real and can be documented in the history of religions. But in contrast to all these possible ways, the Judeo-Christian tradition has taken another path, one that leads through history. It experiences meaning and happiness in history, and historical events are the ones it celebrates, interprets, and repeats. The events by which it lives can be dated: the Exodus of the Jewish people from Egyptian slavery, the resurrection of Jesus from the dead. By "historical experiences" I mean here experiences having to do with the body and society. They have a physical, public relevance. Despite widespread tendencies to spiritualization, this basic materialist thrust of Christianity can be neither denied nor eliminated. A certain fidelity to the earth and to the real experiences of its inhabitants caused the development of certain hopes that appeal to the biblical tradition.

According to the classical view, Christ is God in the conditions of human existence. He renounced the divine attributes that transcend human existence; he stripped himself of them. He willed not to be omniscient, omnipotent, and omnipresent; he plunged fully into the conditions set by the world: he became a slave in a slaveholding society, he experienced hunger and thirst, cold and pain, like all the others who did not have the wealth that would have protected them from such experiences.

The cross is the climactic and clearest symbol of this unique occurrence in the history of religions. It was an instrument of class struggle, wielded from above and used to discipline rebels—that is, runaway slaves and tenants who fled the land and could not pay their debts. It was an atrocious instrument of torture that stripped death of any dignity and reduced sacrifice to torment. We understand the cross only if we have a material understanding of what it meant in physical and social terms. "Were you there when they nailed him to the tree?" asks the spiritual, the religious song of black slaves. Those who sang it had to reckon with the real possibility of being lynched, of hanging on a tree as its alien fruit. "Were you there when they crucified my Lord?" they sang, in order to achieve self-identity and see their own lives mirrored in the old story. "Were you there when the sun refused to shine?" Christianity is a religion of slaves and does not need Nietzsche's exhortation about being faithful to the earth, because its God is not to be found except in the flesh.

A bourgeois theology will inevitably seek to reverse the incarnation. Its tendency is to exalt God more, to set him at a distance, to make the experience of God independent of the material, to separate it from popular piety and to spiritualize it. One example: the development (fostered especially by painters) of the motifs of Christmas is based on the opposition of light and darkness, brightness and shadow; these are symbols of the opposition between the dark powers and forces of earth and the bright powers and forces of heaven. But the materialist interpretation of Christianity as found in songs, popular plays, and crèche tableaux transforms the opposition into one that is perceptible not only by the eye but by all the senses and the organs that perceive cold and heat. Light is materialized and grasped in its physical effects.

Bertolt Brecht made the "great cold" a central motif of his creative work. Even in his early Christmas poems he refers to the darkness and the great cold; fear of the cold dominates. To counteract the great cold of the world there are available only very limited and poorly distributed stores of warmth; wind and snow, which are the messengers of the cold, make the earth almost uninhabitable. But Brecht is a great materialist and never develops his theme in purely natural terms, treating the cold as a "natural" occurrence that affects all equally. In Brecht the cold affects precisely the disabled and the defenseless. In Brecht the cold is not neutral toward class.

Bourgeois theology, with its antimaterialist bent, focuses on supratemporal truths and dehistoricizes its own tradition. Its exegesis of the Bible shows little concern for the sensuous, concrete experiences and struggles of the human beings in the scriptures. Even within the Bible itself "blessed are the poor" is no longer or not very well understood, and the "poor" become the "poor in spirit." Statements such as those found in the Magnificat, which predict that the rich will be dispossessed, are weakened and rendered innocuous. The idea becomes prevalent that a change of mind is all that the rich need in order to enter the kingdom of heaven and that the expropriation of which the Magnificat clearly speaks is not inevitable.

An example of a dehistoricizing, deconcretizing approach came my way not long ago. The Protestant periodical *Radius* asked me to write something on the subject of "existence without suffering—a utopian idea?" The editors of the journal took as their starting point the chapter in the Revelation of John that speaks of "a new heaven and a new earth" and says that God "will wipe away every tear from their eyes, and death will be no more, neither shall there be any mourning nor crying nor pain any more, for the former things have passed away" (21:1, 4). They asked whether the "existence without suffering" that is described here is a utopian notion or whether on the contrary some kind of divine reality lies behind it.

At the time when I began to think about this vision, I was caught up in the same kind of schematic approach to the Bible as were those who put the question to me. That is, I automatically presupposed that the biblical revelation is given to all, including me. I unconsciously assumed that the expectations and desires expressed in the Apocalypse were the same as mine in the twentieth century. Without realizing it I made a carefree appropriation of hopes that as a matter of fact were those of historically determined groups. At that time it was the disinherited and the outlawed who were looking for the city of God. It was Christians persecuted by the Roman state who conjured up this vision of the city of God from the midst of "great tribulation" and distress. Similarly, throughout the history of the interpretation and appropriation of the Bible, the ones who have called for a God who will wipe all tears away have been those who, like the German peasants of the sixteenth century, have been oppressed and persecuted and have had their right to life severely curtailed.

By a "bourgeois appropriation of the Bible" I mean the claim made by a privileged group to all the treasures laid up in history. I regard such an appropriation in our day as impudent and bourgeois because it pays no heed to the underlying distinction of classes and because, although it proceeds historically at its point of departure, it acts ahistorically in its determination of the goal. A life without hunger is promised to the hungry, not to the satisfied.

The concern of the biblical authors was not to make a general statement about a situation as free as possible of suffering for everyone, but rather to console those under persecution and unjustly treated. They pay no heed to the persecutor and the onlooker at this spectacle. But bourgeois theology has ways of interpreting revelation to suit its own pleasure. It passes over in silence the judgment and the necessity that "the former things must pass away" before the tears of the afflicted can be dried (just think of the world that is meant by "the former things"), and it privatizes hope, as though hope were meant for each individual as such, regardless of his or her economic and social position.

To read the Bible in a materialist manner means to resist these tendencies to neutralization and class neutrality. It is true, of course, that Jesus Christ died for all and came in order to liberate all. But we would be interpreting this liberation in a completely schematic, miraculous, and extrinsic way if we thought of it simply as a shifting of objects to another place, where, so to speak, the sun shines brighter. Objects cannot be liberated; they can only change owners. If liberation is just an exodus from injustice, then it need bear little relationship to specific classes; without a transformation in the relationships of ownership and property, it will be just another idealistic expression of individual desires that remain completely unconverted.

As long as the great cold dominates all relationships, it is not possible to speak of liberation in terms merely of enlightenment—that is, of greater light. Theology stands in very great need of Nietzsche's exhortation: "Brethren, be faithful to the earth," because it is in great danger of regarding the human person as a spiritual entity, an individual who is independent of corporeality and society and only accidentally entangled in them. The theoretical idealism of Christianity entails a certain helplessness that many regard as cynical because it accords with the superficial practical materialism with which the history of the human race has been so familiar.

In Western Europe and the United States—the First World—this practical materialism is based on production that is geared to profit, not need, and that must at the same time continually produce incentives to consumption. The most important relationship that persons develop to things in these circumstances is the relationship of having; having determines the relationship of persons to nature ("more sun for the money"), to art, to work, and to interpersonal relationships ("beauty is waiting for you at the beautician's"). Because money is the universal means to this having and getting, all relationships are first quantified in terms of the universal exchange value and then they become interchangeable. They go as far as relationships to things bought and sold can go ("it doesn't look good to go emptyhanded").

Visitors from the Third World have often pointed to a widespread coldness in human relationships as the most significant characteristic of the highly industrialized societies. There exists a deathly kind of reserve; not to touch or be touched becomes the most important of the strategies for living. The empty phrases that appear in Zorn's account of his parental home have precisely the function of avoiding both suffering and life: things are "difficult, I'm afraid" or "not so simple" or "beyond comparison."

Materialism, as it appears in everyday usage, no longer has anything to do with matter or the earth or the senses; exchange-value has swallowed up use-value. This development can be seen in our ravaged language. Eduardo Galeano writes:

> The word "love" is used to define the relationship between persons and their automobiles, and "revolutionary" to describe the effect of a new detergent. "Happiness" is what the gentle soap of a certain manufacturer brings, and the eating of a certain kind of sausage ensures a feeling of bliss. In many places in Latin America "land of peace" really means the peace of a cemetery, and a "healthy person" really means a "powerless person."[2]

It can be said that practical materialism, or the fetishism of commodities (Marx's later name for what he had initially called alienation), accompanies theoretical idealism. Idealism as the liberating philosophy of the rising bourgeoisie decays and dies with the hopes of a cosmopolitan universal emancipation fostered by the bourgeois revolution. What was left of Schiller and Hölderlin—for example, in the educational system of the German *Gymnasium*—has long since surrendered the claim to be liberative and now served only to adorn the unchecked expansion of capital and the nation. The best traditions of German idealism lived on in the worker movement; it was workers trained in materialism who read and memorized Friedrich Schiller, whereas in the schools of the ruling classes Schiller's thought was reduced to a cheap ideology with a Christian trimming and had no effect on the healthy urge to acquisition. Infidelity to the earth went hand in hand with the love of money.

"The earth does not belong to man, but man to the earth"

It is precisely when we take seriously the progressive tendencies of the bourgeoisie that we can learn most, in our situation, from the oppressed peoples and cultures that have offered resistance to economic and ecological imperialism. Seattle, an Amerindian chief of the Duwamish tribe in the state of Washington, wrote a famous letter to the president of the United States who wanted to buy more land from the Indians. This document of 1855 belongs to the history of materialism, the history of a different kind of relationship to matter and the earth:

> We realize that the white man does not understand our ways. To him one part of the land is the same as any other, for he is an alien who comes in the night and takes from the earth whatever he needs. The earth is not his brother, but an enemy, and when he has conquered it he moves on. He leaves behind him the graves of his ancestors—but he does not care. He steals the earth from his children—but he does not care. He treats the earth, which is his mother, and the sky, which is his

brother, as things to be bought and looted, to be sold like sheep or gleaming pearls. His hunger will swallow up the earth and leave nothing behind but a desert.

The earth has become a commodity to be bought and sold, something appropriate for speculation, as though more of it could be produced at will. The capitalist relationship to earth is that of producer and seller; other possible relationships to the earth and to nature and life are not required or permitted in the capitalist mentality. But this economic materialism has deep roots in the dichotomy of spirit versus matter, of shaping, formative power versus mere—and therefore dead—material. Other dichotomies characteristic of this focus on mastery and control are: man and beast, male and female, adult and child, master race and slave race, mental work and manual work. It is in the framework of such relationships as these that there has developed the assumptions that mind is superior to matter and that human beings legitimately dominate and control what is subordinated to them.

Given this understanding of things, it is not possible to depict relationships except in terms of mastery and subjection. *Divide et impera*—divide, disperse, and conquer—is the way to deal with living reality. Here once again is what the Amerindian chief wrote to the great chief in Washington:

The air is precious to the red man, because all things share the same breath: beast and tree and man—all share the one breath. The white man seems not to notice the air he breathes; like one who has been dead for many days, his senses are impervious to the stench. What is man without the beasts? If all the beasts were to disappear, man would die of great loneliness of spirit. What happens to the beasts soon happens to man himself. All things are connected each with the others. What happens to the earth happens also to the children of the earth. For we know that the earth does not belong to man, but man to the earth. Man did not create the fabric of life; he is only a thread in this fabric. Whatever you do to the fabric you do to yourself.

I shall take this guiding principle of a materialist understanding of man as the motto for this part of my essay: the earth does not belong to us as something to be plundered and used as we wish, but rather we belong to the earth. To "belong" means to heed, listen to, be affiliated with, and live in mutual dependence. We belong to the earth; we are its debtor; we cannot live in opposition to it, we cannot live in disregard of the earth; we cannot eliminate day and night, summer and winter, warmth and cold from our lives without inflicting harm on ourselves.

In contemporary feminist writing the expression "to belong to someone" is often criticized as denoting a wrong kind of dependence that is especially dangerous to a woman because it keeps her from becoming self-reliant and makes the male the focus of her entire development. Admittedly, a dependence that is not reciprocal is highly questionable, but this is no reason for rejecting a voluntary reciprocal dependence and for seeking instead an individualistic self-sufficiency. Perhaps the most important message the Amerindians have for us is that we can accept our dependence on the earth and regard it as something good, something we would not exchange for emancipation from material things. The earth does not belong to human beings, who would then be simply exploiters; human beings—female and male alike—belong to the earth.

Like the Bible, this kind of materialism understands human beings as made of earth and belonging to the earth. It tries to remain faithful to the earth—that is, to the sensuous and biological, the economic and social dimensions of reality.

This does not mean that the human person is reduced to the biological and economic, and thus subjected to a rigid determinism. Even if the danger of determinism and of economic reductionism has not always been avoided in the history of Marxism, it would be a naive misunderstanding to identify materialist philosophy, as it developed from Feuerbach to Marx, with determinism. According to Marx, not only does material reality condition consciousness, but there is a dialectical reciprocity as well; the consciousness of, for example, workers who have become aware of their class affiliations changes the meaning of a society.

The central concept (still lacking in Feuerbach) that enables this dialectic to play an active role and makes hope possible within history is the concept of praxis—human engagement that brings about change. An analysis that simply observes and examines objective economic and technological forces at work is not a Marxist analysis. Only when the element of active intervention is added, only when the world is described as capable of being changed—only then is an undialectical materialism transcended, only then does the discussion of anthropology take human needs as its starting point, and only then does the question become not what the human person is as a metaphysical entity, but what its needs and requirements are. Practice is thus the coming to grips, amid struggle and suffering, with our own needs and desires.

Christian theology, too, has repeatedly described the human person in terms of its needs, its desires, its "soul." "Where your treasure is, there will your heart be also." "You are your own deepest desires." "Your god is whatever you rely on and make the central goal of your life." But Christian tradition says something about human needs that Marxism does not say or at least does not say clearly enough. It says that these needs are limitless and cannot be satisfied by anything finite. Only God can satisfy them. Our deepest desires cannot be fulfilled by "having," but only by "being," by becoming different, by entering into communion with others. Here is how Christian tradition expresses this passage from having to being: "Our hearts are restless, O God, until they find rest in you" (Augustine). Only love can satisfy our desire to be loved; only love can satisfy this deepest and most comprehensive need that we can describe in material and spiritual, esthetic and political, religious and social terms.

In Christian parlance, praxis goes by the name of "faith," which is one of those words that have been overworked yet are irreplaceable. "Rise and go your way; your faith has made you well," says Jesus (Luke 17:19; cf. 8:13). Or: all things are possible to those who believe (Mark 9:23). The paralytic gets to his feet, picks up his mat, and walks away, because he now has a practical share in the liberation that is promised in theory. The gospel is described as this kind of praxis: "The blind receive their sight . . . the deaf hear . . . and the poor have the good news preached to them" (Matt. 11:5). Materialism and the Judeo-Christian tradition are at one in seeing human beings as dependent and enslaved and in undertaking the liberation that is practicable. This teaching on liberation is deprived of its true scope when it focuses on spirit and individuality and not on the earth, corporeality, and society.

"The earth is the Lord's"

"The earth is the Lord's"—this watchword from the peasant liberation movements of the later Middle Ages and the early modern period captures the mystery and the power of materialism. The earth is the Lord's: this statement is a critical principle brought to bear against those who make themselves masters of the earth; it is a communistic principle that is spoken and heard against private ownership of land. Contemporary theologies of liberation, especially in Latin America, are reviving this principle.

Occupation of land in Chile, the attempt at a communal cultivation of crops in Peru, the experiments of Jesuit groups in Guatemala—suppressed by violence—are manifestations of the realization that the land belongs to those who till it, because no one can "own" the land in the abstract sense in which we use this term. The earth is the Lord's; it cannot be possessed or sold off. In the eyes of those who till the soil, land or earth or matter is not something dead like a commodity that one produces in order to sell. "I am made of earth" also means that speculation in land is an affront to my being, an ontological mockery of my existence in this world.

To theologize in a materialist way means a refusal to regard the earth as unimportant, as though God and the soul were the subject matter of theology. No, the subject matter of theology is the earth and how it can become God's and be converted to the use of all. The biblical prophecies of the messiah's reign are concerned precisely with this reconciliation between nature, no longer subjugated and looted, and human beings who no longer play the brigand. The wolf will lie down with the lamb, swords will be forged into plowshares: these are images that retain the taste and smell of the earth.

I should like to end this appeal for a biblical materialism by offering a brief exegesis of an author who is hardly suspect of materialism—an exegesis, that is, of some verses of Paul the apostle.

Let sin therefore not reign in your mortal bodies, to make you obey their passions.

Do not yield your members to sin as instruments of wickedness, but yield yourselves to God as men who have been brought from death to life, and your members to God as instruments of righteousness.

For sin will have no dominion over you, since you are not under law but under grace.

The passage is from Romans 6:12–14. The context for these verses is the teaching that through baptism the Christian has "died" (vv. 2, 4, 7) and our old self has been "crucified with" Christ (v. 6) and that we have been "freed" from the domination of sin (v. 7) and are dead to sin but alive to God (v. 11).

I shall present my interpretation in three steps. First, I shall state my interest in this text and formulate my questions with regard to it. Then I shall try to make the statements in the text intelligible to myself. Finally, I shall offer a paraphrastic, interpretive translation of the text and apply it to us, so that its direct and pointed relationship to us emerges clearly.

My interest is in the anthropological statements that Paul is making here. I have difficulty with such terms and phrases as "mortal bodies," "passions," "members," and "members as instruments" (or "weapons"). What presuppositions lie behind these terms and phrases? Can we share them? Can we share them in the light of the axioms that have guided the approach to materialism in this essay: "I am made of earth," "Brethren, be faithful to the earth," "The earth does not belong to man, but man to the earth," and "The earth is the Lord's"?

Does Paul's word "body" have anything to do with the concept of "earth" that I have been developing here? What does liberation mean to Paul? And, in this connection, is our ancient concept of "redemption" an essentially idealist concept that suggests redemption *from* chains and fetters and from earthly reality? "Redemption" as a metaphor means release from illness, imprisonment, or some other evil state, and a transfer to a different and better state. But is that what Paul is talking about? Is he a representative of the dichotomist tradition, of the rupture between spirit and flesh that has promoted and glorified suppression in the history of Christianity?

This dichotomy has played an ideological role in sexism, racism, and domination by one class. It was and still is a tool of empire and the will to power; in this sense, it is imperialistic. In the thought system based on this dichotomy, human beings can only be redeemed, translated, whisked away. But do not our deepest expectations of life for ourselves and our world go far beyond this? Do we not need liberation, not simply redemption? What is the real meaning of *soteria* or "salvation" in Paul? Is "liberation" the best translation of the word because it includes the body and the social dimension, or, in other words, all that we understand anthropologically and sociologically by the word "earth"?

But back to the text. As I see it, Paul is here making three statements.

1) To dwell in a mortal body and to be a body in the proper sense means *to be dependent.* Paul uses the terms "body," "members," "instruments,"

and "you" as parallels; these words stand not for parts of the human organism but for the whole being. Existence means corporeality; it means being controlled, being conditioned, being unfree. "And because I'm human, I need a bit to eat, thank you very much!" But something more is meant than this type of dependence. We are dependent not only on our biological nature but also on those who rule over us, and on their culture, ideas, and laws.

Thus my inability to accept myself as a woman (for example, the shame caused by menstruation) and my attempt to deny a dimension of my bodily existence show me how dominated, controlled, and unfree I am. In commenting on this passage Ernst Käsemann says: "Corporeality means standing in a world for which different forces contest and in whose conflict each individual is caught up, belonging to one lord or the other and representing this lord both actively and passively."[3]

In the shame that has been bred into me and in the fears that I have internalized, I am a representative of a male order of things that is hostile to creation. I am dependent on prevailing ideas. I am dependent on them even in my dreams. My desires too are controlled by alien forces, and they destroy me because they function as instruments of wickedness and exploitation.

Let me clarify this point by an example. In Latin America recent decades have seen more and more farm and pasture land coming into the possession of foreign corporations that use the land to produce luxury exports. Thus, for example, strawberries and orchids are now grown where beans and grain used to grow or could be grown.

"Do not yield your members to sin as instruments of wickedness!" My desire as a consumer to have strawberries regardless of the season functions objectively as an instrument of wickedness. The condition of the economy on which I depend can be easily related to the mythological images used by Paul of the power of sin, which "bursts" into human life, seizes power, and rules. Within a closed economic system that works not to satsify human needs but to make a profit for the owners, sin—that is, this system of injustice—has demonic traits: it is uncontrollable; we do not understand it; and it is all-powerful in two ways: externally, in regard to production, and internally, in regard to desires or passions. In no area has latter-day capitalism succeeded so well as in the matter of manipulating the passions, wishes, and dreams of persons so that they become subject to the domination of capital.

2) Paul's second statement is that *life is in no way neutral*. When we placed our faculties, our powers, our way of life—this is how I understand Paul's metaphorical term "members"—and indeed our very selves at the disposal of the prevailing injustice, then we were dead. Sin—that is, injustice—ruled as despot over us: through our bodies, through our participation in this world, through our conscious or unconscious support of this world. It is impossible to be neutral: we always exist "in the mode of belongingness and participation,"[4] because we are bodies: interrelated, rational beings. To exist as a body means that "no one, at bottom, belongs to himself alone."[5] The fact that we are made of earth raises the further question of whom the earth belongs to;

the earth is not something incidental, nor is it purely economic in its significance.

Acknowledgment of the material fact that we are made of earth leads directly to the further question: To whom does the earth belong? If we were spiritual beings, the question of domination could be disregarded as a purely worldly and extrinsic matter.

Christoph Blumhardt, a pastor, a member of Parliament for the Social Democratic Party in Germany, and one of the fathers of the modern Christians for Socialism, wrote in the 1890s:

> We should not make our question a subjective one: Am I becoming just in God's sight? But instead . . . : How does God's justice come to me? Objectively. . . . The Bible never speaks of "the justice that has value in God's sight"; Luther translated it that way because he had a false idea of it, and the Bible had to yield to Luther. The Bible always speaks rather of "God's justice," and this comes through faith and not through the law.[6]

The dispute is an old one. The justice that has value before God and that is attributed to me as something from outside me is a basic experience that has reference to a subject. It is the passage from despair to praxis. The nonneutrality of life means that there is no state between despair/sin and praxis/faith. There do not exist any other more tranquil, more inoffensive alternatives. The expression "justice that has value before God" reflects this in relationship to a person. But "God's justice" means more than this kind of passage. It refers to the material body and the earth, two things that go together. The earth ceases to be a place of denials of life, a place of exploitation and injustice.

In the bourgeois period of Protestantism "God's justice" was interpreted in profoundly personalist terms. But a contemporary materialist interpretation says that the earth is God's earth. How did this change take place? The same Christoph Blumhardt wrote on New Year's Eve, 1911:

> In earlier decades, around the time of my birth, the famine, the lack of daily bread, was so terrible that many persons were simply unable to help themselves. That era is now past. I regard everything that is happening in our time as part of the Coming. "He is coming on the clouds," and therefore not just to you or to me or to us or to this or that society. He is manifesting himself to human beings everywhere, in accordance with the divine plan and will, and he is doing so in a way that is completely unique and fully material (as, for example, the electric light began to shine in our stables). He is coming in the whole development of the age!

Blumhardt gives a completely material interpretation of God's coming. In taking this approach he makes himself vulnerable, of course, though in a completely different way than does an idealist interpretation that pays no heed either to famine or to the electric light. To make oneself vulnerable is one aspect of fidelity to the earth. It is why Paul is forced, in another passage, to describe the apostles as "fools for Christ's sake" (1 Cor. 4:10).

3) Paul's third statement is in even more decisive contradiction to traditional Protestant thinking than are the first two. This thinking is essentially colored by a pessimism about humankind that believes it capable of everything evil and nothing good. But Paul says here that *we are capable of righteousness in Christ*. We can put our members—that is, our faculties, our powers, our way of life—in the service of righteousness; we can turn ourselves into instruments of righteousness and tools of peace for God to use. It is not true that we are subject to objective compulsive forces that control us whether or not we are Christians. We exist not under the laws of an exploitive imperialist structure but under grace. To believe means that we are not compelled to live as we used to, in iron constraints; we can exchange dependence for a new voluntary fidelity to the earth.

Paul sees this radical conversion as the work of grace. It is a grace for us to pass from dependence on the ruling powers to praxis. It is a grace to live in opposition to these powers; it is a grace to work for liberation.

Henceforth our bodies and our lives exist for the sake of justice, not in an idealist but in a practical and material sense of this word. Justification and sanctification coincide, a point that emerges most clearly in the word *parhistanein* (v. 13, "yield"), which can be translated as "give oneself to God" (with the erotic connotations of "yield") or as "put oneself at God's disposal" (in a military sense): to put oneself at his disposal, to make oneself available (or *disponible,* as the French worker-priests used to say), to undertake an obligation or commitment that transforms my body, my real life. The place where I live will then look different; the time I spend on certain things will be reallocated; my priorities can no longer be this-worldly—that is, they cannot be centered solely on money and consumption.

To be in Christ means to make the great sacrifice. The Taizé Easter Message for 1970 says: "The risen Christ will prepare us to give our lives so that one person may no longer be the victim of another." To give one's life, to make the sacrifice: these are expressions that can be used of martyrdom; I think, for example, of Elisabeth Käsemann who gave her life in order that one person might no longer be the victim of another. But the surrender begins before death; it also embraces the daily surrender of body, reality, money, job security. To say that sin should "have no dominion" over us means that I surrender my life to the point of no return. This point, says Paul, can indeed be reached. Let me paraphrase the text once again:

Therefore let the system of injustice no longer determine your manner of life, causing you to pursue illusory dreams. Do not put your faculties at the disposal of capital, which uses them as instruments of exploitation, but yield yourselves to God as men and women who have ceased to be isolated, powerless beings but have instead become living persons. Put your powers and

EXAMPLES

7

From Criticism to Enmity:
An Interpretation of Mark 2:1-3:6

EKKEHARD STEGEMANN

Our evangelists derive their narrative material from, among other sources, the experience of those to whom they owe the oral traditions, isolated components, and collections that their gospels contain. In bringing these various strands of tradition together to form a general picture of past events—in other words, their gospels—they transmit past experience along with their own. Thus the actual situation of the evangelists as narrators is superimposed on the situation that is reflected in the traditions they use and joins with those traditions to form something new. At the literary level this meshing of situations shows as a complex unity of tradition and redaction.

This later (by comparison with the elements of tradition) and quite independent world of experience as represented by the gospel of Mark, its author, and the first readers for whom he composed his work is my main focus of interest in this study of Mark 2:1-3:6. I shall be asking how the evangelist integrates into the narrated text the experiences of the period in which he is doing his narrative work, and how his text, understood as an interpretation of specific events, functions as his partner in the act of communication.

In pursuing this line of thought, I presuppose that the evangelist was more than an archivist of a respectable tradition about Jesus and that he went on to be an interpreter of it. In other words, I understand the gospel of Mark to be a retelling of old narratives about Jesus, but a retelling that is conditioned by and integrated with the experiences of the evangelist and his audience.[1] These experiences do not exert a purely unconscious influence on the evangelist as he works on his gospel. Rather he makes conscious use of them in an ongoing confrontation with the tradition available to him, his purpose being that in

104

the gospel his audience may discover its own history and draw the proper conclusions from this knowledge.[2]

A New Teaching

From the very first line the reader knows that the gospel of Mark is concerned with the career of Jesus Christ, the Son of God. In the prologue the reader learns that this Jesus is the Lord promised long ago by the prophet, the Lord whose way John the Baptist prepares and whom the Baptist proclaims to be greater than himself and the one who is to come after him. Finally, at his baptism in the Jordan, this Jesus is identified by God himself as his Son. Then in the wilderness he lives up to this sonship despite all of Satan's temptations and he is again approved, this time by the angels (Mark 1:1–13).

Even if it be thought that Mark hardly intended to tell his audience anything new in the story thus far but was simply recapitulating what they already believed, the prologue would nonetheless be important as an acceptance of this basic consensus. In fact, however, Mark intends something more in the prologue. Everything said here about Jesus gives the impression of being something definitive, something that is still (or once again) outside "history." At this point Jesus is still moving in the world of God and Satan, of beasts, angels, and the witness who is his precursor; he is not yet in the public sphere where other persons, enemies and followers, are located. The history that includes all these begins only in Mark 1:14, and it begins, characteristically, with the observation that Jesus came on the scene just when John the Baptist was leaving it. Thus a dark shadow falls on the beginning of the career of the Son of God: the shadow of the death of his first witness, whom they have "handed over."

With this man's fate behind him, but with an eye still on it, Jesus proclaims that the time is fulfilled and the kingdom of God is at hand, and that his own time has come: "Repent, and believe in the gospel." Mark does not say to whom this first preaching in Galilee is directed. It evidently sums up the demands made by Jesus throughout his ministry and thus serves as a general key to an understanding of his story and thus also to the gospel of Mark, inasmuch as it tells the story of Jesus, "the gospel of Jesus Christ." Here again Mark is hardly telling his audience anything new about the preaching of Jesus. He does, however, use the words of Jesus to call for faith in the gospel and for repentance or conversion; he thus expects his readers to read his work in this light.

The first thing Jesus does is to call disciples; but they are more than disciples, they are followers who come after him and snatch Satan's prey from him: they are fishers of men (Mark 1:16–20). It would be of interest to read through the entire gospel keeping in mind the question of whether and how the disciples perceive their task of continuing in the footsteps of Jesus. We would see that in all truth Jesus often had trouble enough in keeping the disciples with him, in bringing them back to the path from which they had strayed, and in encouraging them to continue on when they wanted to stay put. We would see that the disciples found the way increasingly difficult as Jesus drew closer to Jerusalem, the place where he would suffer and die, and that finally, at the moment of greatest danger—the moment of Jesus' arrest—they ran away and left Jesus to suffer and die alone. But we would also see that after his resurrection, through the angels' message and the mediation of the women, Jesus again asked these men, who had failed in their attempt to follow him, if they would follow him once more and that he promised them that such a following would enable them to see him again.

It is impossible here for us to pursue this aspect of the gospel narrative any further, although I am convinced that it represents a basic experience of the evangelist and his readers—namely, their own failure to follow Jesus. "Repent and believe in the gospel": as seen in the light just indicated, this demand that is voiced at the beginning of the gospel would take on a new meaning for its first readers; the gospel would recapitulate their own experience in the history of the first followers of Jesus and at the same time would be a repetition of the offer that Jesus had already made to his disciples.[3]

The first call of disciples is followed by a series of stories that the evangelist has put together to make up a paradigmatic first day of Jesus' activity.[4] The evangelist introduces the series with a summation (Mark 1:21–22) in which he first notes that it was Jesus' custom to teach in the synagogue on the Sabbath. He then gives a concise description of this teaching. The teaching caused astonishment in the crowd because Jesus taught with authority and not like the scribes. "Teaching" in this context does not refer to any specialized doctrine, but is rather to be taken as "instruction"—that is, the kind of schooling in the way to God that the scribes likewise claimed to give, although in a way quite different from that of Jesus.[5]

The element of power, which evidently contributed to the tremendous impression the teaching makes on the crowd, is exhibited by Mark in the subsequent scenes of the first day of Jesus' activity as exorcist and healer. In the very first story, which tells of Jesus' struggle with a representative of the demonic realm (1:23–28), the authority of Jesus, the Holy One of God, over the demonic world is clearly demonstrated. The acclamation of the crowd then expressly states once again that the teaching of Jesus is indeed a teaching with authority: even the demons obey him. Here, almost in passing, but also in a characteristic manner, another facet of the teaching of Jesus is added to the picture: this teaching is new. Thus a new kind of instruction, a new and authoritative teaching about salvation, has come to the synagogue of Capernaum in the person of Jesus.

To this first impressive example of Jesus' power-filled teaching Mark adds a second. Immediately after the exorcism in the synagogue, Jesus shows his power once more. The demonstration is less spectacular this time, but it is no less convincing. He heals Peter's mother-in-law (1:29–31). Thus he shows the power of his new teaching both in conflict with demons and in compassionate aid to the sick. No wonder, then, that the street in front of the house is immediately turned into a hospital and that the demons begin to tremble (1:32–34).

Surprisingly enough, after these deeds of power Jesus takes refuge in an unpopulated solitude in order to pray. His disciples pursue him and try to bring him back, but instead he invites them to come with him and preach in the surrounding villages. It could be that Jesus' example is here being offered to a later age as archetypical of the restless life of an itinerant preacher whose (missionary) work has reached a successful conclusion—or an unsuccessful one due to public rejection (see Mark 6:10–11).[6]

In this series of scenes Mark does not explicitly tell us what the difference was between the teaching of Jesus and that of the scribes. The impression of power given by Jesus' exorcistic and healing activity and by the new mode and manner of his teaching that both astonished and attracted the crowd does allow us, of course, to infer that the teaching of the scribes was quite different: powerless, timeworn, making no impression on the crowd. But Mark does not make the difference explicit until later on—after the paradigmatic first day of Jesus' activity and after a "missionary journey" of Jesus through Galilee (of which we are told in summary form), and when he has returned once more to Capernaum.

But between the end of this journey and the return to Capernaum the evangelist introduces still another act of power: the healing of a leper (Mark 1:40–45). This story once again brings out in the clearest possible way both the compassion of Jesus and his great power. Above all, however, it emphasizes the fact that this power is not directed against the rules laid down by Moses and that it is not meant to inspire a revolution, a rebellion against the religious authority of the law and its official exercise. For Jesus impresses on the healed man that he must remain silent about what has happened and simply submit himself for the official declaration of cleanness by a priest and satisfy the requirement regarding a sacrifice—this as "a proof for them" (Mark 1:44, NAB).

The meaning may be that the man healed is to submit to the legally appointed ritual in order to give "them" a proof of the authority of Jesus, thus convincing them of the new teaching. Because the man does not obey Jesus' order but publicizes what has happened to him, the opportunity is lost. Another interpretation is more probable, however; this understands the phrase "as a proof for them" to mean an eschatological witness for the prosecution against the unbelief of the priests. Then the disobedience of the man healed would be a failure to take advantage not of a missionary opportunity but rather of a situation in which a confession of faith could be made before a tribunal that is hostile to the new teaching (cf. Mark 13:9 and 6:11). The de facto result of the "spreading of the news"[7] by the man healed is that ever larger crowds seek out Jesus and even follow him into the desert places to which he withdraws.

Let me sum up what emerges from Mark 1:1–45. Jesus is the promised "Son" whom John proclaims and whom God himself identifies. After the martyrdom of the Baptist he begins his career in Galilee by preaching the good news in the company of a group of followers. The new teaching that he brings is filled with power, as is proved by the victory over the demons and the compassionate help given to the suffering. This teaching is not directed against the law of Moses, but it is nonetheless different from the interpretation of the law by the scribes and from the implementation of it by the priests, who on this point are clearly hostile to Jesus. But the crowd is attracted by the teaching.

Confrontations

Once Jesus has returned to Capernaum (Mark 2:1), the evangelist picks up again the narrative thread that tells of the profound impression made on the crowd by the teaching of Jesus. So many persons gather in front of the house in which Jesus is staying that it is impossible to enter by the door, and a paralyzed man must be lowered through the roof by his bearers. While in this introductory scene the evangelist is returning to his account of Jesus' authoritative action in behalf of the suffering, he is also beginning here a series of open confrontations with the scribes and Pharisees.

This change of interest can also be seen in the structure of the narrative, which shows a unique mingling of debate and miracle story. A mingling like that in 2:1–12 is also to be seen in 3:1–6, whereas the interval between these two passages is occupied by "pure" debates. This first series of confrontations culminates in the decision of the Pharisees and Herodians to do away with Jesus (Mark 3:6). In the context of the gospel as a whole, this decision is a preliminary one, inasmuch as Jesus and these adversaries will clash over and over again. But from the viewpoint of Jesus' destiny this provisional closure of a series is a clear pointer to the passion, which tells of how the decree of Jesus' death is turned into a reality. Viewed thus, this first series of confrontations takes on a quality of deadly seriousness.

The issue in the conflict is more than a point of theology. A purely theological debate could well be a search for the truth and as such could be a bond between Jesus and his enemies, even, and indeed precisely, by way of criticism. But since in fact these confrontations are a matter of life and death for Jesus, the atmosphere is one of hostility. And because the hostility is directed at the teaching of Jesus, who is Son of God, and at his followers, Mark sees the scribes and Pharisees as evil from the very beginning.

The radical change of atmosphere in Mark 2:1–12 can be gauged from the behavior of Jesus toward those who seek his help. Mark expressly uses the term "faith" to describe the efforts of the bearers, which alone enable them to get through the crowd and make their way to Jesus in such an unusual manner. The ulterior point being made here is probably that those who are to make their way to Jesus himself, to his house, must move beyond the kind of fascination with Jesus that characterizes the crowd. When Jesus tells the paralyzed man, who has come for healing, that God forgives him his sins (the grammatical construction is the *divinum passivum*), he is making it clear that believers can expect a great deal more from Jesus: the healing of their souls and not just of their bodies. The new teaching in power is medicine for the sick but even more for sinners. It effects a restoration of their proper relationship to God.

This new, authoritative teaching manifests the power of God, whose Son Jesus is. But while using the proclamation of forgiveness in order to bring out the close union of Jesus with God, Mark also uses it to introduce the confrontation with the scribes. The theology of the scribes evidently excludes such a close union of Jesus with God, because they see such a claim as a blasphemy against the unity of God and thus against the fundamental Jewish profession of faith in God. But Jesus makes public their hidden thoughts and challenges them to conclude, through a practical syllogism, to his right to act in God's name and behalf on earth: "Which is easier to say to the paralytic, 'Your sins are forgiven,' or to say, 'Rise, take up your pallet and walk'?" Jesus' acts of power should make the scribes conclude to the close union with God that the forgiveness of sins implies. Jesus then reduces the syllogism to practice by healing the man, to the astonishment of the crowd.[8]

It is no accident that later on, in the passion story, the actual sentence of death is pronounced when Jesus answers the high priest, in the presence of the Sanhedrin, with a proclamation that he is indeed the Christ—that is, the Son of God (see Mark 14:62–64). It is this blasphemy that, in the final analysis, makes him deserving of death in the eyes of the Jewish religious authorities, although unjustly so from Mark's viewpoint: Jesus' acts of power have demonstrated that he is indeed the Son of God.[9]

The second confrontation (Mark 2:13–17) is introduced by the call to discipleship that Jesus gives to Levi the tax collector. Here the debate shifts from the "theological" level to the "ecclesiological." As the following scene makes clear, this call was not exceptional. Rather, it was the normal thing for Jesus to accept this kind of follower, as Mark mentions in passing. Moreover, Jesus even welcomes tax collectors and sinners to fellowship at table. We are not told why this practice offends the scribes.[10] But in all likelihood it is the contemptible social and religious standing of such persons that they criticize in a global manner.[11] Jesus answers the reproach not by defending these followers but by stating the real purpose of his mission, which is to call sinners and not the righteous. Just as the physician comes to the sick and not to the healthy, so Jesus comes to the tax collectors and the sinners. Of course, the preceding story about the forgiveness of sins has already made it clear that Jesus grants God's forgiveness to these followers of his. Consequently, the "theological" dispute is closely connected with the "ecclesiological" dispute.

The third confrontation (Mark 2:18–22) again shifts the focus of conflict. Now it is the behavior of his disciples that becomes the occasion for a confrontation with Jesus. The disciples neglect the religious practice of fasting, which is observed by the disciples of John and by the Pharisees. No indication is given of the kind of fasting that is meant: whether private fasting or the public fasting that is obligatory for all Jews on the great day of atonement (once the temple was destroyed, a memorial fast, for it was joined to the fast of Yom Kippur). In any case, the neglect of fasting by his disciples is so conspicuous that Jesus is compelled to justify it.

He does so with the help of an image that portrays the time of his presence as a time of messianic joy, as a wedding celebration, during which it would be absurd to mourn. Another pair of images explains that fasting is one of the religious practices proper to the time before Christ's birth, one of the old instrumentalities that are incapable of containing the new reality that is present with Jesus, just as an old wineskin cannot contain new wine. But Jesus does add a limitation: even for his disciples a time will come when they will fast—namely, after he "is taken away from them." It makes no difference here whether the reference to a future "fasting" is to a specific practice of fasting by the disciples or simply to their felt privation of the presence of Jesus. Nor does it make any difference whether this future period begins directly after the death of Jesus or refers rather (improbably, in my view) to a more distant eschatological future. In any case the fasting of Jesus' disciples is still clearly distinct from that of the Pharisees, because the basis for it is the taking away of Jesus, the sadness caused by his death. Thus this story too contains a clear reference to the passion.

The fourth confrontation (Mark 2:23-38) has also to do with the behavior of Jesus' disciples, and once again it concerns a religious practice. In this case, however, the disciples do not omit something that is commanded but do something that is forbidden. Moreover, this new action concerns a far more important identifying mark of the Jewish religion than that of fasting— namely, the sanctification of the Sabbath. The first reason Jesus gives for the behavior of his disciples would simply justify it as an exception in an emergency. The second argument he uses likewise remains within the same framework, although he formulates it in a much more comprehensive way: according to God's will and the order of creation, the human person is the measure of the Sabbath. But the conclusion drawn from this argument shows that the behavior of the disciples on the Sabbath does not represent the utmost that is permissible, but that on the contrary it quite obviously reflects the power that the Son of Man has even over the Sabbath.

And in fact the real meaning of Jesus' statement is brought out by the final case in this series of confrontations of Jesus with the scribes and the Pharisees (Mark 3:1-6). Here the scene turns into a court, although an unusual kind of court for those who wish to accuse Jesus. They are watching for a reason to accuse him, and they believe it is within reach in the form of a cripple whom Jesus is likely to heal on the Sabbath. And in fact Jesus accepts the challenge. But by calling the cripple forward Jesus makes it clear that the cripple, the human being in distress, be it chronic or acute, is the real subject of the debate. The real issue is not the question of proper Sabbath practice, especially when the man's wretched state is taken into account. No, the real issue is suffering human beings: Are they to be treated rightly or wrongly? Are they to be rescued or left to perish? Jesus confronts his adversaries with these alternatives when he issues his challenge in the form of a question about what is commanded or forbidden on the Sabbath: "Is it lawful on the Sabbath to do good or to do harm, to save life or to kill?" It is the generality (really only apparent) of these alternatives that shows that Jesus' question is being asked from a standpoint located beyond the halakic Jewish discussion of the sanctification of the Sabbath. For this generality implies that there exists no third principle that would assign to the sanctification of the Sabbath an independent, competitive religious value.

Such a principle would in fact be idle—apparently pious but in fact evil, when the alternatives are taken into account. The principle enunciated in the previous story—that the Sabbath is made for humankind and not humankind for the Sabbath—is thus given an unambiguous interpretation. Action in behalf of needy human beings is commanded always and everywhere. An exclusion of such action on the Sabbath or an admission of it with reservations or a prohibition of it in certain circumstances—for example, in the case of chronic invalidism—all these approaches witness to a confusion of priorities. Convicted by this argument, even the adversaries fall silent. But, as Jesus' anger and sadness show, their silence does not signify an interior agreement or even a simple lack of counterarguments, but reflects rather their hardness of heart. This deeper inability to accept the truth, which calls forth the emotions of Jesus and gives his reaction the appearance of a definitive divine judgment, is probably what leads the Pharisees to connive with the Herodians, a politically influential group, to get rid of Jesus once he has, in obedience to his own rule of showing mercy and promoting life, healed the cripple in a miraculous manner. The plot that will lead to the passion has been laid. Its execution is still in the future, but now it is inevitable.

Let me summarize. The new, authoritative teaching of Jesus meets with deadly enmity from the scribes and Pharisees. Their hostility is aroused especially by Jesus' claim to be acting on earth by God's power and in God's name (a claim that Mark sees as amply validated by Jesus' acts of power). The hostility is therefore also directed at specific consequences of the authority of Jesus: his admission to discipleship of sinners and other social outcasts (all of them assured of forgiveness by Jesus), and the practices of these individuals that are not in accord with certain important and characteristic elements of the Jewish religious identity. These deviations by Jesus' disciples are seen (by Mark) as theologically justified in the light of Jesus' mission. The same cannot be said of the enmity that the Pharisees and their disciples show for Jesus. Here the dominant factor is a hardness of heart that inevitably means death for Jesus. The passion story will describe this ultimate result, but the ministry of Jesus and his new teaching with power serve as a lengthy introduction to this denouement.[12]

Radical Hostility

In order to fill out this picture of the hostility of the Pharisees and scribes for Jesus, we would have to move on to other chapters of Mark's gospel and in particular to the passion story.[13] Such a follow-up would not substantially change the impression already gleaned from Mark 2:1–3:6. It would, of course, become clearer that in their rejection of the divine spirit at work in Jesus' exorcistic activity the scribes do not (in Mark's opinion) shrink even from suspecting this activity of being demonic in origin (see Mark 3:22–30). And we would find the Pharisees demanding further signs from heaven as proof of Jesus' authority, despite the many miracles he has worked and continues to work (see Mark 8:11–13 and 11:27–33). We would also see them, of course, continuing their conspiracy with the Herodians for the purpose of eliminating Jesus (Mark 12:13–17), and ultimately meeting with success (Mark 14–15). Finally, we would obtain further evidence that Jesus by no means teaches his fellow human beings to act against God's will and his word as found in the scriptures, but that, on the contrary, he restores to this word its original integrity, which had been overlaid by human tradition and rules (see Mark 7:1–22).

It is clear that the conflict regarding the new teaching of Jesus, as we have seen it in Mark 2:1–3:6, runs like a scarlet thread through the entire gospel of Mark. Why does the evangelist narrate these confrontations? The most obvious reason is that in these stories Mark is coming to grips with experiences that he and his readers have had. But because he is presenting the conflicts as those of Jesus and his first disciples, and because he is evidently doing so with the help of traditional material, we must first ask to what extent the manner and content of the confrontations come from the tradition and what, on the contrary, is to be attributed to the evangelist.

A literary analysis of the relevant sections of the gospel of Mark has led to the clear conclusion that the substance has not been composed independently by the evangelist but has been taken from the tradition. But there is disagreement on details. At which points has Mark changed the tradition he has received? Above all: In what kind of arrangement did the tradition reach him? To take Mark 2:1–3:6 as an example: Is Mark using here an older collection of debates and, if so, what form did it have?[14]

In this essay I can only summarize my own view of the transmission process behind Mark 2:1–3:6, without providing the methodically controlled arguments for my position and without discussing other views.[15] It seems to me demonstrable that the evangelist is responsible for the present form of the series of confrontations to the extent at least that he has deliberately placed 3:1–6 at the end of the series. I suspect, moreover, that 2:1–12 and 3:1–6 were originally transmitted as a single unit and that the evangelist has inserted 2:13–28, which, in essentials, probably already existed as a unit prior to Mark. The literary technique used here, which has quite aptly, even if somewhat frivolously, been described as a "sandwiching procedure," is often found in Mark. The use of the technique in Mark 2:1–3:6 can be shown by arguments from literary criticism as well as from form history and tradition history.

Of course, it is not just the overall arrangement that is to be assigned to the evangelist. He has probably edited details as well and given them an independent formulation. This is most likely true of the formulation of details in 2:1–12 and 3:1–6, especially in 2:10 and 3:6. But the evangelist has probably also introduced revisions into the older collection, especially at the juncture points; in particular, I regard 2:28 as the work of the evangelist. In addition, the identification of the adversaries is only partly traditional; for the rest it is redactional. Finally, the possibility cannot be excluded that the complexes of traditions that Mark puts together to make up 2:1–3:6 already had a history of transmission behind them before his reception of them. In all likelihood, this is especially true of 2:18–22 and 23–27.

But, whatever the relationship between tradition and redaction in Mark 2:1–3:6—and any reconstruction must remain hypothetical—it is probable, in my view, that the tradition behind Mark does not bear witness to the deadly enmity on the part of Jesus' adversaries that we see here. As a general principle, to the extent that the overall context of the gospel as a whole does not first suggest this enmity and then introduce it into the individual strands of tradition in the process of putting them together, it is the evangelist himself who introduces it. In some places, of course, it is possible to discern a process of increasing intensification of conflicts in the course of transmission. But the present configuration of deadly hostility and irresolvable oppositions is the work of the evangelist (or the most recent stage of tradition) and reflects his experience.

Apart from this context the early elements of the tradition do, of course, present a conflict between Jesus (or his disciples) and their adversaries. But there is question here of intra-Judaic disputes, not of a confrontation of enemies. Another essay in the present volume—chapter 8, below—makes out a convincing case for this view in connection with the tradition behind the dispute in Mark 2:23–28; the same could be shown for other passages.[16] The question therefore arises: How did an intra-Judaic criticism of the early disciples of Jesus become in Mark a manifestation of radical hostility and irreconcilable opposition?

Rejection of Israel

The deadly hostility to Jesus (and his followers) that was felt by the Pharisees and scribes and indeed—as the passion story shows—by the political authorities in Israel is in clear contrast to the enthusiasm of the crowd for the new teaching of Jesus and to the positive relationship of this teaching to the religious tradition of Israel (a tradition purified, of course, of its human additions). Broad negative judgments on "the Jews" are therefore not to be found in the gospel of Mark, which differs in this respect from that of John. A desire to make distinctions is clearly present in Mark.

Thus in at least one passage the evangelist is able to pass a judgment that is marked by great sympathy for the scribes (12:28–34), even though shortly after he takes up once again in a very undifferentiated way the hypocrisy of the scribes (12:38–40). He also admits that the crowd was still enthusiastic at the time of Jesus' entry into Jerusalem and that its later shouts of "Crucify him!'' (Mark 15:11ff.) were instigated by the high priest. But not a single positive word is said about the Pharisees, whereas the highest Roman authorities (represented by Pilate) who shared in the condemnation of Jesus are relieved of the primary responsibility for his death (though this is surely contrary to historical probability). In a complete inversion of the real distribution of power and the real legal relationships in Palestine during the time of Jesus, the Romans are portrayed in Mark's passion story as executors of the will of the Jewish authorities. And it is surely no accident that a Roman centurion beneath the cross is the first to confess the divine sonship of Jesus, whereas a few minutes before, the dying Son of God had heard nothing but blasphemy and mockery from the Jews.

In Mark's gospel this deadly hostility of the Jewish authorities evokes from Jesus a decisive and radical rejection of his own. Strikingly enough, its object is not only this particular group of agents but Israel as a religion. Thus after the death of Jesus and the confession of the centurion it is remarked that the curtain of the temple is torn (15:38). In reporting this, Mark is probably saying that God has abandoned the Holy of Holies and thus the temple. After the death of Jesus, therefore, there can no longer be any worship of God, at least not in the temple.

Three other passages are even clearer and more conclusive. In the story of the cursing of the fig tree, which is obviously a symbol of the Jewish religion (see Hos. 9:10-17, where it refers to the people in general), its final withering is predicted: "May no one ever eat fruit from you again" (Mark 11:14). And when Mark introduces, between the cursing and the report of its fulfillment (11:20ff.), the scene of the vigorous cleansing of the temple by Jesus, he makes it clear that the curse is really a response to the perversion of the temple, which God had originally meant as a house of prayer for all peoples (!), into a robbers' den.

The parable of the vinedressers goes even further (Mark 12:1-11). It is said here that God will take the vineyard from Israel and give it to others because Israel has always mistreated God's messengers and finally even put his Son to death. In fact, not only will the vineyard be taken away, but the old tenants will be put to death. The citation of a passage from the psalms at the end of this parable once again states in a metaphorical way that the rejection of Jesus by Israel has made him the cornerstone of a new building.

Finally, in Mark 13 Jesus predicts the complete destruction of the Jerusalem temple and thus makes it clear that in the terrible defeat of the Jews in their first war against Rome, at the end of which the temple was destroyed, his curse and these prophecies had their final historical fulfillment. When the Jewish authorities rejected the new teaching of Jesus, which is the good news of God, and when they put his Son to death, they themselves pronounced sentence on their own now perverted religion and brought God's punishment upon themselves. They still have the power to drag the disciples of Jesus before their tribunals and to scourge them in the synagogues (Mark 13:9). But they are in fact only a withered barren tree, and their vineyard is taken from them, whereas the gospel is now being preached to all nations (Mark 13: 10). Apart from the following of Jesus there is only impenitence (Mark 4: 10–12).

Hostility and the Holocaust

There is no doubt that the anti-Judaism of Mark's gospel is justified in terms of what might be called a theology of history. The terrible suppression of Jewish resistance by the Romans and the fact that the temple and almost all of Jerusalem with it was leveled to the ground are taken by the evangelist as a sign of divine punishment and even as a kind of campaign of revenge by God for the killing of Jesus and as a definitive destruction of the Jewish religion. God has abandoned his people.

The author of 4 Esdras makes this same terrible event an occasion for disputing with God about his administration of justice, but he does not regard Israel as wholly abandoned by God. The gospel of Mark takes a different view: it interprets the Roman victory as marking the end of Israel as a "teaching"—that is, as instruction about the way to God. Thus the hostility of the Jewish authorities to the new teaching of Jesus only mirrors the hostility of this teaching to Judaism. The role of the Jewish authorities in the trial of Jesus (a role that is undoubtedly invented by Mark and presented in an extreme form) and the tradition of conflicts between the early followers of Jesus and their fellow Jews (a conflict exaggerated into an enmity) serve to ground a particular interpretation of a particular historical event. How did the evangelist come to this interpretation?

There can hardly be any explanation that goes beyond conjecture. My own conjecture is that the gospel of Mark is to be seen as reflecting the process in which "Christianity" separated out from Judaism after A.D. 70, and in the course of which after the catastrophic defeat by Rome Judaism united itself behind a primarily Pharisaic and scribal tradition. The community represented by the Markan group was opposed to this consolidation on both theological and ecclesiological grounds. That is, the community opposed it because of its own veneration of Jesus as Son of God, because of its composition (a majority of non-Jews?), and because of its way of life, which was so remote from the elementary practices of the Jewish religion. The confrontations in Mark 2:1–3:6 convey a clear message in this respect.

No less clear, however, is the fact that the members of the Markan group had to render an account of their "faith" before the synagogal judges and that in certain circumstances they were punished. But this punishment probably did not exceed the (permissible) measure that is depicted in Mark 13:9. Jewish courts had no jurisdiction to inflict capital punishment. Even in the passion of Jesus no such jurisdiction is claimed. On the other hand, the trial of Jesus seems meant to portray the kind of behavior the disciples were to show in such synagogal trials. This is especially so inasmuch as Peter's denial of Jesus and his avoidance of a confession of faith, which are interwoven with literary skill into the upright and courageous martyrdom of Jesus, must have served as a surely important example of a following of Jesus that, in the evangelist's opinion, had been a failure. As a matter of fact, in numerous passages the evangelist presupposes that the disciples of Jesus have failed to follow the suffering confessor of their faith. It even seems as if the evangelist is trying to consolidate this desolate and pitiful community against a background of this kind of failure and of much apostasy and erroneous teaching. I mentioned this point at the beginning of my essay.

An analysis of the discourse in parables in Mark 4, of the apocalyptic discourse in Mark 13, and of the great composition that runs from the messianic confession of Peter in Mark 8 to the arrival of Jesus at his goal, Jerusalem, in Mark 11 would support this contention. It seems to me that the gospel as a whole is a "training in Christianity" at a time when the bitter separation from the synagogue has already taken place. Consequently, entry into the group of Jesus' disciples involves more than a simple confession of faith; it means the abandonment of all previous religious and social ties, a change of religions (see Mark 3:31–35; 10:17–31). In this situation hostility toward those outside serves internal stabilization. And it is no accident that the most serious reproach to the disciples in this gospel is that they are no less obdurate and hardhearted toward Jesus than the Jewish authorities are (see Mark 6:52; 8:14–21).

In his gospel Mark breaks a path that Matthew and Luke—the two recipients of his work whom we know of—follow as their own. The intensity of the rejection of Judaism by the early Christian communities increases rather than abates after A.D. 70. The judgment passed becomes ever more unrelenting and the denial of any justification for the independent religious existence of the Jews becomes ever more threatening, while Christians lay claim to the Jewish religious inheritance. Nothing changes in this respect even when the early Christian minorities enter upon a historical course that proves successful.

But did the church rightly invoke Mark, Matthew, and Luke? As far as the content of its theological position in regard to Judaism is concerned, the negative judgments passed by the church do in fact have a basis in the New Testament. But we must also look at the reversal of power relationships that had meanwhile occurred and at the potent instruments that the church acquired in the process and used, or allowed to be used, against Jewish life and limb. How is it, finally, that this same church failed in its mission when faced, less than a generation ago, with the murder of millions upon millions of Jewish children, women, and men, at a time when killing and the doing of evil were just as much the order of the day as were the omission of good and the failure to save lives, although such saving is always and everywhere commanded?

It is the epochal horror of the Holocaust that is forcing Christian theology and the Christian church to reverse its hostile attitude to the Jews and their religion. The search for the roots of this hostility cannot stop short of the

New Testament. But it is not truthfulness alone that makes it necessary to reflect on Christian fundamentals in the light of this real history and especially on the Christian claim to absoluteness. The question is a life-or-death one for the church. A renunciation of "overidentification" on the part of the church in relation to the Jews and their religion[17] might well be a first step in the practice of Christian solidarity with the members of other religions.

NOTES

1. On this point, see L. Steiger, *Erzählter Glaube—Die Evangelien* (Gütersloh, 1978).

2. For more recent literature on the Gospel of Mark, see the two-volume commentary by R. Pesch (Freiburg, 1976–77). On Mark 2:1–3:6 in particular and on the problem of the relationship between the Gospel of Mark and Judaism, see P. von der Osten-Sacken, "Streitgespräch und Parabel als Formen markinischer Christologie," in P. Strecker, ed., *Jesus Christus in Historie und Theologie. Neutestamentliche Festschrift für H. Conzelmann* (Tübingen, 1975), pp. 375–94; T. A. Burkill, *Mysterious Revelation. An Examination of the Philosophy of Mark's Gospel* (New York, 1963), pp. 117–42; T. L. Budenstein, "Jesus and the Disciples in Conflict with Judaism," ZNW, 62 (1971) 190–209; H. W. Kuhn, "Zum Problem des Verhältnisses der markinischen Redaktion zur israelitisch-jüdischen Tradition," in G. Jeremias, H. W. Kuhn, and H. Stegemann, eds., *Tradition und Glaube: Das frühe Christentum in seiner Umwelt (Festgabe für K. G. Kuhn)* (Göttingen, 1971), pp. 299–309.

3. I have dealt with this strand of the tradition especially in my dissertation "Das Markusevangelium als Ruf in die Nachfolge" (Heidelberg, 1974).

4. See Pesch 1:116ff.

5. See Osten-Sacken, "Streitgespräch," p. 377.

6. See G. Theissen, *Sociology of Early Palestinian Christianity*, J. Bowden, trans. (Philadelphia, 1978), pp. 8–16.

7. Mark uses a very disparaging term here for the healed man's spreading of the word.

8. In 2:10, as elsewhere in his gospel, Mark uses "Son of man" as a self-description of Jesus. The term may be a pseudonym for "Son of God."

9. See Osten-Sacken, "Streitgespräch," p. 378.

10. The text speaks here of "the scribes of the Pharisees"!

11. See L. Schottroff and W. Stegemann, *Jesus von Nazareth—Hoffnung der Armen* (Stuttgart, 1978), pp. 16ff.

12. See Osten-Sacken, "Streitgespräch," pp. 375–76.

13. See Pesch 2:319ff.

14. See H. W. Kuhn, *Ältere Sammlungen im Markusevangelium* (Göttingen, 1971), pp. 53ff.

15. I have done this to some extent in my dissertation (n. 3, above).

16. See Schottroff and Stegemann, *Jesus von Nazareth*, pp. 16ff.

17. See Rosemary Ruether, *Faith and Fratricide: The Theological Roots of Anti-Semitism* (New York, 1974), and P. von der Osten-Sacken's epilogue to the German translation, *Nächstenliebe und Brüdermord: Die theologischen Wurzeln des Antisemitismus* (Munich, 1978).

8

The Sabbath Was Made for Man:
The Interpretation of Mark 2:23–28

LUISE SCHOTTROFF AND
WOLFGANG STEGEMANN

The tradition of interpretation of the story of the plucking of the ears of grain on the Sabbath can be very concisely summed up as follows. The focus in the interpretations of the story is on the contrast between the freedom that Jesus gives and the legalistic casuistry (of the Pharisees) from which human beings at times have to suffer. Mark 2:27 is regarded as the central statement in the pre-Markan story of the plucking of the ears (2:23–27) and is often attributed to the historical Jesus. The key phrases in which each interpreter tries to formulate the meaning of the story are usually reflections of Mark 2:27.[1] Here are two important and representative interpretations: "Priority is no longer given to the Sabbath and the requirements of the law; human beings and their needs are valued more highly than the commandment regarding the Sabbath" (E. Lohse).[2] "All scenes dealing with the Sabbath emphasize the importance of the human person as compared with the day of worship" (H. Braun).[3]

Our intention here is not to criticize the various exegetes but to criticize rather an exegetical tradition that in our opinion does not do justice to the meaning of the story. The persuasive power of this tradition is so great that it is undoubtedly very difficult even to attempt to abandon it. But this tradition seems to us to call for two criticisms:

1) It speaks in too general a way of "man" or "human beings" (this is surely a result of the formulation in Mark 2:27).

2) It depends upon a contrast, which in our view is historically incorrect,

118

between "law" and "the human," or between "casuistry" and "humaneness."[4]

The conflicts over the Sabbath in which Jesus is reported as being involved are in fact much more concrete. Furthermore, to the extent that they concern the Jesus movement within the Jewish people, we shall not understand them properly if we apply to them a contrast between "human beings" and "law." A reading of Matthew's version of the same story will help us here to acquire a needed distance from our own habits of thought. For Matthew understands the story in a way quite different from the one to which we are accustomed.

Whether Matthew in fact understands it correctly is a question we will have to answer later on.

Matthew's Interpretation

The plucking of the ears of grain on the Sabbath (Matt. 12:1–8), like the story of the tax collector's supper (Matt. 9:9–13), is *for Matthew* a story about the mercy of Jesus and the central importance of love of neighbor in the Torah. No attack is made either on the Sabbath or on the Pharisees' Sabbath observance. The only thing attacked is an erroneous interpretation of the law by the Pharisees (that is, by the Pharisees of the time when Matthew's gospel was being composed). "If you had known what this means, 'I desire mercy, and not sacrifice,' you would not have condemned the guiltless" (12:7). The Pharisees' erroneous interpretation leads them to condemn the plucking of the ears by the disciples as an impermissible desecration of the Sabbath; Matthew does not agree that this is a valid judgment.

The disciples are hungry (compare Matt. 12:1 with Mark 2:23). Jesus allows them to pluck and eat some ears of grain, even though it is the Sabbath. The fact that they actually eat the grain is stated in the opening verse in Matthew; the same fact is not stated at all in Mark. Moreover, the fact that *they* eat, but not Jesus, is important to Matthew (note the alterations in Matt. 12:4 as compared with Mark 2:25–26). That Jesus allows the hungry to eat is due to his mercifulness, as Matthew indicates with the help of a citation from Hosea, thus adding to the story as it came to him (Matt. 12:7). Here Jesus himself is exercising the mercy toward the hungry that Matthew regards as a central element in practical mercy and love for neighbor, as he makes clear in 25:31–46: to feed the hungry, give drink to the thirsty, and so on. Mercy and love of neighbor are commanded by God and his Torah. In Matthew's eyes love of neighbor is *the* commandment of the Torah and no less important than the commandment of love of God (Matt. 22:39, 40).

When Matthew 12:7 says: "I desire mercy, and not sacrifice," the point is not that the moral law takes precedence over the ceremonial law.[5] Matthew's intention is rather that the entire Torah should be observed (5:17), but in accordance with the consistent interpretation that Jesus gives of it. The "antitheses" of the Sermon on the Mount do not set the commandments of Jesus *in opposition to* the Torah; rather, Jesus is interpreting the Torah. He is explaining what God's intention is in the commandments of the Torah. But in fact in the Torah itself there are already instances in which, in a given concrete situation, one commandment comes into conflict with another. In such cases, one commandment takes precedence over the other. Thus the commandment requiring priestly service in the temple takes precedence over the Sabbath commandment (Matt. 12:5 with the help of Num. 28:9–10). When, in a concrete case, the Sabbath commandment comes into conflict with the commandment of love (as it does in the case of the plucking of the ears), then the commandment of love takes precedence.

In cases of conflict,[6] then, the principle holds: "I desire mercy, not sacrifice." This is not to say that the commandment of love of neighbor cancels out other commandments of the Torah or devaluates them in principle. It says only that in case of a conflict there is a kind of hierarchy among the commandments of the Torah. And in *this* hierarchy the commandment of love of neighbor stands very high, higher even than the commandment of service in the temple. Matthew 12:6 is arguing from the less important to the more important. As compared with the commandment of service in the temple, the commandment of love is "greater." The statement that the Son of man is lord of the Sabbath does not mean for Matthew that Jesus does away with or relativizes the Sabbath, but that as interpreter of the Torah and teacher of God's will he can, in case of conflict, declare the legitimacy of an infringement of the Sabbath.

The Matthean community observed the Sabbath (see Matt. 24:20). For this community the story of the plucking of the ears is not a story of opposition to the Sabbath; when repeated in the story as told by Matthew, even Mark 2:28 loses the element of dissociation from the Sabbath that it has in the Markan story. The fact that at the beginning of the story Matthew immediately identifies the reason for the infringement of the Sabbath—namely, hunger—may be due to a desire on his part to avoid giving the false impression that the Sabbath may be infringed for just any reason at all, even an arbitrary one. No, the reason here is the hunger of the disciples and the observance of the commandment of love. The fact that Matthew omits Mark 2:27 ("The Sabbath was made for man, not man for the Sabbath") fits quite well into this picture. Mark 2:27 *in connection with* Mark 2:28 can only be interpreted as a dissociation in principle from the Sabbath commandment.[7]

Matthew is evidently leery of an *interpretatio christiana* of the essentially valid rabbinical principle given in Mark 2:27; this *interpretatio christiana* was known to him, as it is known to us, from Mark 2:23–28. Matthew does not criticize the Sabbath commandment, but neither does he criticize the Pharisaic observance of the commandment, or Pharisaic casuistry in dealing with the Sabbath. In fact, if the rabbinical interpretation of the law be called casuistic, then Matthew's own argumentation must likewise be called casuistic. Matthew criticizes the Pharisees for not properly interpreting the Torah and for not realizing that in this case of conflict the commandment of love takes precedence over the Sabbath commandment. Because they do not correctly understand the Torah, they condemn the disciples (see especially the formulation at the end of Matt. 12:7 as compared with Mark 2:24). They regard the plucking of the ears as an impermissible infringement of the Sabbath. But it is in fact an infringement allowed by the Law itself. For this reason the disciples are innocent (Matt. 12:7).

The purpose of the story in Matthew is to clarify the *importance of mercy as a commandment of the Torah* through a critical confrontation with the Pharisees who would judge differently in this case and give the commandment of love a lower rank in the hierarchy. If we survey the rabbinical discussion of cases of need that take precedence over the Sabbath, we may well conclude that in a case such as the one discussed here in the gospel they would probably have said that, inasmuch as the hunger in question is not a real danger to life, the disciples can wait until the Sabbath is over.[8] Matthew's view, on the contrary, is that because of the disciples' hunger mercy takes precedence over the Sabbath or, in other words, "it is lawful to do good on the Sabbath" (Matt. 12:12). The reason for the infringement of the Sabbath is thus of decisive importance for Matthew. The disciples' hunger justifies the infringement of the Sabbath.

As the situation is narrated by Matthew, but also by the earliest form in which the story was transmitted (see below), we must picture it as follows. The disciples pick the now almost ripe "rubbing ears," as they were called. The ears were rubbed by hand, the small bristles were blown away, and the grains were eaten raw.[9] This was the kind of modest meal taken by someone who became hungry while working in the fields or by a poor person who might be passing by a field of grain. Did farmers in fact allow strangers to pluck the ears? It is doubtful that they did, because, in the first Christian century, as in later rabbinical interpretation, the Old Testament law that allows the poor to take food in this way (Deut. 23:26) seems no longer to have been understood as a law permitting the "theft" of food. It was understood rather as permission for wage earners working in the harvest to take some food from the field during rest periods.[10] It was probably neither allowed nor forbidden for strangers to pluck the ears. If the farmer were present it would hardly happen. This view fits in with the flow of the story, which does not think to ask whether the plucking of ears is permitted apart from the Sabbath. On the Sabbath itself the plucking was probably prohibited as being a preparation for a meal, just as cooking itself was prohibited on the Sabbath—prohibited, that is, as a form of work.[11]

In Matthew's eyes, hunger is not just any reason for infringing the Sabbath. Hunger calls for mercy and practical love of neighbor. The principle that human needs take precedence over the Sabbath is not one that Matthew would accept *in so general a form*. He would say that the works of love commanded in 25:31–46, or the needs reflected in this list, do take precedence over the Sabbath. Matthew 12:1–8 is part of an intra-Judaic discussion between the Pharisees of the Diaspora after A.D. 70 and the "Jewish Christians''[12] regarding the significance of mercy as a commandment of God. In this discussion ''mercy'' is to be thought of in a concrete way as an exercise of practical works of love along the lines of Matthew 25:31–46.

Matthew's interpretation of the story can obviously help us to achieve the needed distance from the kind of interpretation of it that we bring with us. Furthermore, insofar as the story in Matthew's gospel differs from the version in the gospel of Mark, it can also help us better to appreciate the special character the story has in Mark—both at the level of the interpretation that Mark's gospel gives the story by the context in which it places it, and at the level of the pre-Markan tradition.

Mark's Interpretation of the Pre-Markan Tradition

If we turn from Matthew to Mark, it is chiefly the significance that Mark 2:28 acquires through its context that determines the meaning of the story in Mark. When Mark says that the Son of man is lord of the Sabbath, his meaning is that Christians are not obliged to observe the Sabbath and that new wine should be put into *new* wineskins (Mark 2:22 in the context of 2:18–22). In Mark's view, the dispute of Jesus with the Pharisees over the Sabbath is a dispute that, joined to other conflicts with the Pharisees, leads to the decision that Jesus must die (Mark 3:6). Mark 2:27, taken in connection with 2:28 and with 3:1–6, means that the Pharisees make the Sabbath more important than human beings and their needs, whereas Jesus gives them priority over the Sabbath, which the followers of Jesus now have no reason for observing. The fact that the Sabbath exists for the sake of man is indirectly illustrated by Mark in a new scene (3:1–6) in which Jesus makes a sick man the focus of attention (3:3). Mark 2:27 tells us how Mark sees the positive purpose of Jesus: Jesus focuses attention on human beings and their needs. At the same time, the hardness of heart of the Pharisees, as Mark sees it, becomes clear by contrast.[13]

In Matthew Jesus debates with the Pharisees (12:5–7, 11–12). In Mark (3:1–6) it becomes clear that there is no room for debate; rather there is a hardening of the positions.

In this context Mark 2:23–26 or 23–27 seems an alien body, whereas 2:28 fully expresses Mark's meaning. Mark 2:28 is therefore often, and rightly, taken as Markan. Mark 2:23–26(27), on the other hand, presents the confrontation between Jesus and the Pharisees in a different way than does the context (see esp. 3:5–6). In the story of the plucking of the ears Jesus carries on a discussion with the Pharisees and offers arguments to which it is possible for them to assent.

Mark 2:25–26 proposes the same argument that is found in Matthew 12:5–6: even the Torah allows for the infringement of a divine commandment in a concrete case. If we compare Mark 2:23–26(27) with Matthew 12:1–8 it becomes clear that both texts argue in terms acceptable within Judaism, but also that the passage in Mark represents a less sharp conflict with the Pharisees than does the passage in Matthew. Matthew has turned the question asked by the Pharisees in Mark 2:24 into an assertion *and* a condemnation (Matt. 12:2, 7).

In connection with the question of the Pharisees in Mark 2:24 and with the argument from the Torah in 2:25–26, Mark 2:27—as part of the pre-Markan story—becomes a further argument for the possibility of an infringement of the Sabbath by plucking ears of grain. An appeal is made to the meaning that God gave to the Sabbath at creation. The Sabbath is meant to help persons and promote their well-being. In its pre-Markan context 2:27 represents neither a dissociation from the Sabbath nor a relativization of the Sabbath; it is rather an argument in which the God-given meaning of the Sabbath leads to the conclusion that the disciples' infringement of the Sabbath is permissible.

The negatively formulated half of the sentence ("not man for the Sabbath") is not, in this context, a rejection of an opponent's position. The Pharisees are not saying in Mark 2:23–27 that human beings were made for the Sabbath. This part of the sentence is often wrongly understood as referring to a position held by the Pharisees. Such an interpretation is not supported by the views of the Pharisees either in Jewish history of the first century A.D. or in the pre-Markan story. The negative part of the sentence is meant only to clarify the positive half by restating it negatively and thus to compel the assent of the partner in dialogue. Pious Jews would have no desire to say that human beings were made for the Sabbath, any more than they would be willing to say that David had done wrong. In the context of the pre-Markan story, Mark 2:27 has a meaning that is close to that of rabbinic parallels to this sentence. The rabbinic aphorism "The Sabbath is given to you, not you to the Sabbath"[14] refers simply to another case of permissible infringement of the Sabbath—namely, the supersession of the Sabbath when there is danger to human life. This is not the issue in Mark 2:27, but the thinking of the rabbis is comparable to that in Mark 2:27.[15]

In light of these considerations we may conclude that the pre-Markan story of the plucking of the ears of grain (Mark 2:23–27) derives from a period in which the intra-Judaic conflict with the Jesus movement had not yet reached the point of severity that is reflected in the gospel of Matthew. The story is connected with the Jesus movement in Palestine *before* the destruction of Jerusalem. That it is even to be connected with the very earliest Jesus movement remains to be shown.

If then we compare—as we have done in this section of our essay—the versions of the story of the plucking of grain as told in Matthew, in Mark, and in the pre-Markan tradition, we find significant differences in the attitude of the Pharisees toward Jesus. These differences make it possible to relate each of the *three* stories to a historical context.

The Meaning of the Pre-Markan Story

Hunger and Mercy

In Matthew 12:1–8 the hunger of the disciples is the reason given for the plucking of the ears of grain. Matthew emphasizes this point right at the beginning. In doing so he has not appreciably altered the story in any essential way. In the pre-Markan story, too, the disciples pluck the ears because they are hungry. Mark 2:23–24 clearly presupposes that they have acted out of hunger, and it even presupposes that this fact is perfectly clear to the hearer. Verses 25–26 then go on to make this hunger the basis of an argument.

In Matthew, 12:1–8 the hunger of the disciples is a hunger that calls out for mercy. But the pre-Markan story says nothing about mercy. Neither does it say that one commandment of God (love of neighbor) is here in conflict with another commandment (observance of the Sabbath). It says rather that hunger takes precedence over the Sabbath law because the Torah itself already makes it clear that hunger justifies an infringement of a divine commandment (vv. 25–26).

We must see the hunger of the disciples in the real historical context out of which the story comes. It comes from first-century Palestine, which was subject to the rule of the Roman emperor. Here, as elsewhere in the Roman empire, a sizable part of the population had barely enough to sustain life.[16] The many poor who play a part in the synoptic tradition at all historical levels, and of whom Josephus likewise speaks, are starving. If we keep in mind this historical context, we can understand that the hunger of the disciples is not that of persons who accidentally have nothing to eat, perhaps because they have forgotten to bring food with them. In Matthew's estimation the hunger of the disciples is that of the poor; it calls out for mercy. In taking this view Matthew has doubtless grasped the real situation better than his modern interpreters who consider the reason for the infringement of the Sabbath to be either secondary or replaceable by some other.

There are, then, two reasons compelling us to interpret the hunger of the disciples as the hunger of the poor of Palestine: (1) the fact that Matthew too understands the text in this way; and (2) the real historical context in which the story belongs. A third reason can be seen in the importance that the story assigns to the hunger. We must now go on to ask what connection the story establishes between the hunger of the disciples and the Sabbath.

The Infringement of the Sabbath

The plucking of the ears of grain is an infringement of the Sabbath. Behind the Pharisees' question in Mark 2:24 stands the idea that this infringement is illegitimate, "forbidden," when judged by Jewish theological conceptions of God, the Torah, and the Sabbath. The arguments in Mark 2:25–26 endeavor to show that, on the contrary, when judged by these Jewish theological conceptions of God, the Torah, and the Sabbath, this *infringement* of the Sabbath is legitimate. The type of argument is similar to that which we know from Matthew and from the rabbis. For Matthew this infringement of the Sabbath is legitimate because the commandment of love of neighbor takes precedence over the Sabbath commandment. Many rabbis argue that a danger to life supersedes the Sabbath. Here, in Mark, it is said that *hunger* does so. But what does this mean?

Let us turn again to Matthew for help. In Matthew the plucking of the ears of grain is a symbolic act. The intention is not to justify works of love on the Sabbath but rather to point out the proper order that exists between the commandment of love and the Sabbath commandment. The pre-Markan story likewise tells of a symbolic infringement of the Sabbath. Its ultimate purpose is not to justify a future plucking of grain on the Sabbath. This would be of no use to anyone, least of all the poor of Palestine.

This infringement of the Sabbath is meant rather to show the true *status of hunger* when measured by Jewish theological conceptions of God, the Torah, and the Sabbath. In God's eyes the hunger of the poor is more important than the Sabbath and imposes a more important religious duty than does even the Sabbath. If we reflect on the central role of the Sabbath for the Israelite people, we become aware of the enormous religious claim being made in the story. The hunger of the poor is explained in a symbolic way as setting Israel its *central* religious task, one that takes precedence even over the duty of observing the Sabbath. The intention is not to attack or relativize the importance of the Sabbath, but rather to use the Sabbath in order to bring out the importance of alleviating hunger. The test-case infringement of the Sabbath has a positive, not a negative and critical, purpose. The focus of attention is not on criticism of the Sabbath but on the hunger of the poor.

Whereas Matthew is forced to bring the idea of mercy into the story in a somewhat roundabout way (Jesus gives food to his disciples—an idea that hardly emerges from the de facto scene), the pre-Markan story is much simpler. It can readily be taken as not a literary, fictive story, such as Matthew's is, but as a report of an actual occurrence, of a real test-case infringement of the Sabbath. We can confidently assume that Jesus and his disciples (or members of the Jesus movement after his death), who were themselves poor and lived among the poor, might seek, by means of a test-case infringement of the Sabbath, to bring home to the Pharisees or to other pious Jews willing to listen to them, what the times were saying: that there were now no alternatives left. Anyone who wants to serve God must take the side of the poor. Mark 2:23–27 is saying precisely what the Beatitude on the poor in Luke 6:20–21 says: that everything that God has promised to Israel by way of salvation belongs to the poor. They now take precedence over everyone else.

The nucleus of the tradition regarding the other Sabbath confrontations of Jesus yields the same picture. Noncritical illnesses are healed: the withered hand (Mark 3:1–5 and parallels); the woman bent over for eighteen years (Luke 13:10); the man with dropsy (Luke 14:1–6); a man who had been sick for many years (John 5:6, 10); and a man blind from birth (John 9:1, 14). In all these conflicts over the Sabbath, the infringements of the Sabbath are therefore *symbolical*. The distress of the sick takes precedence over the Sabbath no less than does the hunger of the poor. The distress of the sick imposes a religious duty that takes precedence over the duty imposed by the Sabbath commandment. The gospels of Luke and John interpret these conflicts about the Sabbath in their own ways, and we need not go into them here. On the other hand, we do have to explain the fact that, despite quite different subsequent interpretations, the basic presupposition—de facto conflicts about the Sabbath—is retained throughout.

The explanation is to be found in the central content of the earliest tradition about Jesus. This content is so firmly linked to these symbolic infringements of the Sabbath that it is still recognizable as part of the basic structure of all the stories about Sabbath confrontations. The healings of the sick on the Sabbath are an implementation of what the earliest tradition about Jesus also calls the "gospel of the poor": the blind see, the lame walk . . . (Matt. 11:2–5 and parallels). The miraculous healings mark the beginning of God's kingly reign. Through these healings the poor—for in the last analysis it is chiefly they who make up the sick—come to realize what it means to say that in God's eyes they are more important than the Sabbath. In view of the Sabbath healings and of Matthew 11:2–5 (and parallels) it is perhaps even possible to maintain that in the earliest tradition about Jesus the plucking of the ears of grain on the Sabbath is intended to mark the beginning of God's kingly reign: now the Beatitude on the poor is being fulfilled! In a series of symbolic cases the followers of Jesus have violated the Sabbath by miraculous healings and by plucking ears of grain. They have thus made it clear that God's reign is now beginning and that the poor are at last receiving what has been withheld from them.

The Poor of Palestine

In regard to the earliest, pre-Markan stage of transmission, the interpretation given here of the plucking of the ears of grain on the Sabbath is methodologically different in one important way from the tradition of interpretation that was mentioned at the beginning of this essay—namely, its attention to the historical and social situation in interpreting the text. The story cannot be interpreted apart from the hunger and poverty of Palestine.

In order to test in a further and different way the necessity of this methodological approach, we shall briefly discuss another current interpretation of the same material. H. Braun regards the stories about the Sabbath conflicts of Jesus as productions of the community (he includes Mark 2:23–28), but he also maintains that in these stories Jesus' "critical attitude to the Sabbath" is correctly portrayed.

> All the Sabbath scenes emphasize the greater importance of the human person over the day of worship, and they usually do so by having Jesus effect a healing on the Sabbath . . . and on one occasion by having the disciples pluck ears of grain on the Sabbath. . . . It is quite evident that the situation is artificially constructed and meant to serve as a type. In the earlier stage of transmission the arguments clearly . . . express the superior value of the person as compared with the Sabbath: the Sabbath is made for man, not man for the Sabbath.[17]

In Braun's view Mark 2:27 gets to the heart of the matter; he also considers it to be probably an authentic saying of Jesus. We need not discuss here his particular interpretation of the plucking of the grain as a fictive occasion for a violation of the Sabbath. In any case, Braun maintains that in the Sabbath healings human distress is the reason for infringements of the Sabbath—infringements that bring out the greater value of the human person as compared with the Sabbath.

In our opinion, however, this thesis needs to be made more concrete. The real issue is not the Sabbath in principle or the human person in principle, but the poor of Palestine. No criticism is made of the Sabbath or, for example, Pharisaic observance of the Sabbath. We should not think of the relationship of the earliest Jesus tradition to the Pharisees or comparable Jewish groups as being one of theological confrontation at the level of dogmatic principle. The Sabbath confrontations do deal with dogmatic positions, but only in a concrete context and in the interests of a concrete goal. "The Sabbath is made for man" has a concrete function in Mark 2:23–28, and it is from this function that the principle acquires its specific meaning.

Braun tells of a sermon he gave on this or a related text when he was a pastor in Magdeburg shortly after 1945. During the previous week a freight train carrying cabbages had stood in the station. Individuals who were starving and freezing, most of them women and children, had stolen the cabbages. Braun defended this theft in his sermon: human beings take precedence over the law. Clearly enough, such a concrete application of biblical exegesis is not reached by socio-historical methods. Socio-historical interpretation is meant rather as a help to concrete preaching. But concrete preaching will always be superior in existential terms to any socio-historical interpretation of the Bible.

NOTES

1. In this interpretive essay we are continuing a work that appeared under the title "Armut verdrängt den Sabbat" in a volume of essays presented to H. Thyen (privately printed).

2. "Jesu Worte über den Sabbat," in *Judentum, Christentum, Kirche. Festschrift für J. Jeremias* (Berlin, 1960), p. 85; see also, idem, "sabbaton," TDNT, 7:22, 25.

3. *Spätjüdisch-häretischer und frühchristlicher Radikalismus*, 2 (Tübingen, 1950), p. 70.

4. R. Pesch, *Das Markusevangelium*, 1 (Freiburg, 1976), p. 196, says that the "inhuman casuistry of a perverted religious obedience" is being condemned here.

5. See also the arguments of G. Barth, "Matthew's Understanding of the Law," in G. Bornkamm, G. Barth, and H. J. Held, *Tradition and Interpretation in Matthew*, P. Scott, trans. (Philadelphia, 1963), pp. 82–83.

6. See E. Schweizer, *The Good News according to Matthew*, D. E. Green, trans. (Atlanta, 1975), pp. 276–79.

7. See also R. Hummel, *Die Auseinandersetzung zwischen Kirche und Judentum im Matthäusevangelium* (Munich, 1966), pp. 40–41.

8. It is probable that the Pharisees generally thought of danger to human life as constituting a situation that took precedence over the Sabbath; see esp. Mehilta on

Exod. 31:12, 14; bYoma 85b (Yoma 8, 6); cf. Mark 3:4; Luke 6:9; a collection of material on this question may be found in Billerbeck 1:624ff. See E. Schürer, *A History of the Jewish People in the Time of Jesus*, S. Taylor and F. Christie, trans. (New York, n.d.), div. 2, vol. 2, pp.96–105.

9. G. Dalman, *Arbeit und Sitte in Palästina*, 3 (Gütersloh, 1933), pp. 126–27; S. Krauss, *Talmudische Archäologie*, 1 (Leipzig, 1910), pp. 93–94.

10. bBM 87b.

11. G. Dalman examines this explanation of Mark 2:23–27 in *Arbeit und Sitte*, p. 263. Luke 6:1 adds the phrase *psochontes tais chersin* ("rubbing [them] in their hands") and thus shows the purpose of the plucking of the ears; he thereby relates the action to the prohibition against preparing food on the Sabbath; *any* work is forbidden on the Sabbath. Luke's clarification fits the real situation. The explanation frequently offered, that the plucking of the ears is a kind of *harvesting* and as such forbidden on the Sabbath, does not do justice to the context.

12. More accurately: Jews who are disciples of Jesus and await his coming at the judgment. For the historical situation in the Gospel of Matthew, see chap. 9, below.

13. For further explanation of the Sabbath conflicts in Mark and especially of their concrete significance for the Markan community, E. Stegemann's essay in this volume (chap. 7) and his dissertation "Das Markusevangelium als Ruf in die Nachfolge" (Heidelberg, 1974).

14. Mekilta on Exod. 31:12, 14; see the German translation by J. Winter and A. Wünsche, *Mechiltha* (Leipzig, 1909), p. 336; for parallel traditions, see Billerbeck 1:623.

15. W. Nowack, *Die Mischna: Schabbat* (Giessen, 1923), p. 24, wrongly interprets the saying "the Sabbath is given to you" as an ineffective exception to an otherwise rabbinical interpretation of the law that lays burdens on human beings.

16. See the evidence in Schottroff and Stegemann, "Armut verdrängt," pp. 26–28.

17. *Radikalismus*, 2:70.

9

Human Solidarity and the Goodness of God: The Parable of the Workers in the Vineyard

LUISE SCHOTTROFF

The Social and Legal Situation in the Parable

Presuppositions Derived from the Parable Itself

Like many other parables, the one in Matthew 20:1–16 tells a story from real life. A proper understanding of it requires, therefore, that the real-life situation be explained with as much detail and accuracy as posssible. Above all, we must not tacitly appeal to modern relationships between worker and employer as we try to interpret the parable.

Detailed socio-historical information is extremely important because interpreters set the switches, as it were, for their interpretations precisely at the points at which they see the story as departing from everyday reality. For example, an interpreter who thinks that the continued hiring of laborers until late in the day is improbable in the case of an earthly employer will interpret the parable differently from an interpreter who regards this element in the story as plausible but considers full-time wages for a part-time worker to be improbable. In the one case, God's goodness comes into play in the hiring; in the other, it is manifested in the wages.

The parable itself reveals the following socio-historical presuppositions. First of all, it is an everyday occurrence for the owner of a vineyard to hire workers in the marketplace. Men seeking work wait there for jobs. The owner of the vineyard goes in person to look for workers; such a man is not, of course, a great landowner who assigns slaves in administrative positions to this kind of duty and does not himself pay much attention to the wine harvest.

Pliny the younger was a landowner of this type, and there were some such in Palestine as well. Pliny complains:

> I have just been getting in the vintage—a slender one this year, although more plentiful than I had expected—provided I may speak of "getting in the vintage" when I have simply picked a grape here and there, glanced into the press, tasted the must in the vat, and surprised my town servants who are now supervising the rural workers and have left me to my secretaries and readers.[1]

The owner in Matthew 20 has less land than that; he does have a steward (Matt. 20:8) who supervises the workers and pays them their wages, but he nonetheless goes in person to the market place in order to hire temporary workers.

The day laborers evidently do not expect any long-term contract but only a job for the day. As the story develops, it becomes clear that there are more workers available in the marketplace than are needed and that unemployment, even at harvesttime, is the rule among rural workers. Matthew 20:7 explicitly says that these men are unemployed: "No one has hired us." The degree of unemployment may be gauged above all from the matter-of-fact way in which we are told of workers who are still standing around in the marketplace at 9 o'clock (3rd hour), noon (6th hour), 3 o'clock in the afternoon (9th hour), and 5 o'clock (11th hour).

There is still another sign of unemployment. Harvesttimes are the most work-intensive periods in a rural economy. Day laborers who find work during the harvests are not employed on the farms apart from these periods. We can only guess at how they support themselves. Either they have farms of their own, which are too small to support a family, or they belong to the uprooted whom hunger drives into the countryside at harvesttime but who at other seasons look for occasional work in the cities—and who often enough must beg as well. We should not read into the parable the idea that the laborers who still have no work at midday are lazy and that their claim to have found no employer is a lazy man's excuse. No, the situation of unemployment is clear from the story itself.

The agreements with the day laborers are varied and are reported in detail. With the long-shift workers—that is, those hired at the beginning of the day—an oral agreement on wages is made. The workers agree to the wage and the hours, and are then sent off to work. To judge by the parable, one denarius is evidently the usual day's wage in that area. No such detailed agreement is made with the four groups of short-shift workers. The first three groups are hired, and the amount of the wage is left unspecified: "Whatever is right I will give you." The story presupposes that the precise amount of the wage is not determined in advance. There is no reason to assume that the phrase "whatever is right" refers to a wage usual throughout the area in such cases.[2] For the unemployed are evidently in such a weak position that they go off to work without any clear agreement on wages and accept the risk of having the vineyard owner pay them less than what they hope for. Finally, there is no question of relying on his charitableness, either in the story or in reality.

In the case of the last group of short-shift workers, those hired at the eleventh hour, there is, consistently enough, no mention at all of a wage.

The long-shift workers expected that each group of short-shift workers would be paid less than they and that the wage of these groups would be proportioned to the amount of time spent at work or, more probably, would take the form of a meal and a minimal amount of money. The workday lasts from sunrise to before sunset. During the grape harvest in August or September the workday would be twelve or thirteen hours long.[3] Workers hired at the eleventh hour (of the workday) thus, in all probability, work only a good hour or so.

The story tells us that the vineyard owner hires his day laborers in five stages, but it does not lay any emphasis on this point. If such a procedure were inconceivable or even just unusual in everyday real life, the story would make this clear.

It is obvious enough that the wage given to the short-shift workers is an unusual one. The course of the story itself thus compels us to agree with J. Jeremias's conjecture that at harvesttime vineyard owners do what they can to complete the harvest by evening.[4]

The story speaks of five groups of day laborers, but the second, third, and fourth groups play only a secondary role. In the dispute about the wage paid, these groups make no appearance. There are obviously good artistic reasons for this. The essential thing is the dispute about the wage paid to the two groups furthest apart. To report on the wage paid to the other three groups would be to introduce a detail superfluous from the artistic viewpoint. These other groups have to be mentioned in connection with the hiring, because a vineyard owner would not wait until the eleventh hour to judge that he needs still more workers; instead, he would keep on top of the situation and bring in extra workers in several stages as he determines that those already hired are not enough.

The payment of wages in the evening is likewise taken for granted and is to be regarded as the rule for such day laborers, unless of course the employer is trying to cheat them of their wage (see Lev. 19:13; Deut. 24:15). The relationship between employer and day laborers is to be thought of as a very loose one; the workers do not expect that the same employer will be able to use them the next day.

The story makes it clear that the amount of the wage paid to the short-shift workers is utterly unusual, so unusual that the long-shift workers may well expect so kind an employer to show them the same generosity and pay them substantially more than the agreed wage. It is not said that they expect five or six times as much, in keeping with the length of time they have worked. If a denarius is the usual day's wage, then a wage five or six times greater would be improbably large and even ridiculous in the judgment of hearers. Further-more, such a view of the matter presupposes that work was paid for by the hour, but this is something that cannot be simply assumed to have been the case in antiquity. It is obvious that the vineyard owner is free to give away what is his own. The unusual thing is that in fact he does so.

Such is the extent to which the story itself and its manner of relating events permits us to reconstruct reality and identify departures from it. The story is quite plausible in all its details; only the employer's generosity is unusual. The dispute that this generosity occasions is the point to which the parable is meant to lead.

Socio-Historical Material

Most of the observations made thus far can be confirmed by what we know of social history.

The fact that extra day laborers were hired during the various harvests is not attested solely by this parable, although we should not underestimate the value of the parable as a source of information about social history. The use of day laborers during harvests is also attested for the Roman rural economy; the testimonies so closely resemble those of the parable that the information in the two sources is mutually confirmatory. Consequently, in this particular question at least, we can draw upon Roman writers of agriculture in order to clarify further the situation in Palestine. In addition, the Book of Ruth shows a comparable situation. The reapers who work in Boaz's field and are super-vised by an overseer (Ruth 2:3ff.) are probably harvest workers hired by the day, or else a crew hired for the harvest period, such as is known also from the Roman economy.[5]

Varro (116–127 A.D.) wrote his *Res rusticae* ("On Agriculture") when he was eighty years old. As far as the workers used in the rural economy are concerned, he is interested primarily in the overseer, and he offers the land-owner advice on dealing with this overseer or steward in the interests of greater productivity.

What he says about rural workers themselves is said rather in passing:

> All agriculture is carried on by men—slaves, or freemen, or both: by freemen, when they till the ground themselves, as many poor persons do with the help of their families; or hired hands *(mercennarii)*, when the heavier farm operations, such as the vintage and the haying, are carried on by the hiring of freemen and those whom our people called *obaerarii* [those who are working off a debt], and of whom there are still many in Asia, in Egypt, and in Illyricum.[6]

Cato (234–149 B.C.) also employed freemen as day laborers and recom-mended: "He [the landowner] must not hire the same day-labourer or servant or caretaker for longer than a day."[7]

The point of this last recommendation is that the landowner should try to put day laborers in as weak a position as possible when it comes to wages. Other ways were also tried in an effort to reduce the wage of a day laborer.

Columella (ca. 1–70 A.D.) writes that a farmer should plant various kinds of vines in separate plots:

> One who separates the various sorts by sections has regard to these differences [among vines] as to situation and setting. He also gains no small advantage in that he is put to less labour and expense for the vintage; for the grapes are gathered at the proper time, as each variety begins to grow ripe, and those that have not yet reached maturity are left until a later time without loss; nor does the simultaneous ageing and ripening of fruit precipitate the vintage and force the hiring of more workmen, however great the cost.[8]

With the aid of these sources, which could be supplemented by others, we can to a great extent reconstruct the social situation of day laborers.[9] The picture that emerges is the same as that given in Matthew 20:1–15. During the harvests, and especially the grape harvest, day laborers are hired on larger estates. Even less heed is taken of their health than of the health of slaves. A clever farmer sees to it that the pressures of the harvest do not force him to pay excessive wages to these day laborers.

Modern scholars sometimes assume that contracts with day laborers were of little importance in the Roman imperial age because it was chiefly slaves who did the work.[10] But in all likelihood there were local differences in the number and situation of day laborers. Columella, for example, supposes a dearth of such workers at harvest time, whereas Matthew 20:1–15 supposes an oversupply.

It is not surprising that little attention should have been paid (in the law, for example) to this group of men who were in fact less protected than were slaves. But we may not conclude from this that they were few in number. Their numbers would be directly dependent on the economic situation of the rural population of each time and place. As estates became larger, the number of day laborers would grow.

The fact that we are better informed about the wretched condition of slaves than about the even more wretched condition of day laborers is probably connected with the fact that to the landowners of antiquity slaves were an object of economic and legal concern. In the calculations of such owners the harvest worker and his distress played a secondary role. To this extent the picture usually given of a "slaveowning society" is incomplete, and reflects the consciousness of the ruling class in antiquity. The landowner had an interest in the productivity—that is, the capacity for work and the life expectancy—of his slaves. They were his property and he had to pay for their cost and yield a profit as well. If a slave died too soon or became incapable of work too soon, the owner lost his capital investment.

The day laborer, on the other hand, was a kind of slave at his own risk.[11] The information in Matthew 20:1 that day laborers receive a denarius is difficult to evaluate when we try to reconstruct their living standard. There were fluctuations in the value of money at this period; in addition, it is not easy to determine what a worker could buy for this money and how often he could count on such a wage. On the whole, the attempt made by A. Ben-David to figure out the daily caloric intake of a day laborer's family in the period of the Mishnah will apply also to the situation of the day laborers in Matthew 20:1-15.[12] Theirs too is a life lived at "the lower limit of human nutritional needs."

Jewish and Roman law also confirm our picture of the social situation of day laborers. In the Old Testament the law prescribes that day laborers are to be paid their wage on the evening of the same day (Lev. 19:13; Deut. 24:14-15). The point is that there were employers who tried to withhold a day laborer's wage even though the latter had immediate need of it. The day laborer and his family lived from hand to mouth. The Mishnah contains detailed regulations regarding the day laborer's right to board during the time he is working. For example, he is to be kept from demanding food of too high a quality or, as the case may be, from eating too much of the produce that he is harvesting.[13] On the other hand, the employer is also prevented from failing to provide such board as is customary in the area.

Like the Old Testament, the Mishnah also requires wages to be paid on the evening of the same day. However, the Mishnah allows the employer to withhold the wage if the worker does not ask for it (BM IX, 12b). This represents a serious alteration of the Old Testament prescription: at least such workers as might hope to be hired more frequently by the same employer would under these circumstances not always have the courage to demand their wages immediately. The plight of day laborers is made especially clear by the regulation in the Tosefta: "A worker may not spend the night working for himself and then hire himself out to work for another during the day, because by doing so he robs his employer [by not being able to work as energetically] in the work given to him."[14]

These legal prescriptions show us how compromised in many respects the day laborer's demands for wages really were and how desperate his social situation was on the whole. The oracle of the prophet Jeremiah was probably applicable to the whole of the ancient world: "Woe to him . . . who makes his neighbor serve him for nothing and does not give him his wages" (22:13; cf. Job 7:1; Sir. 34:22).

Legal questions do not arise in Matthew 20:1-15. The wage contract with the long-shift workers is indeed depicted as a legally correct oral contract. But it is doubtful whether in case of a dispute such workers could obtain a legal settlement. The agreement with the short-shift workers, in which no wage is mentioned, would probably not be a legal contract under Roman law,[15] but in Jewish law it seems to have been regarded as validated by the fact that the man begins the work.[16] In any event, the weak position of the short-shift workers in relation to their employer is clear, whether or not one judges that their position is also weak legally inasmuch as no contract has been made. In either case their position is such—and is so described—that the employer can unilaterally determine how much or how little he will give them.

It has sometimes been assumed that the short-shift workers had a right to a full day's wage because there was no payment by the hour in either the Jewish or the Roman economy.[17] A day's wage for hourly workers—it is said—must have been the normal rule.[18] As has been shown, the hiring of day laborers for a single day and not for several favored the employer in every respect. But in addition there was in fact a hiring for parts of a day, as can be seen, for example, from this phrase in the Edict of Diocletian: "A water-carrier who works for a whole day . . ." (VIII, 31-32). These words show that the obligation of a full day's work may not always be presupposed. In Jewish law, too, we find indications that there might be a hiring for only parts of a day (BM IX, 11; bBM 76b). Contracts for an hourly wage, such as those we are familiar with, probably did not exist.

The picture derived from other sources thus matches the one given in Matthew 20:1-15. As the grumbling of the long-shift workers indicates, they take it for granted that the short-shift workers will receive only part of a day's wage. The long-shift workers are not complaining because *here, as usually,* a part-time worker is being paid a full day's wage; they are complaining because *this particular* employer is not following the usual practice.

What the Parable Is Intended to Convey

As we have now seen, the same picture emerges from the course of the story in Matthew 20:1-15 as from observation of the everyday world of day laborers. Matthew 20:1-15 presupposes this real-life situation of workers in every detail but one: the behavior of the employer when he pays the men their wages. This behavior is in sharp contrast with everyday reality. Workers would in fact be afraid that the average employer might ill-treat them by not giving them a wage proportionate to the time they had worked. Employers normally take every opportunity to reduce wages. The parable presupposes this, as do the Old Testament, Cato, and Columella, among others.

Now that the relationship of the parable to reality has become clear, I must try to explain the intentions of the parable as far as possible. To this end I shall begin by restricting myself to the text in Matthew 20:1-15 as a self-contained entity. Two crucial points emerge. The parable intends to speak of the *goodness* or generosity *of God* (see esp. v. 15) and of the *behavior of human beings toward one another* as contrasted with the goodness of God (e.g., the envy and grumbling of the long-shift workers).

Matthew 20:1-15 is meant as a parable of the reign of God (see v. 1). A Jewish listener will realize from the very first sentence that the householder is God. The metaphorical representation of God as an employer is quite popular in Judaism, and this is not the only Jewish parable to explain God's dealings with the human race in terms of the behavior of an employer.[19] The picture is clear. Two levels of representation are simultaneously present: the work world of everyday life and the "world" of God. Interpretation of the parables involves explaining the relationship between these two levels.

Radical answers to the question have not stood up to testing. This parable—and the same is true of many others in the synoptics—is not a "parable" as understood by A. Jülicher and R. Bultmann, nor is it an allegory.[20] The story does not remain on the level of the human picture; it is not connected with the intended reality simply by a *tertium comparationis* (Jülicher), a *single* thought, or a "judgement" (Bultmann), such as would be the case with a "parable" in the sense given this term by Jülicher or Bultmann. From verse 8 on, it is the action of *God* that dictates the logic of the story, whereas up to that point it is everyday reality that determines its logic.

The other radical answer to the question of how parables are to be interpreted is to conceive of a parable as an allegory; that is, to relate almost every detail of the picture to something else—namely, the world of faith. This kind of interpretation breaks down here as it does in many other parables. This insight of Jülicher has proved valid with regard to many of the synoptic parables. The marketplace is a marketplace and not, for example, a symbol of the world.

In my opinion, it is methodologically possible to make use of the (socio-) historical presuppostions that play a role in the development of the picture in order to explain the logic of the story as it unfolds *from sentence to sentence*. Another point to be kept in mind is that in the original historical context of the parables of Jesus, all hearers knew from the outset that they were listening to a parable—that is, that a story was being told that really had God for its object. As applied to Matthew 20:1–15 this means that in verses 1–7 the employer is a real employer, but the hearers know the story is meant to explain an action of God. From verse 8 on, the employer is a different "employer," at least when it comes to the payment of wages. The fact that he has a steward is derived from everyday experience. The employer is thus in certain respects an "employer in quotation marks"—that is, God.

The parable depicts the goodness of God. Because it depicts the goodness of God through the image of an employer, the parable makes it clear that God is different by showing his goodness to be the source of experiences not normally to be had amid life's hardships. The world of toil provides the dark backdrop for a luminous picture of God. The contrast with this backdrop is a further source of light. Even the everyday world becomes more clearly visible; one is better able to see what makes it such a grim place. Matthew 20:1–15 is not intended as social criticism, but as a discourse about the goodness of God. But the picture used in conveying this is not of something "neutral" (Bultmann); reflection on the goodness of God as highlighted in a parable from the work world will obviously shed light on the reality of life itself and cause it to be seen more clearly.

The goodness of God is not depicted as unconnected with anything else; rather its consequences for the life of human beings in community are immediately brought out, as the scene of the grumbling long-shift workers shows. These men have in fact done more than the short-shift workers have. It is not their desire as such for a just wage that puts them in the wrong, but the way in which they deal with this desire—that is, they turn their desire for a just wage into a weapon against others. They are envious (v. 15); they begrudge the short-shift workers their denarius; they would be satisfied if the short-shift workers were to receive significantly less than they themselves received. What is being criticized here is not any abstract views on wages or any demands for a just wage, but rather behavior that is uncompassionate and lacking in solidarity. God is kind and merciful; the long-shift workers lack solidarity and compassion.

These are all thoughts that can without difficulty be garnered from the parable. But what does it all mean concretely? Who are the grumblers? To what does the goodness of God refer? What behavior is singled out? The concrete application of the thoughts cannot be discerned in the parable itself when it is taken as a self-contained entity. A context is needed: the context provided by texts *and* the context provided by concrete life—that is, in this case the precise historical situation to which the parable is related.

The attempt is usually made to concretize the parable by locating it—and rightly so, in all probability—in the context provided by the situation of the historical Jesus. But before I attempt this kind of concretization once again, I must take a critical look at a widespread kind of interpretation. It can be said of the exegetical tradition in the interpretation of Matthew 20:1–15 that the theological emphases are in almost every case open to criticism, even if one finds oneself in agreement with many observations on details. Moreover, they are open to criticism not only from the theological viewpoint but also from the viewpoint of the story itself. The parable is almost always understood as being in principle a critique of the Jewish "concept of recompense" (*Lohngedanke*) or even a complete rejection of this concept.[21] In all likelihood it is chiefly Paul Billerbeck's commentary on the New Testament with its explanation of "the teaching of the ancient synagogue on *recompense*" (4/1:490ff., 495) and of "the thirst for *recompense* among the [Jewish] people" (pp. 496ff.) that has swayed many interpretations of the parable in this direction.

Here I can only assert that in such pictures of the Jewish religion completely inadequate categories are used that do neither theological nor historical justice to the reality. As far as the parable in Matthew 20:1–15 is concerned, this kind of interpretation can be subjected to detailed criticism. The parable is not concerned with the concept of recompense, however the latter may be concretely understood, but rather with the use of the sense of justice (which requires that recompense should match the work done) as a *weapon* against other human beings. In other words, the parable deals with a concrete function of the concept of recompense. The idea that the Pharisees are being attacked here, or that the Christian concept of God is being opposed to the Jewish concept is completely erroneous.

The development of the parable is clear: its ultimate intention is not to criticize persons like the long-shift workers. Its ultimate intention is rather to win hearers over, to address those whose behavior is reflected, in exaggerated form, in the behavior of the long-shift workers.[22] Those addressed are to be able to recognize themselves even in this negative guise and, because they see the depicted behavior to be wrong, to change their way of acting. The purpose of the parable is not negative (criticism) but positive: to teach solidarity.

To read into the parable a difference, of whatever kind, between "Judaism" and "Christianity" is to miss the point of the parable. The parable rather presupposes that "short-shift workers" live in close proximity within a community and that nothing divides them but a lack of solidarity on the part of certain "long-shift workers."

The parable is a Jewish parable, told to Jews by a Jew. It is based on the idea of God in the Old Testament and Judaism, and specifically on the notion of God's goodness that is found therein. "The lord is merciful and gracious, slow to anger and abounding in steadfast love" (Ps. 103:8; 86:15; Exod. 34:6). The comparison repeatedly made by exegetes between this parable and that of the short-shift worker in the Jerusalem Talmud (jBer 2, 3c; see Billerbeck 4:493) is misleading. The rabbinic parable is meant to show that the rabbi who dies prematurely is not at a disadvantage. He receives a full reward from God because he accomplished more in a short life than others do in a long life. The parable thus presupposes that God rewards accomplishments—but so does the parable of the workers in the vineyard! The intention of the two parables is so different, however, that a comparison of the two is irrelevant. The rabbinic parable is about the distress of a young man faced with death; Matthew 20:1–15 is about solidarity.

These observations on the intention of the parable and on the history of its interpretation can be summed up as follows. The parable has two focuses: the goodness of God and—as a consequence of this goodness—solidarity among human beings. The goodness of God is not being opposed to another picture of God in which God rewards according to works or results. What the good God is implicitly being contrasted with is the employer in everyday life who keeps his wages as low as possible. The theological statement made by this parable is not to be understood as a challenge to another theology but as a challenge to the lives of human beings. The parable seeks to foster solidarity among human beings who share the same idea of God as merciful.

The questions of what the concrete context of this solidarity is and of what accomplishments the short-shift workers lack can be answered only by placing the parable in a concrete historical context. One must, for example, look for the reality behind the statement of the long-shift workers: "You have made them equal to us." This search can be carried out, on the one hand, in the historical context of the earliest traditions about Jesus (or of the historical

Jesus himself—the distinctions in one that need not be thematized here)[23] or, on the other hand, at the historical level of Matthew's gospel.

I shall first consider Matthew's application of the parable in the context of his gospel as a whole and in the context of the historical situation discernible in his gospel. This first step will make it easier to look then for the concrete meaning of the parable in the situation of the earliest Jesus movement, because we see that if we want to understand the parable we cannot neglect its concretization in Matthew. Matthew does not use the parable to explain general and even supratemporal theological ideas, but rather to cope with a painful and pernicious conflict within his own community.

The Meaning of the Parable in the Context of Matthew's Gospel

As in the other gospels, so too in that of Matthew the tradition of the stories and sayings of Jesus that are taken from (for example) the gospel of Mark or the Logia source (Q) is made part of a train of thought that is new and relevant to the disciples of Jesus at the time of Matthew. First, then, I shall follow Matthew's train of thought in the proximate context of the parable (19:16–20:28). Then I shall look for substantive parallels in the total context, which is Matthew's gospel in its entirety, and I shall ask what the real meaning of Matthew 20:1–16 is for him.

Matthew 19:16–20:28

Matthew is here following the text in Mark 10:17–45, which includes: the story of the "rich young man"; the subsequent conversation with the disciples regarding the wealthy; the prediction of Jesus' passion; the desire of the sons of Zebedee to sit at Jesus' right and left; sayings about the order of precedence among the disciples. In Mark 10:31 as in Matthew 19:30 the conversation about the wealthy ends with the saying: "But many that are first will be last, and the last first." This saying evidently gives Matthew an opportunity to introduce into the Markan sequence an addition (Matt. 20:1–16) that ends with a slightly altered repetition of the saying about the first and the last (v. 16).

Interventions in the Markan text, which in themselves are to some extent minimal, profoundly alter Mark's original train of thought in the process of relating it to the situation of Matthew's community. The rich man is *young* only in Matthew, and, unlike in Mark and Luke (whom I cannot discuss here), he is pert and unserious in Matthew. The changes from Mark, slight though they seem when taken in isolation, give rise to a new story.

In Matthew the young man asks Jesus: "What good deed must I do . . .? " Jesus answers by criticizing the question: "Why do you ask me about what is good? One there is who is good." For Matthew this response means: the question was a superficial one, because the necessary consequence of God's goodness is love of neighbor, and the concrete need of the neighbor shows what ought to be done at the moment (Matt. 25:31–46). The most powerful presentation in Matthew of the imperatives that God's mercy lays upon human beings in their relationships with one another is the parable of the scoundrelly servant (Matt. 18:23–35).

In Matthew's story Jesus continues: "If you would enter life. . . ." If you are serious, then keep the commandments. Again the young man responds with a question that really represents an intention of avoiding the burden of the commandments: "Which [ones am I to keep]?" This question is just as unserious as that of the lawyer in Luke 10:29 who asks who his neighbor is. Matthew is saying: this young man is trying to engineer a theological discussion on which commandments one should keep, instead of going off and practicing love of neighbor. Jesus sums up the commandments for him and then, in Matthew's story, explicitly adds: "And, You shall love your neighbor as yourself." The young man now makes a rash claim: "All these I have observed; what do I still lack?" Once again he tries to avoid the radical demands of love of neighbor by asking superficial questions. The claim that he is perfect—and this claim is implicit in his rhetorical question—anticipates God's finding at the last judgment. This is an intolerable act of religious arrogance in Matthew's eyes; in his view the final judgment will produce great amazement among human beings (Matt. 25:31–46). Jesus does not here, as he does in Mark, look at the young man with love, but simply answers him once again in a quite objective way: "If you would be perfect. . . ." If you want to set out on the way to perfection—for you are not yet at all on this way—then act as love of neighbor demands, "sell what you possess and give to the poor." Do not talk; act! (cf. Matt. 7:21 or 21:28–32).

Stories of pert young men whose prattling makes it clear to a teacher that they are not really serious were often told in antiquity. For example, it is told of Zeno that "to a young man who was indulging in a good deal of idle talk he [Zeno] said: 'Your ears have run together with your tongue.' "[24] Matthew calls the rich man a young man because he can thus characterize the role the man adopts in relation to Jesus: that of an impertinent questioner.

In Matthew, therefore, the young man is an unlikeable rich man. After he leaves, Jesus converses with his disciples about the rich (as he does in Mark). The assertion that it is difficult, even impossible, for a rich person to enter the kingdom of God does not make the same strong impression in Matthew that it does in Mark, who several times reports the dismay of the disciples at this severity. Matthew mentions their shock only once. Matthew 19:16–26 seems to reflect painful experiences of the Jesus community with the rich, although this problem does not receive as much attention from Matthew as it does especially from Luke.[25] For Matthew the rich are not an internal problem of the community.

As in Mark so in Matthew, after this depressing scene Peter speaks to Jesus about the disciples. In Mark there is an almost arrogant self-assertiveness

("We have left everything"), to which Jesus responds with a warning (Mark 10:28, 31). In Matthew, however, Peter's statement is followed by a question: "Lo, we have left everything and followed you. What then shall we have?" For Matthew this question is not an expression of arrogance, but a legitimate question to which Jesus gives a positive answer by his promise of twelve thrones (19:28). In Matthew the story ends with the statement that "many that are first will be last, and the last first"; in other words, those who in this world are rich and "first" will be last in the kingdom of God if, like the rich young man, they do not keep the commandments. On the other hand, those who are poor in this world because they have left everything for the sake of Jesus and who are therefore "last" as far as money and prestige are concerned, will be first in God's kingdom. Unlike the same statement in Mark 10:31, Matthew 19:30 is not a warning to the disciples but a warning to those who act like the rich young man and prove faithless to the commandment of love of neighbor.

In 20:1 Matthew takes up a new theme. The problem now is that some of Jesus' disciples want to be first in relation to the other disciples (20:1–28 deals with the theme of *protos en hymin*, "first among you"). The theme is proposed in the story that follows at this point in Mark (Mark 10:33–45; Matt. 20:20–28), and is evidently very important to Matthew. The theme is another that is illumined by the saying about the eschatological reversal of first and last (Matt. 20:16).

In Mark the sons of Zebedee had asked that in glory they might sit at the right and left of Jesus. Matthew seeks to shift the onus somewhat from the sons of Zebedee themselves. He has their mother ask the ugly question about a special reward for her two sons, an extra reward that will put them in an advantageous position in relation to the other disciples. Matthew does not want to show the two disciples themselves in this negative light, but he does regard as important the problem of the desire for religious privileges within the community. Consequently he can conclude the story taken from Mark with almost the identical words that Mark uses: "Whoever would be great among you must be your servant, and whoever would be first among you must be your slave (20:26–27).

Matthew 20:1–16 is already linked to this theme of the religious claims that Christians make at the expense of other Christians. Matthew 20:16 is a warning to those who should recognize themselves in the long-shift workers. The long-shift workers act like the mother of the sons of Zebedee, with whom the disciples are justly angry (20:24), because the desire of these two men for an extra reward is a form of opposition to the other disciples, with whom they are unwilling to live on equal terms.

In my opinion it is not possible to interpret 19:30 as another warning to the disciples and thus to create a more obvious connection between 19:30 and 20:1–16.[26] Matthew 19:28 militates against such an interpretation. The question that the disciples ask in 19:27 about their reward is not criticized but is given a positive answer. I must agree with E. Schweizer (in his commentary on this passage) in seeing a certain material difference between 19:30 and 20:16: Matthew 19:30 criticizes the rich young man and others like him; Matthew 20:16, on the other hand, criticizes persons like the mother of the sons of Zebedee and the long-shift workers.

Lack of Love in the Matthean Community

Matthew 20:1-28 shows what an important place the gospel of Matthew gives to the problem of counteracting the desire of being *protos en hymin*, first in the community. There are some texts in Matthew that make possible a fuller picture of the lack of love in the Matthean community and of the way in which Matthew deals with this problem. I refer especially to Matthew 18:1-14 and 23:8-12. Each text might have as its title the bitter saying: "Most men's love will grow cold" (Matt. 24:12).

Matthew 23:8-12 is part of a lengthy discourse of Jesus against the Pharisees. Matthew puts a great deal of himself into it as he constructs it out of material in Mark and Q and perhaps in another tradition as well. It is directed against the Pharisees of Matthew's own time. There are grounds for thinking that Matthew is living somewhere in the Jewish Diaspora during the period after the destruction of Jerusalem. The Pharisees with whom he is at odds are probable Pharisees in the same Jewish Diaspora community (perhaps Antioch) to which the Matthean Christians belong.

The fact that Jews have persecuted the disciples of Jesus is for Matthew now past history; otherwise why should he have put the prediction of persecution by Jews (from Mark 13:9-13) into the mission discourse (Matt. 10:17-25)? This striking transposition can mean only that the persecution of the disciples by Jews is in the past. The condemnation of Israel (in Matt. 23:1ff), from Q, means this to Matthew: to the extent that the Jewish people persecuted Jesus and his disciples, it has since been punished by the destruction of Jerusalem. Matthew has sharp criticism for Judaism, but we must not lose sight of the fact that he and his "Christian" community are *also* Jews. The Christians are probably a kind of sectarian group within the Diaspora community and carry on a keen ideological debate with other Jews while emphasizing the fact that the followers of Jesus regard themselves as Jews, that the God of the Old Testament is on their side, and that they observe the law to the full (see 5:17).

It would be an error to think of the passage as one in which *Christians* are speaking against Jews. Christianity in this sense does not yet exist here. This is certainly true in the minds of the "pagans" who persecute "Christians" (Matt. 24:9b-14). Persecutors might indeed harass the disciples of Jesus, but because they were, for example, a messianic group of *Jews*; the Matthean community emphatically confesses Jesus as son of David. The disciples of Jesus understand the persecution as persecution for the sake of Christ (see, e.g., 24:9b), but the persecutors understand it as a measure aimed at counteracting the political danger that Jewish messianic movements represented to them.

The historical state of affairs just described is one with which we are quite familiar, even if not as one concretely related to the gospel of Matthew. In Eusebius, for example, there is a citation from Hegesippus that may serve as an illustration of this historical situation:

> "And there still survived of the Lord's family the grandsons of Jude, who was said to be His brother, humanly speaking. These were informed against as being of David's line, and brought by the *evocatus* before Domitian Caesar, who was as afraid of the advent of Christ as Herod had been. Domitian asked them whether they were descended from David and they admitted it. . . ."
>
> Then, the writer [Hegesippus] continues, they showed him their hands, putting forward as proof of their toil the hardness of their bodies and the calluses impressed on their hands by incessant labour. When asked about Christ and His Kingdom—what it was like, and where and when it would appear—they explained that it was not of this world or anywhere on earth but angelic and in heaven, and would be established at the end of the world, when He would come in glory to judge the quick and the dead and give every man payment according to his conduct. On hearing this, Domitian found no fault with them, but despising them as beneath his notice let them go free and issued orders terminating the persecution of the church.[27]

Of course, the special problem of the descent of some disciples of Jesus from David, as presented in this text, is not comparable to anything in Matthew, but the theological and political situation is indeed comparable. Matthew could well have used the same eschatology to defend himself against the accusation of political messianism.

In the framework of the polemic against the Pharisees in chapter 23—the historical situation of which I have been trying to elucidate—Matthew suddenly digresses in 23:8-12 to criticize his own people—that is, disciples of Jesus. Having criticized the Pharisees for preferring the places of honor at feasts (23:6-7), he turns directly to a criticism of the same phenomenon within the Christian community. There are Christians who like to be called "rabbi," "father," and "master" (23:8-10). They regard themselves as teachers of the community and demand a special precedence on this account. Jesus tells them: "You are all brethren," "You have one Father, who is in heaven," and "You have one master, the Christ." Preferential treatment, which is to be thought of as analogous to *protoklisia* ("places of honor," v. 6), and the social claim this expresses should not exist among Christians. This abrupt digression against Christians in the midst of a discourse against the Pharisees shows how important a role the claim to privilege plays in the Matthean community.

Matthew 18:1–14 gives a similar picture. Here Matthew is following Mark 9:33–37, 42–50. From there he takes the theme and the key terms, but he sets the emphases differently in dealing with the problems of the disagreement about status. In 18:10–14 Matthew is using material from the Logia Source (parable of the lost sheep) in order once again to discuss ill-treatment of the "little ones," a subject he had already raised in 19:6 where he is dependent on Mark 9:42. The disciples' question about who is the greatest in the kingdom of God is immediately criticized in Mark (9:35) and treated as the expression of a wrong attitude. In Matthew, however, it is answered in a more nuanced way.

First, we are told who are in fact the greatest in the kingdom of God: those who humble themselves and become childlike.[28] Then Matthew shows the wrong way of giving vent to a desire to be greatest in the kingdom of God: by causing the "little ones" to take scandal (which probably means: to leave the Christian community) and by despising the "little ones" (Matt. 18:6–9, 10–14). It would be better to mutilate oneself than to become a source of scandal (18:6–9); one ought to go after the "little ones" as one goes after a lost sheep.

For Matthew the "little ones" are those who are "low" on the social scale—that is, both in regard to social prestige and in regard to economic status: they are in need of active mercy. The *elachistoi*, or "least," in Matthew 25:31–46 are, from a social and economic standpoint, identical with the *mikroi*, or "little ones," of Matthew 18. This means that there are "little ones" both inside and outside the community. In 25:31–46 the "least" are not presented as coming solely from among Christians, for if they were, their benefactors would not be so astonished at the final judgment.[29]

Insofar as dealing with those who are "low" on the social scale are concerned, Matthew 18:1–14 and 25:31–46 may be summarized as follows. Within the community social distinctions *must* be eliminated (18:1–14); independently of whether or not they belong to the community, all who are in distress must be the recipients of active mercy (25:31–46). In Matthew's eyes the behavior of Jesus shows him to be the teacher of this kind of mercy. In the stories of miraculous healings he has pity on the sick; he has pity on the tax collectors and sinners; he has pity on the hungry disciples who pluck the ears of grain. All these stories about Jesus are for Matthew—and usually for him alone among the evangelists—stories about mercy (see 9:13; 12:7).

Within the community the "little ones" are obviously being treated as outsiders. The community to which Matthew belongs is not a community of the poor. Even the problems of the day laborers in 20:1–15 are not presented in such a way as to suggest that the readers had personal experience of them. Nonetheless the distress of human beings confronts this community—made up of persons who are not perhaps "rich" but who at least do not experience material want—with the question of truth: whether they are truly on the side of the Jesus who calls those "who labor and are heavy laden" (11:28–30);

whether they are truly on the side of the God who takes pity on the "short-shift workers."

For Matthew, then, 20:1–16 means: there are Christians who claim privileges in God's sight because in fact they do more than the "little ones" in the community. Such are the teachers, who shape and maintain the public image presented by the community. Their claim to privileges before God and therefore in the community as well offends against solidarity. "You are all brethren." For Matthew, the measure of how seriously Christians take their faith is their behavior toward the lowly inside and outside the community.

The Meaning of the Parable in the Earliest Jesus Tradition

Although it is not possible to *prove* that Matthew 20:1–15 as a whole is older than the gospel of Matthew, there are nonetheless grounds for surmising that the parable stems from the earliest tradition about Jesus.[30] The most important indication that Matthew has taken the parable from another source is the abrupt transition from 19:30 to 20:1. The connective *gar* ("for") in 20:1 is meant to effect a transition, but its meaning can be grasped only from 20:1–28 as a whole. The statement that the first will be last has a different sense from the one it has in 19:30. The *gar* in 20:1 connects one meaning of the saying about the first and the last (its meaning when directed against the rich in 19:30) with its other meaning: a warning against claims to precedence within the community (20:16).

Matthew 20:1–15 yields a sense when placed in the context of the earliest tradition about Jesus. We may regard the pre-Markan stories about the plucking of the ears of grain on the Sabbath (Mark 2:23–27), about the tax collector's feast (Mark 2:13–17), and about the gospel of the poor (Luke 6:20–21; Matt. 11:2–5) as the central texts of the earliest tradition about Jesus and take them as our point of departure here.[31]

Matthew 20:1–15 would fit quite well into the situation of dialogue between the disciples of Jesus and the Pharisees as this is reflected in Mark 2:13ff. and 2:23ff. The disciples of Jesus are poor. They claim that their need takes precedence over the Sabbath. They refuse to be standoffish toward tax collectors and criminals. They do not deny that criminals are sinners, but they regard them as called by Jesus no less than are the righteous (Mark 2:17). The Pharisees should accept this attitude as a logical conclusion from the Torah and from God's mercy, for they attach as much importance to these as do the disciples of Jesus.

There must no longer be a separation within the life of the Jewish people between sinners and nonsinners. "You have made them equal to us": the grumbling of the long-term workers, precisely because it takes this extreme and alienating form, should bring home to the Pharisees the truth that their justified claim to have accomplished more may not be used as an argument against tax collectors and sinners. As elsewhere in the earliest Jesus tradition, theological thinking is directed by a vision of the Jewish people as destined to be remade before God as a new community to which *all* human beings belong.

As part of the discussion that went on between the disciples of Jesus and the Pharisees long before the destruction of Jerusalem, Matthew 20:1-15 is *not* a criticism of and attack on the Pharisees but an effort to bring them to the point of joining the disciples of Jesus and accepting solidarity with the poor, the tax collectors, and sinners. The point of entry at which this approach to the Pharisees is made is their conception of God as merciful. The discussion with the Pharisees in that earlier time is of an entirely different kind from the discussion that Matthew carries on with (a later) Pharisaism. Matthew 20:1-15 shows the same friendly courting of the Pharisees that is to be observed elsewhere in the earliest Jesus tradition.

NOTES

1. Pliny the Younger, *Epistulae* IX, 20, 2.

2. In addition, there was a good deal of flexibility in calculating the "usual" wage to be paid when no prior agreement had been made; see bBM 87a.

3. See G. Dalman, *Arbeit und Sitte in Palästina* (Gütersloh, 1928ff.), 1:1, 44; 4:936. On the length of the workday, see also Ps. 104:22-23 and bBM 83a.

4. See J. Jeremias, *The Parables of Jesus*, S. H. Hooke, trans. (New York, rev. ed., 1973), pp. 136-37.

5. *Corpus Inscriptionum Latinarum* 8, Suppl. 11824.

6. Marcus Terentius Varro, *Res rusticae*, I, 17, 2-3, in *Cato and Varro: De re rustica*, W. D. Hooper and H. B. Ash, trans., Loeb Classical Library (Cambridge, Mass., 1960), p. 225. Cf. Columella, *Res rustica*, I, 7, 4 (note 8, below).

7. Marcus Porcius Cato, *De agri cultura*, 5, 4, in *Cato and Varro*, p. 15. The text is translated in W. Krenkel, "Zu den Tagelohnern bei der Ernte in Rom," *Romanitas*, 6/7 (1965) 141, with whose arguments against the interpretation of H. Gummerus, *Das römische Gusbetrieb* (Leipzig, 1903), pp. 26-27, I am compelled to agree.

8. Lucius Junius Moderatus Columella, *Res rustica*, III, 21, 9-10, in *Columella: On Agriculture*, vol. 1, books I-IV, H. B. Ash, trans., Loeb Classical Library (Cambridge, Mass., 1960), p. 347.

9. For further discussion, see the works cited in n. 7, above, and P. A. Brunt, "Die Beziehungen zwischen dem Herr and dem Land," in his *Zur Sozial- und Wirtschaftsgeschichte der späten römischen Republik* (Darmstadt, 1976), pp. 124ff., esp. 133-34.

10. Thus, for example, F. van der Ven, *Sozialgeschichte der Arbeit*, 1 (Munich, 1971), pp. 98-99. M. Kaser, *Das römische Privatrecht*, 1 (Munich, 2nd ed., 1971), p. 568, is more cautious.

11. On these questions, see Krenkel "Zu den Tagelohnern."

12. A. Ben-David, *Talmudische Ökonomie* (Hildesheim, 1974), pp. 300-301.

13. BM VII, 1-7. On the rabbinical interpretation of Deut. 23:26-27, see chap. 8, above.

14. Tosefta on BM (Zuckermandel, p. 387, line 25); German translation and

further information in D. Farbstein, *Das Recht der unfreien und freien Arbeiter nach jüdisch-talmudischem Recht* (Frankfurt, 1896), p. 45, line 5.

15. *Corpus Iuris Civilis: Digesta*, 19, 2. 2; 19, 5. 22.

16. bBM 76a; on these questions, see also M. Silberberg, "Dienstvertrag und Werkvertrag im talmudischen Rechte" (dissertation, Frankfurt, 1927), p. 19.

17. E. Wolf, "Gottesrecht und Menschenrecht. Rechtstheologische Exegese des Gleichnisses von den Arbeitern im Weinberg (Mt 20, 1–16)," in H. Vorgrimler, ed., *Gott in Welt. Festgabe für Karl Rahner*, 2 (Freiburg, 1964), pp. 640–62; J. B. Bauer, "Gnadenlohn oder Tageslohn," Bib, 42 (1961) 224–28.

18. The Edict of Diocletian (A.D. 301) also assumes that "a rural worker" is hired "by the day and given his board" (VII, la). Further material on work by the day as normal case is to be found in Bauer, "Gnadenlohn"; Krenkel, "Zu den Tagelohnern," p. 141; T. Mayer-Maly, *Locatio conductio* (Vienna, 1956), p. 124.

19. See the parables in Billerbeck 4/1:492–93.

20. A. Jülicher, *Die Gleichnisreden Jesu*, 1 (Tübingen, 1910); R. Bultmann, *The History of the Synoptic Tradition*, J. Marsh, trans. (Oxford, 1963), esp. pp. 174, 198.

21. A (purely random) selection of interpretations that show the validity of this statement: G. Eichholz, *Gleichnisse der Evangelien* (Neukirch-en-Vluyn, 1971), esp. pp. 99–100; Jeremias, *The Parables*, esp. p. 139; H. Braun, "Die Auslegung Gottes durch Jesus, dargestellt an der Parable vom gleichen Lohn für alle," *Der Evangelische Erzieher*, 16 (1964) 346–56.

22. Eichholz, for example, rightly emphasizes this point.

23. See L. Schottroff and W. Stegemann, *Jesus von Nazareth—Hoffnung der Armen* (Stuttgart, 1978), chap. 1.

24. Diogenes Laertius, *De vitis . . . philosophorum*, VII, 21; cf. VII, 22–23.

25. See Schottroff and Stegemann, *Jesus von Nazareth*, chap. 3.

26. Thus, e.g., Eichholz, *Gleichnisse*, pp. 101–3; H. Frankemölle, *Jahwebund und Kirche Christi* (Münster, 1974), p. 154. For a different interpretation, E. Schweizer, *The Good News according to Matthew*, D. E. Green, trans. (Atlanta, 1975), pp. 394–95.

27. Eusebius, *The History of the Church*, G. A. Williamson, trans. (Penguin Classics, Baltimore, 1965), pp. 126–27. The Latin word *evocatus* means "veteran," but the precise meaning here is not known.

28. The logion on self-humbling is used in Matt. 23:8–13 to convey the same point.

29. On these questions, see P. Christian, *Jesus und seine geringsten Brüder* (Leipzig, 1975).

30. The old argument of the form-critics that Matt. 20:16 is secondary in relation to Matt. 20:1–15 (and that the parable is thus from the pre-Matthean tradition), because in it Matthew has incorrectly turned the temporal sequence of payments in the parable into the key point, can no longer be maintained. As I have shown, 20:16, in the context of Matthew's gospel, has its own substantial content and accurately captures the meaning of the parables.

31. See Schottroff and Stegemann, *Jesus von Nazareth,* chap. 1. In what follows I draw especially on the interpretation given there of Mark 2:13–17 and the interpretation of Mark 2:23–27 that is given in chap. 7, above.

10

Vagabond Radicalism in Early Christianity?:
A Historical and Theological Discussion of a Thesis
Proposed by Gerd Theissen

WOLFGANG STEGEMANN

A New Interest in Exegesis

In recent years exegesis has led a kind of shadow existence as far as theology is concerned. All the more surprising, then, that several interpretative studies of the Bible by Gerd Theissen should be attracting great attention even among theologians who are concerned with practical life. Especially in his *Sociology of Early Christianity*,[1] which concludes "a series of sociological studies of primitive Christianity,"[2] Theissen addresses himself to those working in practical theology and endeavors to give a coherent presentation of his detailed analyses in a "contribution to the history of the origins of primitive Christianity."[3] We owe it to the author's ability that his work, though historical and exegetical in its orientation, lives up to the title, now richly freighted with tradition, of the series in which it appears: *Theologische Existenz heute* ("Theological Life Today").

Theissen is able to move beyond the usual dissatisfaction felt with exegesis and to locate his analyses of New Testament texts in the context of a living past that renders eloquent once again stories and sayings that had long since become trite and drew little attention. He makes an impressive attempt not only to interpret verses and half-verses in the New Testament writings or even just individual writings of the New Testament, but to understand the whole range of the New Testament tradition within the framework of a history of early Christianity. He starts with the beginnings of Christianity in the "Jesus movement" in the Syro-Palestinian world and goes on to study the effects of this movement on the established, sedentary Christian communities of the Hellenistic world-civilization in the Roman imperial age.

This comprehensive task is made all the more difficult by the fact that Theissen's aim is not an isolated picture of Jewish Christian "religious history," which would have an existence of its own, as it were, apart from and above the real history of individuals in their time and their society. His approach is that of the "sociology of religion"; this means that he looks for and seeks to bring to light connections between religious ideas and subject matters, on the one hand, and the sociological situation of those who hold these ideas, on the other. Thus Theissen sees it as the task of his sociology of the Jesus movement "to describe typical social attitudes and behaviour within the Jesus movement and to analyse its interaction with Jewish society in Palestine generally."[4] The task set here for New Testament exegesis is thus both historical and sociological, and to this extent it goes beyond customary historical critical exegesis, but without any intention of disdaining the information it supplies.

Theissen's sociological interest in the history of early Christianity compels him to provide a methodological discussion of the specific approach taken in his analyses. He distinguishes three tasks within his religio-sociological approach: "An analysis of roles investigates typical patterns of behaviour; an analysis of factors [investigates] the way in which this behaviour is determined by society; an analysis of functions [investigates] its effects upon society."[5] This sociological interaction model deliberately avoids a onesidedly dogmatic handling of the connection between religion and society in terms of the cause-effect principle, and instead takes into account that "economic, ecological, political and cultural factors cannot be separated in their reciprocal interaction."[6] Theissen's method is to use "constructive," "analytical," and "comparative" inferential procedures in order to elicit from the sources the sociological information that they do not directly offer us.[7]

Although Theissen aims at a comprehensive treatment of the history of early Christianity, it is chiefly his picture of what he calls "vagabond radicalism in early Christianity" that has made his historico-exegetical studies so unusually influential. The influence is not due solely to the welcome sight of a New Testament scholar (once again) attempting to throw light on the *life* of the earliest followers of Jesus. No, there is also and above all the theological fascination of his thesis that wandering charismatics formed the most important group among the carriers of the tradition regarding Jesus of Nazareth. The thesis is fascinating if for no other reason than that the dynamism that once characterized these wandering charismatics and apostles makes us more conscious of the immobility, evident in so many areas, of our institutionalized Christianity.

Even before Theissen published his analyses, Rudolf Bohren in this *Predigtlehre* ("Art and Science of Preaching") had already shown his preference for the early Christian "wandering preacher": between their "Spirit-inspired wandering and a Christianity that finds expression in churches, chapels, pulpits, and parish houses there is a contrast we prefer to ignore."[8] And when this contrast is no longer ignored, people look to the wandering preachers of

early Christianity for new directions that may turn Christianity into a historical movement once again.

It is this theological fascination exercised by early Christian "vagabond
radicalism" that moves me, a theologian engaged in practical parish work, to
test the historical bases of Theissen's views and to look into the reasons for
their exceptional influence. My discussion is inspired by an interest in the
same subject that has attracted Theissen: the study of early Christianity. The
discussion is not meant as an end in itself but is intended rather to serve our
present self-understanding: What kind of Lord shall we Christians confess,
and what kind of life shall we lead, if we consciously align ourselves with the
tradition represented by the earliest confessors and disciples of Jesus? Discipleship is in fact the hidden theme of Theissen's researches. In his first essay
on vagabond radicalism he attempted to take literally the "ethical radicalism" of so many sayings of Jesus and to shed light on the "lifestyle characteristic of the transmitters" of those radical directives.[9]

At this point indeed Theissen was concerned primarily with the "conditions for the transmission" of this ethical radicalism, and it was only the
results of his early analyses that led him to the more comprehensive task of a
"sociology of the Jesus movement." In this more rounded study, vagabond
radicalism, seen as the sociological background of the rigorist ethical directives of the synoptic tradition, is only one of the three "roles" that, by their
interaction, determine the inner structure of the Jesus movement.[10] Theissen
also investigates the role of the "bearer of revelation" and that of the "sympathizers in the local communities." The three roles complete the sociological picture of the Jesus movement. But Theissen still regards the role of the
wandering charismatics as the most striking aspect of the Jesus movement. It
is the chief expression of the "renewal movement within Judaism brought
into being through Jesus."[11] Sociological conditions prevalent when disciples
began to follow Jesus are thus the historical and thematic focus of Theissen's
analyses. My own observations will be limited to this same theme.

Theissen's Thesis on Vagabond Radicalism

"In the beginning, discipleship was something concrete. The disciples left
home and family, possessions and trade."[12] As Theissen pictures it, "the
decisive figures in early Christianity were travelling apostles, prophets and
disciples who moved from place to place and could rely on small groups of
sympathizers in these places." It was they who "shaped the earliest traditions
and provide the social background for a good deal of the synoptic tradition,
especially the tradition of the words of Jesus."[13]

Theissen does not deny that this radical change in the lifestyle of the first
disciples—a change to which the "vocation stories" point—had "primarily
religious motives" and, above all, that it presupposed a "call from Jesus."[14]
But for this "call over which he [the charismatic] had no control,"[15] there
must have been sociological presuppositions in the lives (individual and social) of those so called. As Mark tells it, the "rich young man" refused Jesus'
call to discipleship precisely because he had great wealth (Mark 10:17ff. and

parallels). Theissen has no intention of restricting himself to the purely religious aspect of the discipleship of these first followers of Jesus; he is concerned primarily to bring to light the sociological circumstances in which the disciples decided for Jesus and followed him after their decision. Here we have the chief merit of his analyses. It is a merit that no criticism of the way in which he carries out these analyses can allow us to forget.

The unsuccessful call to the "rich young man" might lead us to suspect that the wandering beggars of the Syro-Palestinian world were the individuals most likely to follow Jesus because of their social condition. Theissen himself sees a hint of the validity of this supposition in the story of blind Bartimaeus.[16] In his opinion, however, the followers of Jesus were not recruited exclusively or even chiefly from this lowest stratum of society, just as they did not come, in any notable degree, from the "upper classes."[17] "The information we have on the wandering charismatics of early Christianity points to a *middle class,* [but one] whose situation was hardly very secure."[18]

Theissen lays a great deal of emphasis on the fact that the situation of the earliest followers of Jesus does not justify "an idyllic picture of life among the lowly folk."[19] Simon Peter and his brother Andrew—to take but one example—were fishermen and as such did not belong to the lowest strata of society.[20] They did have something to leave behind when they followed the call of Jesus. But then it becomes all the more interesting and necessary to show the radical change of behavior that discipleship entailed. Theissen undertakes to do this with the help of a sociological category.

He regards the disciples' following of Jesus as being, from a sociological viewpoint, a "form of social uprooting."[21] Despite the meager information given in the synoptic texts, this interpretation becomes more persuasive when seen against the background of "manifestations of social uprooting in the Jewish society of Palestine" in the age of Jesus.[22] This part of the world was at that time in a state of drastic crisis, as can be seen especially from the "emigrants, new settlers, people at Qumran, bandits, resistance fighters, vagabonds, and prophetic movements,"[23] all of which are embodiments of social uprooting. Theissen counts the disciples of Jesus among the "movements of renewal in Judaism," which adopted the behavior patterns associated with social uprooting, creatively reshaped them, and filled them with religious meaning.[24] They attempted in this way to find new directions amid the general disorientation of their society.

Like other movements, the Jesus movement

> drew its recruits chiefly from marginal groups, i.e., groups on the periphery of a given social class which were threatened with disappearance or had to find their way under changed conditions, as well as from outsiders of various kinds and, to some extent, from the young. In all these groups there was an opportunity for those deviant and often eccentric forms of behavior that were practiced in renewal movements within Judaism and in which widespread deviant behavior—emigration, brigandage, begging—was taken over and creatively modified.[25]

In the case of the Jesus movement beggary was transformed into a "life as a wandering charismatic."[26] Logically, then, Theissen finds in the wandering Cynic philosophers the most striking non-Judaic analogy for the early Christian wandering charismatics. The Cynic philosophers, too, "seem to have led a vagabond existence and also to have renounced home, families, and possessions."[27]

Source-Critical Problems Affecting Theissen's Analyses

Theissen's presentation of the life and circumstances of the earliest followers of Jesus may at first seem quite plausible to one who approaches the synoptic gospels (Mark, Matthew, and Luke) with the intention of finding out what picture they give of the *life* of Jesus' disciples. For in the synoptics too we find a crowd of adherents who for his sake have abandoned their previous social ties and now follow him wherever he goes.

Even a first comparison, however, of the pictures given us in Mark, Matthew, and Luke soon raises the question: What were these disciples of Jesus really like? Were they as fearful and naive, as unprepared to follow Jesus in suffering, as Mark suggests? Or were they the thoroughly praiseworthy "heroes" of the first days of Christianity that Luke evidently considers them to have been? And whereas a reading of Matthew and Mark gives the impression that the disciples regarded the social consequences of their following as of purely secondary importance, Luke on the contrary considers their renunciation of possessions, which makes them "poor" (*ptochoi*), to be the decisive criterion of their discipleship.

A critical analysis of the Jesus movement *as committed to writing* may therefore not accept without examination the pictures given of the disciples in the synoptic gospels. Such an analysis must take into account that from a literary viewpoint the synoptic writers are themselves the provisional end result of a complicated history of transmission. In addition, the evangelists are not simply "collectors" and "transmitters" of a tradition that precedes them; rather it is under the guidance of interests determined by their specific situation and task that they hark back to earlier tradition, modify and correct it in the course of their work, and unhesitatingly introduce views of their own at various points.

Theissen has no intention of subsequently proving that the synoptic pictures of the disciples are historically correct. His purpose is rather to sketch a picture of the Jesus movement as it was lived out "in the areas of Syria and Palestine between A.D. 30 and A.D. 70."[28] The synoptic gospels are indeed the most important source for our knowledge of this historical movement, but they came into existence only after the year 70 and were composed in Greek.[29] More importantly, they were written at the distance created by the experiences of the Christian communities, which in these gospels give expression to their present faith and current problems with the help of events that were supposed to have taken place formerly in Palestine.

Just as the gospels cannot and do not intend to give an authentic picture of Jesus according to the criteria of critico-historical writing, neither is the story they tell of the first adherents of Jesus—whom they call *mathetai* ("disciples"; literally, "learners")—to be taken as a historically faithful account. In other words, we now possess the attestation of the historical Jesus movement only in literary contexts (the synoptic gospels), which arose in historical and objective remoteness from this movement. For this reason a *source-critical* analysis of the texts at our disposal is indispensable.

Theissen is therefore correct in not taking the synoptic tradition in its entirety as the source for his investigations, but in turning rather to the "earliest traditions" contained in it, and especially to the "tradition of the words of Jesus."[30] But we should like to know how he isolates these "earliest traditions" from the remainder of the material in the synoptic gospels, and whether he regards the "tradition of the sayings" or "tradition of the words" as belonging without exception to these earliest traditions. For the only criterion of source criticism that he offers—"In the case of the synoptic gospels we have to remove material which is of Hellenistic origin"[31]—is so general that it really sheds no light at all.

In offering this criterion Theissen is evidently referring to influences on the synoptic tradition that derive from the sociological situation and theological role of so-called Hellenistic Christianity.[32] But in fact even the earliest traditions are given to us only in a form that itself derives from this context. The need therefore is to proceed in the inverse direction and to separate out from the synoptic gospels whatever of the earliest traditions has survived in them.

In referring to a "Hellenistic origin" Theissen is therefore only indicating the task to be carried out; he is unable to carry it out himself or propose a method for doing so. For Theissen's analysis of the Jesus movement a source-critical testing of the synoptic textual basis to which he appeals is indispensable.

Theissen's "Cynical" Interpretation of the Jesus Movement

Even in his evaluation of the sources, Theissen already gives the impression that he largely accepts the state of synoptic scholarship represented by Rudolf Bultmann, although hardly taking any account of the approach known as "redaction history," which analyzes the theological context of these gospels. And yet when the purpose is a historico-sociological reconstruction of the Jesus movement, a high degree of importance attaches to the fact that in the work of the evangelists far more numerous interventions, independent alterations, and explanations of the older tradition are to be expected than even Bultmann accepted. If we read in this light what Theissen has to say on vagabond radicalism under the heading of "constructive conclusions," we are confirmed in our suspicion that he attaches little if any importance to the personal theological contribution of the New Testament writers.

From the Acts of the Apostles in particular but also from the letters of Paul and the noncanonical *Didache*, Theissen concludes that traveling apostles and teachers or preachers were the "decisive authorities" in early Christianity at least until as late as the middle of the second century (*Didache*).[33] According to Theissen's conclusion, the competing mission in the Pauline communities and what we learn in the Acts of the Apostles about the "Stephen group," Antioch, and the Jerusalem community presuppose wandering charismatics. This line of development can be followed through the history of the church where "down the ages, countless others have renounced the idea of a home for the wandering life of an apostle."[34] In any case, "we may assert that what information we have about the first early Christian authorities points to wandering charismatics."[35]

But we must ask whether in principle the history of the influence of the Jesus movement allows unqualified conclusions regarding the history of the movement itself. As Theissen is aware, "the early Christian literature which came into existence in the Hellenistic communities (above all the corpus of epistles in the New Testament) is primarily oriented on interactions within the local community as far as ethical instructions are concerned."[36]

It is surprising, moreover, that Paul, a traveling preacher, nowhere refers to the radical ethics of the disciples of Jesus, even though it might have thrown a favorable light on his own controversial way of life. And it is quite remarkable that in the nonsynoptic literature of the New Testament (with the exception of John) the lifestyle of the first followers of Jesus plays no role at all. In fact, even the picture that the Acts of the Apostles sketches of the first community at Jerusalem by no means indicates that wandering charismatics had any authority. The aim of the author of Acts is to describe the consolidation of the former group of disciples at Jerusalem; and it is the authorities in this community—the apostles—who alone remain in the city when everyone else is driven away (Acts 8:1–4). The missionary activity of Peter gives very much the impression of being an exception to the rule.

In addition, it must be noted that the author of Acts gives a systematic presentation of the spread of the gospel and does not at all portray the chief "missionary personality"—Paul—as playing a role analogous to that of the disciples of Jesus. The picture given in Acts is consistent with that of the Pauline letters when it tells us that Paul earned a livelihood for himself and his fellow workers (Acts 20:33–34). He was evidently a traveling apostle, but one who had a trade even if he did not have a home. But neither he himself nor the vocation stories in Acts place any ethical emphasis on the social consequences of Paul's preaching of the gospel.

This is all the more remarkable inasmuch as it is the author of Acts (Luke) who lays such an exceptional stress in his gospel on the renunciations made by the disciples. Luke is thus aware of a difference between the theological significance and accompanying lifestyle of the disciples of Jesus and the significance and lifestyle of later preachers of the gospel. Thus the very man who in his own way wrote a history of early Christianity from its beginnings in Palestine did not think of showing the persistence of wandering charismatics in early Christianity.

This is by no means to question the existence of traveling missionaries and preachers until well into the second century. But it is very doubtful whether they were the "decisive authorities" of the Christian movement. Even Paul himself does not exercise an unchallenged authority, and the *Didache* is evidence that the *vita apostolica* could be abused (*Didache* 11, 3ff.). Above all, it is questionable whether the lifestyle of the later preachers and missionaries can be compared with that of the disciples of Jesus. The different ways in which Luke's two works present the lives of the two groups should at least have alerted Theissen to this point.

As a matter of fact, Theissen encumbers his analyses with an exegetical task that in his explanation anticipates the central historical section of his investigation (i.e., the analytical conclusions to be drawn from the synoptic texts regarding the role of the wandering charismatics). In his analytical conclusions the author intends to look chiefly to "ethical norms" from the Jesus tradition, "since they relate directly to the attitudes of Jesus' followers." Theissen refers especially to "the pattern of giving up home, family, possessions and protection, which we find in this connection [in the synoptic tradition]."[37] The concept of "ethical norms" (or "ethical radicalism")[38] assumes that *voluntary renunciations* are in question here, even though the social situations—individual and communal—encouraged deviant behavior along these same lines.

Thus (for Theissen) the "pattern of giving up home" is neither the result, elevated to a moral principle, of a flight for social reasons (emigration) nor the result of the passively tolerated homelessness of vagabond beggars. The "lack of possessions" means for Theissen a "renunciation of possessions"[39] and not simply the situation of the poor person who has nothing. The abandonment of family ("the pattern of giving up family") is not the result of some social constraint but an "ethical" consequence of the call to discipleship. For this reason Theissen justly compares the early Christian wandering charismatics to the wandering Cynic philosophers.

These two movements, as Theissen sees them, did not make an ethical virtue out of social necessity (beggary), but rather took real beggary as the model for their own deviant behavior and made this kink of life serve them in the preaching of their message. For this reason I suggest "Cynical interpretation" as a shorthand name for Theissen's interpretation of the historical Jesus movement. The name is intended to bring out the fact that Theissen understands the Jesus movement as that of a group of social outsiders who lived a life like that of beggars, although this was, of course, "beggary of a higher order,"[40] inasmuch as the adherents of the movement freely adopted this lifestyle and made it part of their message.

Critical Examination of Theissen's Sources

My opinion, contrary to Theissen's, is that his "Cynical interpretation" of the historical Jesus movement is incorrect. It is the authors of the synoptic gospels who suggest this interpretation to Theissen. Luke goes furthest in this direction and even gives grounds for suspecting that he consciously understands the lifestyle of the disciples of Jesus against the interpretive background provided by the wandering Cynic philosophers. But this interpretation has no basis in the historical reality of the Jesus movement or, rather, in the testimonies to this movement that have come down to us. In Luke the interpretation is put at the service of a critical "explanation" of the present situation of the community as seen in the light of the history of Jesus and his disciples.

To some extent Luke has a predecessor in Mark the evangelist for his "Cynical interpretation" of the Jesus movement. However, he gives much sharper contours to the "idealizations" already clearly discernible in Mark, especially in the matter of an ethical rigorism among the disciples.

I shall return to Luke's interpretation of the Jesus movement in connection with my own theological reflections. Here let me say only that I exclude on source-critical grounds such texts as Theissen uses for his interpretations that are undoubtedly to be ascribed to Luke himself. The same holds for texts that are to be ascribed to Matthew or Mark. This exclusionary procedure remains within the limits of the source-critical restrictions set by Theissen himself, because all these texts are of "Hellenistic origin." Admittedly, Theissen himself often does not follow his own criterion.

Discrimination must also be exercised in considering Theissen's use of texts usually ascribed to the Logia Source (Q). For reasons that evidently belong to history and not to literary criticism, Theissen does not take into account the source-critical Q-hypothesis. For his historical location of the Jesus movement (A.D. 30–70, in Syria and Palestine) already includes the Logia Source. Given this presupposition, it is unnecessary for him to differentiate between "earliest traditions" and Q. But on methodological grounds such a distinction must in fact be made. For, from a historical viewpoint, once Jesus had died on the cross, no further persons could experience that call of Jesus to discipleship over which they had no control. And because the Logia Source reflects the death of Jesus (as the murder of a prophet), thus indicating that it has taken over and interpreted a still earlier Jesus tradition, there must remain open the question of whether the pre-Q stage of tradition may not have presupposed other sociological conditions of discipleship than those presupposed by Q itself.

I shall show later on in greater detail that there is in fact an important difference here, perhaps not with regard to society at large but certainly with regard to the self-understanding of the groups that are the representatives of the various traditions. At this point it is worth mentioning that for the time being I also exclude the texts that Theissen uses from Q. Given these restrictions, what are we to make of the textual basis in the synoptics for the analytical conclusions Theissen draws as to the role of the wandering charismatics?

1) For the pattern of homelessness, Theissen refers to Mark 1:18 and 10:28–30. Matthew 8:20, 10:5ff., and 10:23 may be left out of consideration for the moment;[41] they will be dealt with in connection with the interpretation of the Logia Source.

2) For the pattern of lack of family, the texts in question are Mark 1:20 and 10:29. All other texts are to be interpreted in connection with Q or else they are of some value to Theissen's thesis only if his presupposition regarding

them is correct (e.g., Matt. 16:17). And precisely the central text to which Theissen appeals for his interpretation regarding the pattern of lack of family shows clear evidence of having been reworked by Luke (Luke 14:26).

3) The texts that Theissen uses for the lack-of-possessions pattern bring out with exceptional clarity the dilemma that his interpretation faces from the viewpoint of literary history. For his interpretation of the most diverse synoptic texts (and even texts from Acts) can only be regarded as amounting to a kind of "lack of possessions" entry in a "harmony of the gospels." Texts from the most varied stages of tradition and the most varied origins are juxtaposed without distinction. For example: the story of the "rich young man" (Mark 10:17ff.); the "camel logion" (Mark 10:25), which occurs in this story but is probably older than the story and, in any case, was not originally connected with it; and the notice in Acts about Barnabas selling his field (Acts 4:36–37). Barnabas is indeed depicted later on in Acts as a traveling preacher and fellow worker of Paul. But in the context of Acts 4 the field is sold in the interests of *equalizing property ownership in the Jerusalem community*. In other words, renunciation of possessions here acquires its meaning from the equalization of property ownership among sedentary individuals and is in no way connected with discipleship that takes the form of vagabondage.

Another example: the Lukan "woe-sayings" with regard to the rich and the satiated (Luke 6:24–25) are correlated with the story of the rich man and poor Lazarus (Luke 16:19ff.) in a way that is indeed correct in its general tendency. But precisely when one grants that (at least down as far as 16:26) the Lazarus pericope contains very early tradition, then the origin of the woe-sayings is no longer explicable (do they come from Luke himself?). Moreover, nothing is said here about lack of possessions or renunciation of possessions in the context of wandering disciples of Jesus. It is Theissen himself who makes this connection.[42] Once again, I leave out of consideration for the moment such texts as come from Q (especially Matt. 6:25ff.).

4) The texts which Theissen uses for the pattern of defenselessness (Matt. 5:38–39; 5:41; 10:17ff.) are all to be discussed in connection with Q.

Consequently, only two passages remain to serve as a textual basis for describing the historical Jesus movement: Mark 1:18–20 (part of the "vocation" stories) and Mark 10:28–30 (part of the unsuccessful call to the rich man). Theissen appeals specifically to Mark 10:28–30 for his interpretation.[43] Can this text in fact support his thesis?

Critical Remarks on Mark 10:28–30

Theissen dispenses with a study of the context of Mark 10:28–30. This is understandable: if no critical analysis is made of the immediate literary context, the text does in fact support his thesis on vagabond radicalism. But closer investigation shows that this main support of the vagabond radicalism thesis will hardly bear the weight put upon it:

Peter began [again] to say to him, "Lo, we have left everything and followed you." Jesus said, "Truly, I say to you, there is no one who has left house or brothers or sisters or mother or father or children or lands, for my sake and for the gospel, who will not receive a hundredfold now in this time, houses and brothers and sisters and mothers and children and lands, with persecutions, and in the age to come eternal life.''

The arrangement of these verses in fact suggests that the social renunciations named are to be understood as a voluntary consequence of the following of Jesus. The same is indicated by the context with its unsuccessful call to a rich man (10:17ff.). In addition, the section 10:17-31 fits into the "framework of the story of Jesus"—or his disciples, as the case may be—in Mark, in such a way that the reader is led to think of Jesus and his disciples as leading a wandering life. And in fact the rich man asks Jesus about eternal life just as the latter "is setting out on his journey" (10:17).

But the integration of 10:28-30 into the overall scheme of the gospel of Mark that is thus effected by 10:28 should be enough to make us skeptical. All the more so because the second half of Jesus' saying promises a present substitute for the surrendered social ties, but a substitute that is problematic in the context of vagabond radicalism. How are we to imagine that those who have renounced their previous social ties for the sake of Jesus or the gospel will recover them—in this life?

Theissen responds with his thesis on the "sympathizers in the local communities." But Mark 10:30 is not speaking of *temporary support* for the wandering prophets, but of a substitute for the social milieu these men have given up. The thesis on vagabond radicalism must therefore take the second part of Jesus' saying as purely symbolic (as, for example, in the saying about authentic relatives in Mark 3:31-35).

It is noteworthy that Luke and Matthew are more cautious in their formulation of the second part of Jesus' saying. They promise only an unspecified "manifold" in this life as a replacement for the abandoned house, family, and possessions; nor do they mention "persecutions" (see Matt. 19:29; Luke 18:30). This makes the concrete statements in Mark all the more interesting. The analogy between what is surrendered and what is given back undoubtedly points to a *community situation*. It cannot be understood of the situation of wandering charismatics, but only of the situation specific to *sedentary persons who "change their religion."* In other words: Mark 10:29-30 reflects in principle the situation of a grown man who abandons his previous community and family when he passes to a different religious communion (*heneken tou evangeliou*, "for the gospel"). Such a change of religion certainly entailed the social consequences described in these verses of Mark.

This interpretation is confirmed by two passages from Philo and Tacitus that deal with the situation of Jewish proselytes. Philo discusses the problem on the basis of an instruction of Moses. Moses grants proselytes the same rank and honors as those born into Judaism, and he admonishes the latter to receive proselytes with special friendliness: "And rightly so. For, as he [Moses] says, inasmuch as these persons have abandoned their native land (*patris*) and friends (*philoi*) and relatives (*syngeneis*) for the sake of virtue and piety, they should not be deprived of new cities (*poleis*) and family (*oikeioi*) and friends (*philoi*)."[44]

Tacitus sees only the negative side of this transition to Judaism: "Anyone who embraces their ritual accepts this practice [circumcision]; and the first thing required of him is that he show scorn for the gods, reject his fatherland, and deny his parents, children, brothers, and sisters."[45]

In view of the two authors' opposite interests (polemical and antisemitic in the one case, apologetic in the other), their coincident testimony on social losses suffered by a proselyte is an important argument for the historical credibility of such consequences of a change of religion.

The same situation—a change of religion on the part of someone resident in a particular place—lies behind Mark 10:29-30 as well.[46] Not only does it explain the wording of the verse better than does the thesis on vagabond radicalism, but in addition—this may seem surprising at first hearing—it fits in better with Mark's own intention. It shows not only that 10:29-30 is pre-Markan and open only to the interpretation just given, but also that its reception by Mark represents a second stage in the experience of *sedentary* Christians. Thus 10:29-30 reflects not the earliest tradition but one that is relatively older than that of Mark himself. These claims need some verification.

The context for Mark 10:28-30 is the unsuccessful call given to a rich man. The man asks Jesus about eternal life. Because he refuses the call to discipleship, on account of his possessions, he goes away sad as one who is evidently unfit for eternal life. In a subsequent conversation with the disciples, Mark derives a principle from this incident. Wealth as an impediment is only an example of a more inclusive point: "Children, how hard it is to enter the kingdom of God!" (v. 24c). It is *this* theme that renders intelligible the bewilderment of Jesus' disciples (*ethambounto*, v. 24), and not the connection between wealth and discipleship. In other words, the "astonishment" of the disciples (or even their "very great amazement," *perissos exeplessonto*) and their worried question: "Then who can be saved?" (v. 26) are connected with the assertion of Jesus that it is difficult under any circumstances to enter the kingdom of God. After all, given their own renunciation of possessions (which is expressly mentioned in Mark, v. 28), the disciples would hardly have been shocked at hearing only that a rich man will certainly not enter the kingdom (v. 25).

This is also how Luke understands things, and accordingly emphasizes the reactions of the disciples. In Luke, of course, the whole emphasis is on the renunciation of possessions, a renunciation that the disciples have made, so that they are not affected by the diatribe against the rich. In Mark Jesus speaks to the *disciples* (and not, as in Luke, to the rich man) and thus from the incident of the rich man he draws a conclusion that applies to the disciples.

The worried, self-centered question of the disciples about who can be saved is answered by the statement that it is impossible for humans but not for God (v. 27). This answer brings Peter into the picture as spokesman for the disciples. He points out the social renunciations they have made: "Lo, we have left everything and followed you" (v. 28). In this way he tries to get Jesus' negative statement discussed further (*erxato legein*). But in reply Jesus relativizes Peter's claim. This relativization of the social renunciation made by the disciples of Jesus is completely in the service of Mark's intention here. With Peter's reference to renunciation Mark now connects a saying of Jesus that Mark has inherited from the tradition (vv. 29–30). It is incompatible with the situation in the story in two respects.

For one thing, the saying presupposes the situation not of wandering disciples of Jesus but of sedentaries who change their religion and become Christians. For another, this traditional logion quietly promises once again the very thing that previously had been called into question (under the form of "entering the kingdom") even for the disciples—namely, "eternal life." These tensions exist because Mark is here grappling with the fact that the recovery of houses, family, and possessions is taking place "with persecutions" (*meta diogmon*). This short remark, which introduces a roughness into the rhythm of the passage, is like an alien body in the flow of 10:29–30 and is doubtless a Markan addition. It says that the "baptism of fire" for Mark's community of disciples consists of persecutions and that no determination has yet been made as to who will enter "eternal life," because "many that are first will be last, and the last first" (10:31).

What Mark is saying here fits into the larger picture of the "discipleship of suffering" that, as shown by Peter's confession, is *the* Markan theme. This theme is then immediately continued in the reference to the passion and death of the Son of man and the corresponding "fear" of the disciples (Mark 10:32–34) and in the reference to the martyr "baptism" of the sons of Zebedee (Mark 10:35ff.).[47]

It is interesting that Mark obviously represents what is already a second stage of Christian experience in the communities. The pre-Markan logion in 10:29 envisages the problem of those who convert to a community of Christians and must, for the sake of the gospel, give up their previous social infrastructuring. Mark turns this "consolation saying" into a critical admonition to his community; the admonition places the disciples' social renunciation under the sign of persecution and adds an "eschatological question mark." At no stage of its history does this logion reflect the situation of wandering charismatics.

Critical Interpretation of Theissen's Texts from the Logia Source

The Q texts that Theissen uses are the ones most likely still to reflect the *social* situation that he has analyzed as being the historical and sociological context for the Jesus movement. But the representatives of this Jesus tradition in Q are not identical with the earliest Jesus movement, nor does a "Cynical" interpretation square with their way of life. For, although the texts from Q reflect (also) the homeless existence of wandering prophets in Syria and Palestine before A.D. 70, they do not advocate a pattern or ethos of homelessness. These individuals do indeed live the desperately poor life of the starving, but not as a result of an ethical principle that calls for a lack of possessions. It is indeed probable that many of these Q-prophets have left their families, but they themselves regard this separation as an unalterable and bitter necessity, and not as a free choice to do without a family. Similarly, they practice defenselessness and the renunciation of force. But this is evidence of the positive character of their message to all Israel ("love of enemies") and not of the specific situation of wandering prophets.

Theissen has in fact painted a largely accurate picture of social reality in Syria and Palestine, a picture that fits the situation of the Q-prophets. But this critical situation naturally affects the various strata of the population of Palestine in different ways, just as these strata differ in their "responses" to their given social situation.

In evaluating the "reaction" of the Q-prophets to the social situation in Palestine it is therefore not irrelevant how we locate them in terms of social status and how we then evaluate this location in relation to the situation of the majority of the people. But if we take as our starting point the fact that throughout broad sectors of the Palestinian people at this time an anxiety about the basic necessities of life and a fear of death by starvation were predominant, then of course the problem of hunger directly decides what the social situation of these persons were, and no analysis of specific strata will be informative if it does not pay attention to this problem of survival.

From this point of view it makes little sense to discuss Theissen's surmise that the Jesus movement drew its members primarily from the middle class of society. The difficulty is aggravated by the fact that he identifies the movement with *marginal* groups. This position contradicts his own analysis of Palestinian society as a whole (an analysis that sees the crisis as widespread) and obeys rather the exegetical constraint exercised by his ethically oriented theses on vagabond radicalism. This can be shown also and especially from the relevant Q-texts.

It is important here, from the viewpoint of method, to interpret these texts first of all in their own literary context—that is, without reference to other texts of the synoptic tradition. This is true even if such a procedure is especially difficult here inasmuch as we must begin by reconstructing the Logia Source from the gospels of Matthew and Luke. But here as elsewhere the principle *Scriptura sui ipsius interpres* ("scripture is its own interpreter") must be maintained on *historical* grounds. Otherwise it will hardly be possible to determine in a critico-historical manner the specific situation of the carriers of this tradition. Admittedly, the literary level of the Logia Source is only *one* level of interpretation. What it says must also be interpreted in the context provided by the social reality.

The admonition of Jesus that Theissen cites: "Do not be anxious" (Matt. 6:25ff.) makes it clear that the problems of the Q-prophets are those of the majority of the people: anxieties about the bare necessities of life. It is to be assumed, therefore, that the representatives of this tradition belong to "the lowly" of Palestine who, despite their different trades and callings, share *one* problem: the problem of hunger. The message of these prophets is therefore an alternative to the life of the lowly and thus of the majority of the population. Their lifestyle is inseparably connected with this message. The Q-prophets were undoubtedly *wandering* prophets. The question, however, is whether they understood this lifestyle as an ethos, a deliberately chosen pattern, and whether we may understand it as such.

The "outfitting rule" (Matt. 10:8–10 and parallels): "Take no money, no bag of provisions, no two tunics, no sandals, no traveller's staff," *distinguishes* the Q-prophets at least from beggars. Vagabond beggars would not voluntarily have refused to outfit themselves. It might be said that this kind of existence, which is even more indigent than that of a beggar, shows a concern on the part of the Q-prophets to differentiate themselves from beggars and to manifest their own ethical and religious intentions by this distinction. But this interpretation can explain only the lack of money, of provisions, and possibly of a second undergarment, but not the lack of sandals and staff. Even a prophet who wants to make it clear that he is not a beggar would see to it that he had staff and sandals as a protection against animals and rough roads.

The important thing, therefore, in this lack of outfitting is not the individual items but rather the overall image given by such a prophet. In their rejection of outfitting these prophets are not taking the image of the beggar and modifying it in the service of their own unmistakable image as prophets. The point of projecting such an image (rejection of outfitting) is to give radical backing to their message of unqualified trust in God; this trust involves a lack of anxiety about even the bare necessities of life and a lack of fear with regard to their own lives:

> Matthew 6:25–33Q, the outfitting rule, and the significance of anxiety about the bare necessities of life on the part of extensive sectors of the population must be seen as related to each other. Matthew 6:25–33Q does not describe the special lifestyle of itinerant messengers of Jesus as opposed to that of sedentary Christians, nor is the anxiety about the bare necessities of life a problem limited to Christians. Refusal of an outfit is a way of putting Matthew 6:25–33Q into practice, according to which it was just as possible for sedentary Christians to rid themselves of anxiety.[48]

In other words, the Q-texts that Theissen uses do not give evidence of an *ethical* radicalism, nor does their content play a determining role in vagabond radicalism. They are rather to be understood in the context of the social situation, which was one of poverty and hunger for the vast majority of the people in the Syro-Palestinian world at about the middle of the first century. In this context the message of the Q-prophets offers an alternative to the anxiety of the poor for their survival. Theissen correctly sees that Jesus' words about not being anxious express "an unconditional trust in the goodness of God,"[49] but he connects this text only with the experience of the wandering charismatics and is unable to interpret it as a message to others as well.

As a matter of fact, however, the lifestyle of the wandering prophets differs in only small ways from that of the poor and the beggars. The prophets have in all likelihood freely decided not to be sedentary—not, however, as a result of a sublime renunciation of possessions but in order once and for all to rid themselves of the daily anxiety about the bare necessities of life and to throw themselves on the loving care of God. The Q-prophets do not adopt the lifestyle of starving beggars and then creatively adapt it, for they were already threatened with death by starvation. What they do now is rather to rely wholly on God's loving care and reject openly any attempt to lengthen their lives in the slightest by their anxieties. Their lives have all along been in God's hands and they trust that he will take care of them no less than he takes care of the birds and the flowers. It is his power and goodness, and not their own anxiety for daily food and their own fears, that will determine the course of their lives.

In this same context belongs the call for "love of enemies" and for renunciation of revenge. The call reflects the experience these prophets have had of persecution. It relates the rejection, persecution, and slaying of Jesus to their own experience of enmity. But neither their open refusal of a traveler's staff nor the call to renounce violence and love their enemies justifies our connecting them with the "peace party" that was urging reconciliation with the Roman occupiers.[50] The "peace party" of which Josephus speaks was a movement of well-to-do citizens (especially in Jerusalem) who because of their possessions collaborated with the Romans.[51]

Finally, the example of Theissen's "pattern of lack of family" makes it clear once again how important a source-critical classification of the synoptic text material is for the historical and sociological interpretation of these texts. For this pattern of lack of family Theissen refers in particular to Luke 14:26: "If any one comes to me and does not hate his own father and mother and wife and children and sisters and brothers, yes, and even his own life, he cannot be my disciple." The parallel text in Matthew (10:37) reads: "He who loves father or mother more than me is not worthy of me; and he who loves son or daughter more than me is not worthy of me."

Beyond any doubt, the Lukan version of this saying of Jesus from Q bears the mark of Luke the evangelist. He formulates the saying in dependence on Luke 18:29b (as can be seen from the Lukan peculiarity of mentioning women explicitly). The context (14:25–35) also makes it absolutely clear that Luke is here concerned with setting down the exceptional conditions required for following Jesus as a *mathetes* ("disciple"). For Luke these conditions culminate in the voluntary renunciation of possessions. The hatred of relatives mentioned in 14:26 is therefore not to be claimed as part of the tradition regarding the Jesus movement. The original intention of Q is preserved rather in Matthew's variant of the saying. As far as Q is concerned, the abandonment of family is likewise not an ascetical norm but a bitter necessity to the extent that the family opposes a confession of Jesus by one of its members. This division in the family is understood as a fulfillment of the prophecy about apocalyptic distress (Matt. 10:35 makes explicit reference to Mic. 7:6).[52]

In summary: the Q-texts that Theissen uses cannot be claimed as supporting a "Cynical" interpretation. They reflect not an ascetical ethos but the radicality of a life situation in which poverty, hunger, and violence are the dominant factors. The Q-prophets counter the radical suffering of the majority of the Palestinian population with their own radical trust in God.

Prior to the Logia Source there was no vagabond radicalism, based on a rigorist ethics, in early Christianity. All the texts that Theissen uses in his analysis of a Jesus movement thus interpreted are either excluded on text-critical grounds or else must be interpreted differently.

Vagabond Radicalism as a Criticism of Rich Christians

Theissen's "Cynical" interpretation of the Jesus movement can appeal to a famous precursor: the author of the gospel of Luke. As no other before him, Luke depicts the disciples of Jesus as wandering charismatics who in responding to the call to discipleship practice an ethical radicalism that assimilates them to the wandering Cynic philosophers. The ethical pattern of homelessness, lack of family, and, above all, lack of possessions characterizes the extraordinary social renunciation practiced by the disciples of Jesus in Luke's work. Of course, this "Cynical" interpretation of their life of discipleship is the contribution of Luke himself; in other words, the claimed radical behavior of the disciples is a literary fiction. It has for its vital context (*Sitz im Leben*) not a vagabond radicalism but the particular situation of a Christian community to whose internal social constitution this theological interpretation of a disciple's existence is a passionate response.

In Luke's portrayal of them, the disciples voluntarily become "poor" (*ptochoi*) as part of their following of Jesus. Luke regards complete renunciation of possessions as a constitutive element in discipleship (Luke 5:20, 28; 12:33; 14:33; 18:22). Like Mark, Luke interprets separation from family as a voluntary social renunciation on the part of the disciple. However, he extends this interpretation further than Mark does, insofar as he also expressly mentions the leaving of a wife and calls for hatred of (i.e., complete social separation from) the entire family as a consequence of discipleship (Luke 18:29; 14:26). The same holds for the homelessness of the disciples. In particular, the lack of possessions and celibacy point to a conscious assimilation of the lifestyle of the disciples to that of the wandering Cynic philosophers. But as a matter of fact:

> The *entire* lifestyle of the disciples, as described by Luke, can be understood by analogy with the life free of desire that the Cynics led. The disciples renounce their possessions, break all ties of human communal life, wander from place to place, are active in preaching and healing, and enter homes in order to preach and heal there. If they are not given lodging, they are to sleep under the open sky—worse off, in this respect, than the foxes and the birds. Their outward dress too is like that of the Cynics, in that it is equally unpretentious. Their own life means nothing to them.[53]

It is possible to see the ethical radicalization of the behavior of Jesus' disciples taking place in Luke if we make a step-by-step comparison of this gospel with the other two synoptic gospels.

At the same time, however, Luke leaves no doubt that he regards this special lifestyle of the disciples as a thing of the past. He does not call for an imitation of their radical behavior. But in thus picturing the lifestyle of the first disciples as a thing of the past, Luke is not acting exclusively as a historian. He has quite another purpose in mind here in depicting the exceptionally poor life of the disciples: it represents the extreme alternative to the life of the rich (Luke 12:13–33). Luke thus connects the description of the disciples' life with a central concern of his gospel. For he is very much preoccupied by the material distinctions within his Christian community and by the social tensions that these distinctions entail. He gives expression to this concern in his presentation of the life and message of Jesus and his disciples.

For Luke, Jesus is the savior of the poor and the despised, and as such he takes a critical attitude to the rich and the self-righteous. Jesus praises his poor disciples and speaks "woe" to the rich. He keeps company with the outcasts of society (tax collectors, prostitutes, sinners) and tells the self-righteous (represented by the Pharisees) that like these sinners they too need conversion (*metanoia*). The gospel of Luke is a sustained call to repentance—and it is addressed to Christians of wealth and repute. These must change the direction of their lives: from riches that are desired for their own sake but make life burdensome, to a life that is rich in relation to God, a life of good deeds and acts of mercy. They must practice solidarity with the Christians they have been looking down on. The desired end result of this "call to repentance" is depicted by Luke in his description of the life of the first community at Jerusalem. The members of this community held everything in common (equality of ownership within the community) and were one in heart and soul (elimination of social tensions).[54]

The fact that Luke thus incorporates the "vagabond radicalism" of the disciples of Jesus into a program of social criticism and social ethics for the communal life of Christians among themselves and with others gives Theissen's analyses a *theological* justification. Independently of whether or not his analysis of the historical Jesus movement is correct, it is capable of spurring theological reflection on the many felt tensions between the message of Jesus and the way this message is preached in our affluent churches. It sets up an irreconcilable contrast between wandering preachers and office-holding pastors, between a hand-to-mouth life and a life of abundance, between a carefree attitude and a self-satisfied security, between a lack of excessive desires and the possession of superfluities. We can sense a boundless difference between ourselves and those who began the Christian movement.

Our attention is caught, however, by the fact that Theissen is expressly concerned to distinguish the Jesus movement, as he portrays it, from any "idyllic picture of the life of the lowly." Why the concern to make such a separation? What would it mean for us theologically if the historical Jesus movement had in fact drawn its recruits from among the lowly? What if the first followers of Jesus, like their master, were from the poor and hungry, not as the result of any renunciation of possessions but because in fact they possessed nothing? What if the historical Jesus movement had been made up of poor beggars and outlawed criminals? What if the desired goal of their criticism of the rich was that in the kingdom of God present relationships would be reversed? What if they had claimed that God's action and the mission of Jesus were directed to precisely such a goal? Would this kind of radicality, which has nothing to lose but much to gain, still win our sympathy? The criticism leveled at us would then probably become even more radical. It would be voiced not by ethically motivated heroes of renunciation but by probably very unattractive characters. We would then be part of the history of a movement that would be excluded from what so effectively determines our lives—namely, prosperity—and that had on the contrary set its hopes on Jesus and on God.

As thus viewed, the "Cynical" interpretation of the Jesus movement becomes a promise of mercy when we come to be judged. And perhaps it is our very prosperity that makes it impossible for us to conceive of the poverty of the first followers of Jesus as other than a form of social renunciation. It is not that we are unwilling but rather that we are unable to imagine the followers of Jesus, and Jesus himself, as belonging to the poorest of the poor, to the lowly of Palestine. On the other hand, the simple, carefree life that even we sometimes dream of manifests to a dangerous degree the traits peculiar to the daydreams of the rich.

For this reason, too, it is important to reconstruct the history of Christian origins as accurately as possible. Such knowledge makes it more difficult for us to take refuge in these attractive daydreams. This is another lesson that history can teach us. For it makes a difference whether, for example, Seneca, the "millionaire" among the philosophers, dreams about the simple life lived in the past or whether, on the contrary, an "authentic" Cynic philosopher, clad in filthy rags and persecuted by political authorities, invokes and lives the simple life as a criticism of persons like Seneca.

The reader should turn to Seneca's fantasy about society and compare it with Luke's social utopia. Both may say the same thing, but the meaning is completely different. Seneca is writing about an idyllic antiquity:

> In those days no one could have too much or too little, for all shared everything without disagreement. The strong man did not yet lay hands on the weaker, nor was there as yet any experience of the avaricious man who withdraws goods from circulation in order to let them lie unused and thus deprive others of what they need. All cared for their neighbors as for themselves. . . . In their forests and under their simple roofs of branches, they passed peaceful and unworried nights. We, on the other hand, toss restlessly on our purple beds, and the sharp prick of care robs us of sleep. But what slumbers they enjoyed on the hard ground! . . . Fresh air and free passage through the open spaces, the

soft shade of rock or tree, a clear spring or stream freely flowing—not stagnant or confined in pipes and artificial conduits—meadows beautiful without the efforts of art, and, amid all this, a rustic hut adorned in a simple rustic way—truly, a dwelling in accordance with nature![55]

Luke is not dreaming of any such rustic idyll. And yet he takes the same kind of conditions as his starting point. He too is familiar with the avaricious person who withdraws goods from circulation to let them lie unused. But such a one—the rich farmer of Luke 12:13-21—dies of his antisocial behavior. In direct contrast to him stand the disciples who possess nothing. Similarly, their concern for the reign of God is contrasted with the greedy precautions of the rich farmer. Luke, too, wants possessions to be distributed equally among the prosperous and the needy, so that there will no longer be any needy persons in the Christian community. For this reason he uses the model provided by the Hellenistic social utopia in describing the first Jerusalem community. And in Paul he shows us a man who remembers the Lord's words: "It is more blessed to give than to receive," and who therefore takes care of the weak.[56]

Luke by no means calls the state of poverty blessed, but he does call blessed the poor disciples who meet the needs of the moment. For the same reason he does not forget to heap "woe" on the rich and the satiated. In his single-minded concern he finds in his picture of the vagabond radicalism of Jesus' disciples and of the continuation of this movement in the first Jerusalem community a way that leads not to a barren social romanticism but that, instead, uses the past to show up present defects of the Christian church so that they may be changed. We must learn from his use of the "Cynical" interpretation of the Jesus movement.

NOTES

1. Gerd Theissen, *Sociology of Early Palestinian Christianity*, J. Bowden, trans. (Philadelphia, 1978). The title of the German original is *Soziologie der Jesusbewegung* ("Sociology of the Jesus Movement").

2. *Sociology*, p. iv.

3. Subtitle of the German original.

4. *Sociology*, p.1.

5. Ibid.

6. Ibid., p. 2.

7. See ibid., p. 3.

8. Rudolf Bohren, *Predigtlehre* (Munich, 2nd ed., 1971), p. 438.

9. "Wanderradikalismus. Literatursoziologische Aspekte der Überlieferung von Worten Jesu im Urchristentum," ZThK, 70 (1973) 245-71.

10. *Sociology*, p. 7.

11. Ibid., p. 1.

12. G. Theissen, " 'Wir haben alles verlassen' (MC X 28). Nachfolge und soziale Entwurzelung in der jüdisch-palästinischen Gesellschaft des 1. Jahrhunderts n. Ch.," NovTest, 19 (1977) 161.

13. *Sociology*, pp. 8 and 10.
14. "Wir haben alles verlassen," p. 165.
15. *Sociology*, p. 8.
16. "Wir haben alles verlassen," pp. 165–66.
17. See ibid., p. 167.
18. Ibid.
19. Ibid.
20. Ibid., p. 166.
21. Ibid., p. 161.
22. Ibid.
23. Ibid.
24. See ibid., pp. 188–89.
25. Ibid., p. 195.
26. See ibid., p. 186.
27. *Sociology*, pp. 14–15.
28. Ibid., p. 1.
29. Ibid., p. 3.
30. Ibid., p. 10.
31. Ibid., p. 3.
32. See ibid., pp. 114ff.
33. Ibid., p. 9.
34. Ibid., p. 10.
35. Ibid.
36. Ibid., p. 115.
37. Ibid., p. 10.
38. The term occurs frequently in his essay "Wanderradikalismus."
39. "Wanderradikalismus," p. 251.
40. See ibid., p. 260.
41. For the actual texts, see *Sociology*, pp. 10–11.
42. For the interpretation of Luke 16:19ff., see L. Schottroff and W. Stegemann, *Jesus von Nazareth—Hoffnung der Armen*, UTB, 639 (Stuttgart, 1978), pp. 38–41, 133–35.
43. See "Wir haben alles verlassen."
44. Philo, *De specialibus legibus*, I, 52.
45. *Historiae*, V, 5.
46. The same situation is probably reflected in Origen, *Contra Celsum*, III, 55.
47. On this subject, see E. Stegemann, "Das Markusevangelium als Ruf in die Nachfolge" (dissertation, Heidelberg, 1974).
48. Schottroff and Stegemann, *Jesus von Nazareth*, p. 64. On the question of the interpretation of Q, see chap. 2 of the same work.
49. *Sociology*, p. 13.
50. See ibid., pp. 112–14.
51. See Josephus, *De bello judaico*, II, 338 and 417ff.
52. Schottroff and Stegemann, *Jesus von Nazareth*, pp. 85–86.
53. Ibid., pp. 111–12. On the interpretation of Luke, see chap. 3 of the same work.
54. See Acts 2:41–47 and 4:32–37.
55. Seneca, *Epistulae*, 90, 36ff.
56. Acts 20:33–35.

Index of Scriptural References

OLD TESTAMENT

Reference	Page	Reference	Page	Reference	Page	Reference	Page
Genesis		15:21	34	24:4	56	2:10	73
1-50	17, 64	15:33	34	24:8	56	2:11	66, 73
Exodus		16:6	34	25:22	56	2:12-14	76
20:22-23:33	38	16:8	34	**1 Chronicles**		2:13	66
21:2-11	38	16:9	34	1-29	64	2:18	68
21:7-11	36	16:15	34	**2 Chronicles**		2:21	68
21:19	36	16:17	34	1-36	64	3:9	66
21:22	36	16:23-24	34	26:1-23	31	3:11	60
21:30	36	16:24	38	26:16-21	28	3:12	69
21:33-34	36	20:26-30	32	34:8	56	3:19	67
22:25	36	20:34	32	34:15	56	3:20	67
31:12	128	21	36	34:16	56	3:21	67
31:14	128	21:1-19	38	34:18	56	3:22	67, 69
34:6	138	22	32	34:20	56	4:1	71
Leviticus		**2 Kings**		**Ezra**		4:2	72
19:13	131, 134	1-25	17	10:2-3	10	4:3	72
Numbers		6:8-23	32	10:12	10	4:4	68
26:52-56	37	6:24-7:20	32	**Nehemiah**		4:5-6	76
28:9-10	120	8:1-6	38	2:20	37	4:9ff.	66
33:54	37	8:7-15	32	**Esther**		5:2	71
Deuteronomy		8:13	32	1-10	65	5:6	77
1-34	65, 75	8:28-29	31, 32	**Job**		5:8	66, 70
22:19	36	9	48	1-42	61, 62, 63	5:9	70
23:26	121	9:1-3	28	7:1	134	5:9ff.	69
23:26-27	146	9:1-16	32	22:6	36	5:15	66
24:10-13	36	9:14-15	31	24:9	36	5:17ff.	69
24:14-15	134	10:32-33	31, 32	36:22	44	5:19	69
24:15	131	13:3	32	**Psalms**		6:3	68
24:17	36	13:7	32	37:25	61	6:10	60
25:5ff.	68	13:12	41	49:16	67	6:10-12	77
Joshua		13:17	32	73:24-25	67	7:1ff.	69
17:14-18	37	13:20-21	32	86:15	138	7:12	65, 66
Ruth		13:22	32	103:8	138	7:13	60
2:3ff.	132	13:24-25	31	104:22-23	146	7:16	72
1 Samuel		14:8-15	41	**Proverbs**		7:16ff.	72
1-31	17	14:21-22	31	1-9	77	7:17	72
8:10-18	38	14:23-29	31	1-31	61, 62	7:18	72, 77
14:47-52	38	14:25	31, 33	7:16	44	7:21	72
22:2	37	14:27	42	8	76	7:22	72
25:2-3	37	14:28	31	10ff.	60	7:23ff.	77
31:10	50	15:1-7	31	24:11ff.	72	7:24	60
2 Samuel		15:5	28	**Koheleth**		7:26ff.	66
1-24	17	22:3	56	**(Ecclesiastes)**		8:2	70, 71
4:12	50	22:8	56	1:2	57	8:3	71
8:15-18	38	22:9	56	1:3	66	8:3-4	71
20:23-26	38	22:10	56	1:4-8	64	8:4	71
24:18-25	38	22:12	51, 56	1:9	64	8:5	71
1 Kings		22:14	51, 56	1:9-11	64	8:6-7	77
1-22	17	23:15-18	41	1:10	64	8:9	69
4	38	23:34	50	1:11	64	8:14	60
13	41	23:35	49	2:1ff.	69	8:15	69
14:17	34	24:1	52	2:6	73	8:17	77

169

NEW TESTAMENT

Abbreviations

ATD	*Das Alte Testament deutsch*, W. Eichrodt et al., ed.
AThANT	Abhandlungen zur Theologie des Alten und Neuen Testaments
b	Babylonian Talmud
BA	*Biblical Archaeologist*
Ber	Tractate Berakoth in the Mishnah
BEvTh	Beiträge zur Evangelischen Theologie
BHTh	Beiträge zur historischen Theologie
Bib	*Biblica*
Billerbeck	*Kommentar zum Neuen Testament aus Talmud und Midrasch*, H. L. Strach and P. Billerbeck, eds.
BK	Biblischer Kommentar, Altes Testament, M. Noth, H. W. Wolff, and S. Herrmann, eds.
BL	*Bibel und Leben*
BM	Tractate Baba Metzia in the Mishnah
BRL	*Biblisches Reallexikon*, K. Galling, ed. (HAT, 1/1)
BZAW	Beiträge zur Zeitschrift für die alttestamentliche Wissenschaft
EvTh	*Evangelische Theologie*
FRLANT	Forschungen zur Religion und Literatur des Alten und Neuen Testaments
HAT	Handbuch zum Alten Testament, O. Eissfeldt, ed.
HK	Handkommentar zum Altem Testament, W. Nowack, ed.
HSAT	*Die Heilige Schrift des Alten Testaments*, 2 vols., E. Kautzsch and A. Bertholet, eds.
HUCA	Hewbrew Union College Annual
j	Jerusalem Talmud
JNES	*Journal of Near Eastern Studies*
KAT	Kommentar zum Alten Testament, E. Sellin, ed.
KBL	L. Köhler and W. Baumgartner, *Lexikon in Veteris Testamenti Libros* (Leiden, 2nd ed., 1958)
KHC	Kurzer Hand-Commentar zum Alten Testament, K. Marti, ed.
KuD	*Kerygma und Dogma*
NovTest	*Novum Testamentum*
NZSTh	*Neue Zeitschrift für systematische Theologie*
OrAnt	*Oriens Antiquus*
PEQ	*Palestine Exploration Quarterly*
SAT	Die Schriften des Alten Testaments in Auswahl übersetzt und erklärt, H. Gunkel, ed.
SUNT	Studien zur Umwelt des Neuen Testaments
TDNT	*Theological Dictionary of the New Testament*, G. Kittel, ed., G. W. Bromiley, trans. (Grand Rapids, 1964–74).
ThB	Theologische Bücherei
UTB	Uni-Taschenbücher
VF	*Verkündigung und Forschung*
VT	*Vetus Testamentum*
VTSuppl	Supplements to *Vetus Testamentum*
WMANT	Wissentschaftliche Monographien zum Alten und Neuen Testament
YCS	*Yale Classical Studies*
Yoma	Tractate Yoma in the Mishnah
ZAW	*Zeitschrift für die alttestamentliche Wissenschaft*
ZDPV	*Zeitschrift des deutschen Palästina-Vereins*
ZNW	*Zeitschrift für die neutestamentliche Wissenschaft*
ZThK	*Zeitschrift für Theologie und Kirche*